Literacy as Conversation

Pittsburgh Series in Composition, Literacy, and Culture

David Bartholomae and Jean Ferguson Carr, EDITORS

LITERACY as CONVERSATION

Learning Networks in Urban and Rural Communities

ELI GOLDBLATT and **DAVID A. JOLLIFFE**

University of Pittsburgh Press

Published by the University of Pittsburgh Press, Pittsburgh, Pa., 15260
This paperback edition, Copyright © 2024, University of Pittsburgh Press
Copyright © 2020, University of Pittsburgh Press
All rights reserved
Manufactured in the United States of America
Printed on acid-free paper
10 9 8 7 6 5 4 3 2 1

Cataloging-in-Publication data is available from the Library of Congress

ISBN 13: 978-0-8229-6698-2
ISBN 10: 0-8229-6698-0

Cover art: Photograph by Sang Cun
Cover design: Joel W. Coggins

To all our partners, allies, and friends,
who have taught us through conversations
about the collective future.

Contents

ix	Acknowledgments
Part I	**Introducing Our Terms**
5	1. How to Read This Book and Why
9	2. How to LEARN and What to Do about It
26	3. Literacy Needs in Two Regions
44	4. Conversation on Attitudes
Part II	**Learning Networks in Philadelphia**
57	5. Out-of-School Literacy Centers
78	6. Community Arts
107	7. Urban Farms
Part III	**Learning Networks in Arkansas**
129	8. Health
146	9. Performance
180	Conclusion: Constructing Hope through Conversation
201	Bibliography
211	Index

Acknowledgments

Eli

First of all, my thanks go to David Jolliffe. We began our friendship while David was still in Chicago—in those days we were both occupied with writing pedagogy and program administration—but when he moved to Arkansas our talk became more focused on community literacy projects and the people we met along the way. This book emerges from our intense and wide-ranging discussions, which serve as one model for our notion of "literacy as conversation." I'm deeply grateful for his wisdom, ease with all types of people, and unflagging energy to make a difference in his state.

Both of us have too many people to thank to name more than a small sample, for we have learned so much for so long from so many. Thanks to Josh Shanholtzer and Jean Ferguson Carr at University of Pittsburgh Press for their cooperation and patience on a book project a long time in the making. I want to mention here the people who were immediate partners in the topic of the book: Mike Reid, Lauren Macaluso Popp, Darcy (Luetzow) Staddon, Nyseem Smith, Jon Weiss, Danielle Mancinelli, Grimaldi Baez, Beth Feldman Brandt, Meei Ling Ng, Gayle Issa, Rosalyn Forbes, Ann-Therese Ortiz, Adam Hill, Dale Mezzacappa, Greg Windle, Alex Epstein, and Sonia Galiber. I talked to many staff members and participants at literacy centers, urban farms, and community arts organizations who were welcoming and helpful. I've also learned a great deal from foundation-related folks such as Ellen Wert, Helen Cunningham, and Bill Adair. Sue and Bob Wieseneck deserve much praise for supporting New City Writing over many years. Special thanks to Melody Wright, friend and co-conspirator on all issues related to making Philly a more livable place, and Jess Restaino, who has built her comp/rhet career alongside her commitment to Planned Parenthood and women's health issues.

Thanks to Temple University for a sabbatical during which I got a good start on this book. I'm especially grateful for friends at Temple and in the field of composition/rhetoric who have helped me on the way. I can't praise each individually, nor is the list comprehensive enough: Sue Wells, Kate Henry, Michael Kaufmann, Rachael Groner, Shannon Walters, Stephanie Morawski, and Daniela Curioso at Temple; Steve Parks, Paula Mathieu, Lauren Rosenberg, Ellen Cushman, Linda Flower, Carmen Kynard, Amy McCleese Nichols, Brad Jacobson, Veronica House, and many others in the field of community literacy; Russel Durst, Linda Adler-Kassner, Keith Gilyard, Bev Moss, Dominic DelliCarpini, Dylan Dryer, John Duffy, and the University of Wisconsin alumni crew, among many in the larger discipline of writing studies. Paul Feigenbaum, one of the reviewers of this book, gave us invaluable advice on bringing forward the threads that got lost in our zeal to tell stories. Both David and I owe a debt to Deborah Brandt for the beacon of her work and her continued friendship.

Conversations among friends in our neighborhood of Mt. Airy have helped me immeasurably: Chris and Ellen Hill, David Bushnell, Alan Wohlstetter, Frank Griswold, Mark Lyons, among many. Long talks with my brother, Aaron, and our brother-friend John Landreau figure in my approach to literacy, too, as do years of conversation about education with my longtime interlocutor Bill Lamme. My wife, Wendy Osterweil, is my constant support and companion. I'm grateful every day for our lives together.

David

I begin by echoing Eli and offering him heartfelt thanks for being a brother in the community literacy work that has filled the last third of our academic careers with such joy and surprise. What I have learned by working with Eli and getting to know his friends and colleagues could not be contained in even the most robust graduate seminar. And speaking of friends and colleagues: my thanks as well go to the roster of outstanding rhetoric and composition scholars and teachers whom Eli acknowledges.

Throughout the book, I name the folks throughout the state of Arkansas who helped me launch the work of the Brown Chair in English Literacy, but special thanks must go to Joy Lynn Bowen and Steve Collier, who invited me into the ARCare family and helped me make Augusta my home away from home, and to Marie Clinton Bruno, who was the first literacy professional to welcome me to Arkansas and who remains a constant go-to person in Little Rock.

Even just listing the people who worked on the projects described in this book fills my heart: Anne Raines, Krista Jones Oldham, Catherine Roth-Baker, Laine Gates, and James Anderson from the Arkansas Delta Oral History Project; Julia Paganelli Marin and Jonathan Green from Students Involved in Sustaining Their Arkansas; Hung Pham of Razorback Writers and the Arkansas Studio Project; Kassie Misiewicz, Erika Wilhite, and Rodney Wilhite on Team Shakespeare; Ashley Edwards, Michael Landman, Vicente Yepez, and Kathleen Trotter of the LatinX Theatre Project; and Kathy McGregor, Matt Henriksen, and Troy Schremmer of the Prison Story Project.

I have benefited from the counsel of great colleagues at the University of Arkansas, particularly Elias Dominguez Barajas in the Department of English and Chris Goering and Sean Connors in the College of Education and Health Professions.

My family has always constituted a great corps of cheerleaders for my work, so I offer my thanks to my sisters, Joyce Wilcox and Judy Fox, and I remember with deep affection the two family members we lost while I was working on this book, my sister Ruth Ellen Parks and my brother-in-law Steve Fox.

My wife, Gwynne Gertz, has been my constant companion and source of both inspiration and pride since we launched our grand endeavor in 2005. Our love knits us together.

Literacy as Conversation

PART I

Introducing Our Terms

1 How to Read This Book and Why

David Jolliffe

This is a book of essays about communities, learning networks, and literacy. And in that sentence sit two chunks of terms that are necessary for potential readers—and we hope they are many, from a wide array of professional and personal walks of life—to preview before launching into the book.

First of all, to get a grasp of how to read it, consider that *Literacy as Conversation* is "a book of essays." The two authors, Eli Goldblatt and David Jolliffe, have known each other for nearly three decades, and we ourselves have engaged in more hours of conversation about our work in community literacy than we can possibly count. Both of us have written articles, chapters, and books designed to be read primarily by our colleagues in departments of English, rhetoric, writing studies, and education; by graduate students—current or former—in those fields; and perhaps even by undergraduates interested in these areas. Our intention in *Literacy as Conversation* is not to exclude any of those readers but to expand our desired audiences beyond the boundaries of our previous works. We fervently hope that the book will be read not only by academics in higher education but also by teachers and administrators in K-12 schools, by school board members, by professionals in not-for-profit organizations that strive to influence quality-of-life issues, by government officials and policy makers who aim to effect positive changes in communities both rural and urban, and by "everyday folk" who share our interest in the ways reading, writing, and conversing can influence the empowerment and enrichment of citizens, now and in the future. We want all of these folks to resonate with the concept of literacy that we sketch out here and flesh out in the rest of the book.

With this hoped-for audience in mind, we consciously decided to write with more of a person-to-person approach than one typically finds in academic treatises. We have written what we call "honest-to-goodness essays"—so designated to contrast them with thesis-driven, argumentative, analytic academic articles. The noun *essay* comes from the French verb *essayer*, which means "to try"—not "prove" or "argue." The great progenitor of the genre was the sixteenth-century French writer Michel de Montaigne, whose 107 wonderfully discursive and often rambling *essais* invite readers (and to an extent lead them) to forge conclusions, sometimes tentative ones, about the thorny subjects that occupied Montaigne's mind: friendship, for example, or vanity, or lying, or sex, or aging. Montaigne's essays allow the reader to participate in the mind's *ongoing thinking*, not its completed *having thought*.

The essays in this book may not be completely open-ended, discursive essays in the mold of those written by Montaigne. But ours are certainly not essays like those school-based composition instruction has taught students to write for the past three centuries—texts with a quick "hook" for an introduction followed by a thesis statement that announces the piece's central idea and then maps its development—a genre that generally shows itself in "grown-up" form in academic articles, chapters, and books. The essays in *Literacy as Conversation* fall somewhere between these two poles, but if we had to stake a spot on the continuum between them, I'd say we fall closer to Montaigne than to Sheridan Baker (1962) or Jane Schaffer (n.d.), two modern pedagogues who teach the glories of the sharply focused, thesis-driven academic essay—which in the Montaignian sense is not an essay at all but more of a *theme* or a *position paper*.

Three stylistic features emerge from our decision to write honest-to-goodness essays. First, we invite our readers to participate in the thinking, the rumination, and the conversations that have undergirded our work with community literacy, so our essays are shot through with the personal: anecdotes and narratives abound. Second, the first-person pronoun is unabashedly present. If you're the kind of reader who is put off by discovering *I*, *me*, *we*, *us*, *my*, *mine*, *our*, and *ours* in a book published by an academic press, you might want to simply put *Literacy as Conversation* aside. We hope, however, that you'll stay with us as we speak out of our own experiences. In that spirit, we include a short chapter that enacts a conversation between the two of us because we want to emphasize that the book grew from hours of talk between us, talk with those we've worked with over the years, talk with colleagues and friends and our life partners. Third, we try hard to keep citations and references to a minimum. Those who know the literature on literacy will recognize ideas and theoretical orientations from many authors, but those coming to our book from other fields and endeavors should not be bothered by too much academic language (our reference to Montaigne aside). The introductory essay on definitions necessarily refers to other literacy scholars, and we do throw in an occasional footnote throughout, mostly to indicate places readers might explore if they are intrigued by one or another detail.

No doubt, the terms in our opening sentence that most strongly need unpacking come at the end of it: *communities*, *learning networks*, and *literacy*. These terms invite the question, "why should you read this book?"

Literacy as Conversation represents our collaborative effort to accomplish three goals. First, we show the fecund territory of community-based projects we have traveled for the past several years, in the hope that our readers might feel compelled to explore similar terrains and develop their own initiatives. Communities come in many sizes and shapes, and sometimes the people in them don't even recognize themselves as a social unit. In our experience, activities that bring people into collaboration can define a "community" for the participants. Second, we characterize the multivalent terms *communities*, *learning networks*, and *literacy* by showing how they are defined and fleshed out in two seemingly different but actually similar community contexts: urban North Philadelphia and largely rural Arkansas. Third, and above all else, we urge our readers to see the human energy, both individual and collective, that sits at the center of vibrant community literacy projects.

This energy is a hallmark of what we mean by literacy as conversation, a conceptualization that we introduce in the next two chapters and illustrate in the essays about Philadelphia and Arkansas that follow. To us literacy is more than tests and test scores, and we are frustrated by the discourse of many fields that insists on seeing it this way. Taking a cue from our friend Deborah Brandt, we see literacy as embedded in ongoing conversations that enable people to *do* things to make their worlds better (Brandt 2014). People want more than to succeed in school and get a decent (or better) job. They want to build relationships with their children and grandchildren by reading stories to them at night. They want to participate in their churches and their civic organizations. They want to help feed the hungry, clothe the naked, shelter the homeless. Literacy engages human beings in significant conversations that lead to *action*, involving them with the world of the word, connecting them to intellectual resources sometimes called technology or theory, information or knowledge, insight or wisdom. These resources grow and morph as their users develop agility and flexibility with the world of words. Scholars and observers of our culture seldom see literacy as integral to the actions of people who want to solve problems. *Literacy as Conversation* aims to correct this shortsightedness.

The stories in this book focus on "ordinary people" growing the abilities to read, write, think, and converse while at the same time helping to improve the quality of life for themselves, their families, their neighbors. As these stories demonstrate, literacy learning doesn't only happen in an official space like a school. We use the term *learning network* to name the web of public institutions, nonprofit organizations, and neighborhood centers that regularly sponsor activities in which people learn literacy through action and through human interaction, even if literacy is not the stated mission. We invite you to immerse yourself in these stories—to experience literacy as conversation.

2 How to LEARN and What to Do about It

Eli Goldblatt

My wife and I taught in Temple University's Rome program during the fall 2013 semester. When we returned to Philadelphia after seven months of exploration and wonder, we were both more than a little lost. We each taught our classes and fulfilled our duties on campus, but so much of our minds were back in our beautiful and tumultuous temporary home, where we had lived near the Colosseum and taught around the corner from the Piazza del Popolo. In Rome I worked with Italian teacher Daniela Curioso to develop a program in which American college students visited English classes in an Italian high school named Liceo Statale Terenzio Mamiani once a week. Suddenly, in November, my students and I witnessed the Italian teens take over their school in protest against austerity cuts in the budget that had left their building in disrepair. Mamiani was a grand but neglected hulking pile that reminded me of unloved Philadelphia high schools built in the early twentieth century. It was great fun talking politics with Daniela and other Italian colleagues, who took the protest as a manifestation of normal political life, and my American students, who were aghast at the audacity and aggressiveness of youths otherwise well behaved by contemporary American standards of obedience and decorum in class. But now I was home, and I wanted to bring that sense of active challenge to the static institutions in my region and that sense of inquisitiveness I had felt in Rome back to the American urban landscape I thought I knew so well. How was I to reengage with my own city now that I had been paid to spectate so deliciously far away?

The answer came in the early morning as I was coming out of a dream. In sleep I'd been gazing at the word *learn*, and I realized it could stand for Literacy Education Audit of Resources and Needs. A crazy, wonky thing to dream on a spring morning, but strangely it gave me hope. I realized that I was thinking in the wrong direction about initiatives I could start or people I could meet. Before I started anything, I needed to assemble two active lists: one naming the issues that were most pressing in Philadelphia neighborhoods related to literacy and a second enumerating all the organizations, churches, programs, and projects that could address those needs. Once I was fully awake and could scrutinize the gift of this insight, I saw that really I already knew many elements on both lists. Although I had often worked with academic programs and nonprofits on SWOT analyses—Strengths, Weaknesses, Opportunities, and Threats—I had never taken the process so personally before. The dream shocked me into looking at agencies and urgencies right before my eyes. The dream challenged me to explore my own city anew, with humility, curiosity, and gratitude. Yes, the city had needs, but it also had a tremendous catalogue of resources.

When I told my friend David Jolliffe about my dream, he recognized his own version of LEARN in Arkansas. Since he had accepted the Brown Chair in Literacy at the University of Arkansas–Fayetteville in 2005, he had been developing literacy projects in the northwestern corner of the state as well as in the Delta, the eastern region that borders the Mississippi River and Tennessee beyond. On trips through the state with David, I'd witnessed him listening to residents about needs they wanted to address, and he regularly sought allies with whom to form productive coalitions. We had long talked about doing a book together that identified similarities and differences of literacy projects in our two environments—mine decidedly urban and his primarily rural. LEARN presented itself as a way to lay out comparisons and contrasts, to pose literacy not as a problem in need of solution but as an ongoing process of human communication, inquiry, advocacy, and collective identity that is always situated within systems, institutions, and polarities: public and private, nonprofit and business, educational and recreational, oppressive and liberating. Because our experiences have usually been with programs outside the grounds of traditional schools, we focus our book especially on sites of informal learning, or ways through which a great range of people develop literacy abilities in out-of-school and non-standardized activities.

LEARN isn't a formalized method, nor is it particularly new. It's asset mapping with a personal flavor, more DIY than Department of Education. I described something similar in my earlier book *Because We Live Here*, focusing on the links and disjunctions of writing instruction in schools, college programs, and nonprofit community centers in Philadelphia. But that was an earlier time in the city and in my career, when I still framed literacy primarily in terms of formal programs and certified instructors. For this book, we wanted to recognize and highlight the power of literacy learning where most people don't look for it—in gardens and art studios, theaters and local health clinics, any place where people are making and doing together. LEARN is meant to identify gaps and strengths in literacy education available to residents of all backgrounds and means. We use this acronym because—after years of watching programs succeed and fail, receive funding or wither for lack of resources—we want to rededicate ourselves to the basic insight that an activist or public educator needs to search out what's going on and what people want before designing "innovative" curricula and building pedagogical castles.

We also want to emphasize *learning* rather than *teaching* in our discussion of literacy. Each of us has taught for more than forty years, and we have a deep commitment to teachers and teachers in training. The name LEARN, however, adopts the verb that matters most in any educational environment. Our most potent influences have been educators who focused on *people learning while doing meaningful activities in group settings*: John Dewey and Paulo Freire, Ann Berthoff and Peter Elbow, David Bartholomae and Linda Flower, Keith Gilyard and Ellen Cushman, Elaine Richardson and Carmen Kynard. The purpose of this book is to make literacy learning outside of traditional classrooms more visible, from docent tours in museums and workshops in art centers to vocational training at work sites, health-care information campaigns, and gardens in vacant lots where immigrants raise vegetables they remember from home. We recognize that today people of all ages are learning about reading and writing, or learning about the world through symbol systems and codified knowledge, in ways that revise our old classroom image of second graders reading primers aloud in tracked groups called the Blue Birds or the Penguins.

We write this book in order to assemble a picture of literacy in action and movement for our two locations, with the hope that our efforts will model a more comprehensive understanding of any region's literacy health and potential. We chose Philadelphia and Arkansas simply because we know them best, and we trust that readers will LEARN about their own regions in their own ways. We have come to see that one promising outcome of LEARN is to identify and enhance what we call *learning networks of literacy sponsorship*. All too often, literacy learning happens in centers or programs isolated from other places where informal or formal learning can or does occur, and an explicit focus on networks can encourage cooperation and circulation that would increase the effectiveness of literacy experiences for all participants. Before we can describe networks that support literacy, however, we need to define what we mean by *literacy*.

What Is Literacy?

We hope in this section to define *literacy* based on the New Literacy Studies orientation toward this human behavior as a "social practice"—embedded in interaction and purpose rather than frozen in rigid rules and specified skills. As David noted in the previous chapter, we also hope to describe literacy in a way that does not require readers to be scholars or educational experts. Despite the rise of literacy studies in anthropology, linguistics, and English in the 1960s and intense research on both reading and writing in education schools and composition and rhetoric programs in the last forty years, the term *literacy* still commonly conjures up elementary lessons in sounding out words and forming block letters. While literacy scholars discuss their subject with nuanced terminology, public debate searches for simple and direct ways to measure literacy rates and articulate standards in school and civic life. We need a way for researchers and policy makers to confer effectively.

UNESCO (2019) defines a "functionally literate" individual in a rather circular way: a "person who can engage in all those activities in which literacy is required for effective function of his or her group and community and also for enabling him or her to continue to use reading, writing and calculation for his or her own and the community's development." This definition strikes us as having the virtue of recognizing that literacy is not only a quality associated with an individual but a range of functions and activities that connect individuals to their community. Still, we need a less bureaucratic-sounding definition, one reflecting people's daily lives, to serve as a foundation for a discussion of literacy learning in urban and rural out-of-school environments.

Over the last twenty years, the US federal government has made an effort to measure and compare literacy rates in the American adult population. In 1992 the National Center for Education Statistics (NCES) sponsored the National Adult Literacy Survey, and in 2003 NCES sponsored a second comprehensive measure of adult literacy called the National Assessment of Adult

Literacy. Both of these surveys asked participants in their homes "to spend approximately an hour responding to a series of diverse literacy tasks as well as questions about his or her demographic characteristics, educational background, reading practices, and other areas related to literacy" (Kirsch et al. 2002). Based on the results, participants were scored on three scales: prose, document, and quantitative literacies. The National Adult Literacy Survey surveyed more than thirteen thousand adults and the National Assessment of Adult Literacy surveyed more than nineteen thousand across the country and in state and federal prisons. Then in 2012–2014 NCES administered the Program for the International Assessment of Adult Competencies, an instrument that investigated "basic skills and the broad range of competencies of adults" in thirty-three countries ("What Is PIACC?" 2018). The program had four domains for assessment: literacy, numeracy, problem solving in technology-rich environments, and reading components. The program added the feature of testing participants on laptop computers, though it also offered a pencil-and-paper version for those unfamiliar with computers.

These broad standardized tests are useful in giving us some baseline information about relative rates of literacy. They are properly rooted in the recognition that literacy is complex, involves rhetorical knowledge about genre and audience, and requires cognitive abilities to solve problems embedded in everyday situations. Such testing also allows a relatively large sample size so that valid inferences might be drawn. Yet approaches based on standardized tests don't help us understand the habits of mind that learners across age groups and ethnic identities most need to develop, nor do they suggest intrinsically rewarding activities that could motivate reluctant or alienated learners. We will have reason to refer to standardized tests such as the National Assessment of Adult Literacy, as well as others that reflect school performance, in our later discussion of the regions we studied. However, such tests alone don't contribute to a definition of literacy as an intimate and all-encompassing element in the daily lives of everyone who works and plays, loves and strives in a culture founded on written symbol systems.

I have written elsewhere that literacy is generated within the dialectic between the group and the individual—on the one hand, the broad socialness of language habits, dialect, and national history and, on the other, the private intimacy of writing or reading alone or with a few like-minded friends and mentors (Goldblatt 2012, 243). This leads us to our working definition for *literacy*: *the ability to engage in a conversation carried on, framed by, or enriched through written symbols*. By *conversation* we mean everything from a passionate argument between friends in a bar, to a Twitter flurry after a public event, and to a leisurely exchange of information about parenting among adults watching their kids at a neighborhood playground. We also mean written debates among microbiologists about experimental ethics, Instagram traffic among fashion enthusiasts over the latest celebrity creation, or sharp disagreements within a major league baseball coaching staff about who to send to the minor leagues. In whatever mode the conversation takes place, it is often sparked or tacitly provoked by some written text or at least touches on the participants' experience with newspapers and websites, manuals and guidebooks, statistical analyses, or fictional narratives. Sometimes conversations can be purposeful, suffused with emotion, or fraught with anxiety while other times chat can be meandering, speculative, or fanciful. And yet, within any given topic or situation—or what the Russian language theorist Mikhail Bakhtin calls "speech genres"—discussions of all types draw on past knowledge, cement shared attitudes, or challenge assumptions with new facts or perspectives. In a literate culture, these *conversations* contribute to the grand fabric of collective understandings.[1]

One consideration that drew us to the idea of conversation has to do with race and other social categories that often isolate or stigmatize specific populations. Both of us work in regions where race is a primary factor in the way civic resources are distributed, education is funded, and penalties for crime are meted out. Despite the fact that both Arkansas and Philadelphia have a significant black middle-class, a great many people of African descent are poor and experience unfair treatment from the justice and medical systems. Spanish speakers from a variety of Latin American countries, as well as immigrants from the Middle East, Africa, and elsewhere, face similar barriers to their well-being that white citizens do not encounter. Fair treatment according to gender, sexual orientation, and disability all depend on freely available and truthful information as well as the cultural will to build an inclusive and just social system. Meaningful conversation across class and race, exchanges that persuade lawmakers and regional planners to prioritize the needs of marginalized people, can improve lives in so many communities. Literacy as conversation isn't just a pleasant metaphor. As David said in chapter 1, in our work

---

1. Following Walter Ong, a great many scholars of literacy and language have noted the constant interaction between oral and written cultural practices. James Gee (1989), for example, goes so far as to privilege *Discourse* as a larger umbrella term within which literacy and other communicative behaviors fall. He famously defines *Discourses* as "identity kits": "ways of being in the world; they are forms of life which integrate words, acts, values, beliefs, attitudes and social identities as well as gestures, glances body positions, and clothes" (6–7). Two other influences we must mention are Kenneth Bruffee's (1984) link between ongoing human conversation and collaborative learning as well as James Britton's (1994) insistence on the interaction between speech and writing.

we have been particularly concerned with *conversations that enable people to do things to make their worlds better.* We believe that candid exchanges and explicit statements about oppression and neglect can be a crucial step toward greater social justice.

Other definitions of literacy may be more precise or technical, but this definition allows us to focus particularly on aspects of literacy we highlight throughout this book:

- Live and unfolding meanings emerge from webs of relationship
- Multiple conversations, characterized by specific purposes and contexts, generate distinctly different literacies
- Oral and interior utterances may be "literate" if they draw on knowledge or orientations associated with written texts.

We discuss each of these aspects in turn because they matter when we consider activities and groups outside of traditional schools. In this book, we investigate learning in non-school environments because we are convinced that much intrinsically motivated education goes on in theaters, clinics, gardens, art studios, and other places where people pursue activities they care about deeply. Especially for marginalized people in rural or urban areas who have not been well served by established agencies like school and social welfare systems, more creative means of drawing on community strengths can foster greater literacy gains and enhanced quality of life.

Live Meanings

When people get together at family reunions, block parties, protest meetings, or funerals, they must make meaning out of complex social situations. People shed tears and laugh—sometimes simultaneously—but they walk away from a group event with some kind of conclusion about how they want their lives to be. Sometimes an event precipitates a major change, like a choice to stop drinking or a reengagement with an estranged relative, but more often than not such events simply reinforce old behaviors or steel participants to losses that come with age or bad weather or peremptory government decisions. Meanings emerge from interactions among characters we admire or like or disdain or avoid. A funeral may teach us something about cancer or environmental hazards, unfair economic conditions, or the strengths and weaknesses that emerge when people encounter tragedy. A protest meeting might form new alliances between aggrieved parties who did not know about their common complaints. A family reunion may reveal secrets and unrecognized histories to the young or inflame old feuds among elders. In every case, participants young and old confirm or expand their impressions of the group, develop in subtle or blatant ways the connections that define their identities and make meaning in their lives. Too often, school—with its fill-in-the-blank lessons and arithmetic drills—isolates students from compelling events and cannot help them develop new insights or perspectives that might come out of direct experience with other people or current conditions.

David has written extensively about the Arkansas Delta Oral History Project he sponsored in a small eastern Arkansas town (2016). Helped by undergraduates from the University of Arkansas, high school students collected stories about life in their town before they were born. Similarly, students who attended the after-school program at Tree House Books (chapter 5) pursued a summer oral history project to collect stories about a barber shop half a block from their meeting place. At Don's Doo Shop, the owner, Don, did the hair of famous singers such as Michael Jackson and Jackie Wilson, who headlined around the corner at the Uptown Theater during the hall's heyday in 1950s and 1960s. In both cases, the interaction between written histories, oral storytelling, photo albums, and visits to historical sites produced for the young people a deeper and more convinced investment in the neighborhoods they thought they knew.

Perhaps the experience that first drew me to think about the unfolding nature of literacy took place in the little urban alternative high school where I taught in 1988–1989 (Goldblatt 1995, 92–93). A vibrant and playful fourteen-year-old whom I'll call Stephen Jones died suddenly that February. As far as anyone knew, neither gun violence nor drugs were involved; all at once he was simply gone. We announced the news the morning after Stephen died, and the entire school population of about a hundred kids went deathly silent. My senior English students felt they needed to do something, and two students in particular (I call them Maria and Tita in 'Round My Way [1995]) decided they would devote all their energies that day to writing a memorial document. Maria and Tita received permission from the principal to skip their classes and work on the project instead. They went around to classrooms and collected written statements from middle and high school students who wished to contribute. They typed up the statements, edited and arranged the text in the primitive word-processing program the school used at the time, and passed out a two-page commemorative document to students by the end of the day. I noted in the book that "their goal was to produce a public representation of grief that could be used to substantiate the private emotional reality of the loss" (93). Now, from the distance of more than thirty years, I still remember the tremendous excitement and gratitude kids felt in receiving the memorial for Stephen, as well as the remarkable maturational moment it was for Maria and Tita to work on such a vital project for the community. The mysterious loss of a child cannot be summed up or consoled away with high words, but a colloquy of grieving voices can affirm the continuity of life just when living seems most fragile. It took a suspension of academics as usual to respond to a reality too real for school.

Multiple Conversations

If readers open volume 6, issue 6 of the journal *Mathematics*, they'll find an article on "Gray Codes" that "focuses on a Random Walk in a N-cube where a balanced Hamiltonian cycle has been removed" (Contassot-Vivier et al. 2018). A nonspecialist can decode every word of this sentence from the first paragraph but can only imagine a bicycle in a long-running Broadway show reported missing during somebody's accidental stroll around a block on N Street. A specialist may make a great deal out of the same sentence, but for perfectly understandable reasons most of us are left out of the conversation.

According to the Flesch-Kincaid Grade Level, a standard readability scale, "*New York Times* articles have a tenth-grade reading level" (FullMedia 2019). Yet a teenager needs considerable background knowledge about politics and union procedure, not to mention ideological clarity on questions about journalistic standards and biases, to appreciate a sentence like this one, printed on the *Times*'s front page: "By a 5-to-4 vote, with the more conservative justices in the majority, the court ruled that government workers who choose not to join unions may not be required to help pay for collective bargaining" (Liptak 2018). Similarly, in an article on the relative chances of India beating England in an international cricket competition, author Ian Chappell (2018) comments that two "classic Cook double-centuries can't mask the fact that in his last 29 Test innings—a period of 12 months—he has had 19 scores under 20, including ten single-figure dismissals." Chappell's incisive prose won't enlighten the average baseball fan in Philadelphia or Little Rock. A reader misses thousands of conversations in the welter of published voices on any given day.

The phenomenon of multiple simultaneous conversations produces the common intuition that literacy comes in many flavors. We regularly talk about media, sports, financial, pop, civic, and nutritional literacies. Membership in an academic discipline or a sports fanbase depends first of all on being able to "talk the talk" in departmental meetings or local watering holes. At a minimum, graduate faculty subject their PhD candidates to qualifying exams to ensure their students don't embarrass their advisors at conference cocktail parties. No matter what their private principles, politicians running for office must speak the lingo of their region and demonstrate that they connect with the speech and conceptual framework of their core constituents, even when that speech may include racist "dog whistles" or idioms from certain ethnic groups. Although differentiation by party and education level makes for factional solidarity and efficient stereotyping, this specialization by jargon and argot can also divide people who might share common causes or prevent an idea from contributing more widely to the common good. Indeed, this dynamic is what Bakhtin identified as the centripetal and centrifugal tendencies in language use: specialized functions spin words off into particular meanings while standardized conventions force language into rigid but roughly shared public discourse. Language proceeds in both directions at once, and literacy codifies and popularizes either tendency.[2]

Max Weinreich, sociolinguist and Yiddish scholar, once famously observed: "a language is a dialect with an army and a navy." In the context of contemporary conversations that define literacy, both public and private languages are reinforced and shaped by publications, websites, billboards, and text messages. If the pen is mightier than the sword, literacy is more powerful than military armaments. But literacy isn't cast in iron the way cannons are; the fluidity of words and conceptual orientations makes teaching writing and reading infinitely challenging. The navy can train a young recruit to pilot a battleship in a few months, but teaching a child to engage in multiple conversations necessarily takes years. A pilot needs standard procedures under specified conditions, while a speaker needs flexibility and imagination beyond a prescribed vocabulary. For this reason, we focus this book's discussion on people acquiring literacy abilities through and within local practices like health care, gardening, theater, and other collective efforts that require language learning in action.

Oral and Interior Utterance

Sadly, few pure oral cultures exist on the planet anymore. Yet habits associated with "orality" by the scholar Walter Ong in his landmark study *Orality and Literacy* persist today within our hyperliterate Western culture. We tell each other stories about family or friends that don't come from books or articles or even websites; one could make the argument that social media, with all its speedy texts and pictures, binds us to a chain of "he said, she said" that has

---

2. Researchers and theorists interested in the interaction of multiple languages, or what has become known as *translingualism*, have noted that, even though non-native English speakers are often dismissed or demeaned in American culture, multilingual speakers bring rich resources to communication. For example, Alyssa Cavazos (2016) has investigated the oral and written practices of multilingual university faculty. She notes that one of her participants, a professor she names Martinez, emphasizes the power of "platica" or conversation "as a strategy he enacts to negotiate his knowledge of different language practices" (8).

an uncanny likeness to the dynamics in a tiny village that make it susceptible to momentary panics and scandals. And yet, as Ong noted in his work, "we have interiorized the technology of writing so deeply that without tremendous effort we cannot separate it from ourselves or even recognize its presence and influence" (Cushman et al. 19). We are fish who cannot understand water.

Our public and private dialogues and monologues, shaped and framed by the written word, go far beyond what we say to our neighbors over the fence or in the bowling alley. We speak to ourselves in times of stress, elation, reverence, and anger out of the playbooks and prayer books of our intimate acquaintance. My childhood reading encompassed Tom Swift and the Hardy Boys, a patchwork of Jewish liturgies, and the box scores of bad Washington Senators teams; David started as a Methodist, sings now with his Episcopal choir, and he followed the Pirates from his home in West Virginia. Because David has appeared in or directed a myriad of Renaissance and modern plays, he frequently quotes from dramatic works, while I tend to reference twentieth-century American poetry because I write poems out of that tradition. Our literate experience not only shapes what we say in formal and casual daily speech but informs our dreams and yearnings, our moral inclinations and political persuasions. Russian psychologist Lev Vygotsky argued that children internalize the speech they hear from the older folks around them. In a literate world, we are always internalizing the discourse we encounter, even if we choose to pattern ourselves after some speakers and writers more than others as we come into greater command of our influences. Then, of course, there are the silly melodies and rhymes that stick in our heads for no apparent reason. (Who would *wish* to hear "God didn't make little green apples" on repeat in the brain if the execrable little earworm weren't so tenacious?) Obsessive humming is the price of a literate mental life.

But Vygotsky and others Russian cognitive researchers in the 1920s and 1930s also thought about thought outside the brain. Following their line of investigation, various conceptual camps have grown up and become especially influential in the development of artificial intelligence and human-computer interactions. Philosophers of mind and cognitive scientists such as Andy Clark (2008) investigate *externalized* mental function, expanding and amplifying human consciousness through computational and compositional tools as varied as pen and paper, laptops, and virtual reality. This echoes Ong's emphasis on writing as a technology, but the analysis now goes much further. Proponents of the "extended mind," says Clark, "paint mind itself (or better, the physical machinery that realizes some of our cognitive processes and mental states) as, under humanly attainable conditions, extending beyond the bounds of skin and skull" (76). Clark refers to this as "the suggestion that *mind it-*

self leaches into body and world" (30) through our machines, our physical alterations in the environment, and language or symbol systems that can be handed down over time. Clark's work grows out of the concept of "distributed cognition," a way of describing thinking not as confined to a brain that must make its own representations of every outside object the individual wishes to manipulate, but instead the individual embedded in a culture depends on artifacts and social knowledge to amplify the power of the brain. The sailor at the helm of an aircraft carrier, for example, only needs to know certain protocols and procedures to call on the vast amount of cognition built into the hardware of the ship. The human mind, as Clark characterizes it, "emerges at the productive interface of brain, body, and social and material world" (219). Thus Clark poses individual biological, mental, and emotional life as always in relationship to the larger outside world, both physically and culturally.

In the same way, researchers in our field of composition and rhetoric recognize that writing and reading facilitate connections. The literacy of individuals takes place within larger institutional and cultural settings, which enable meaningful contributions but can also hinder greater accomplishments.[3] For example, Sue Doe and her colleagues (2011) use daily logs kept by nontenured faculty from many different academic departments to understand the contributions and tribulations of nontenured instructors, who serve their students and their profession without the high status and rewards of their tenured colleagues. Doe and her coauthors establish the richness of their subjects' teaching while also highlighting their marginalization from crucial aspects of academic life. In a remark that resonates with our definition of literacy, they say that the purpose of their study is to provide "context for purposeful cross-disciplinary conversations" (433) that could improve the overall effectiveness of higher education and help educators "understand how we might work together to bring about a more equitable workplace" (447). In this case, the conversation informed by literate practice could underwrite significant change.

We mention this embodied orientation toward extending minds because we too envision education aimed at involving learners of all ages in the construction of the society they belong to. We hope in the following chapters to focus particularly on instances when learners encounter literacy experiences rooted in social connection, inventive activities, and goals that do not depend on grades or abstract rewards for motivation. We turn now to a consideration

---

3. The distributed cognition approach composition and rhetoric colleagues often take is called activity theory (see Bazerman and Russell 2003). Also arising out of early twentieth-century Russian research, activity theory is a way of portraying the complex social context for any person's effort to accomplish a goal.

of the organizations and institutions most likely to support such informal learning environments.

Learning Networks

The idea of a "learning network of literacy sponsorship"—or "learning network" for short—is based first of all on Deborah Brandt's (2001, 19) often cited definition of literacy sponsorship: "Any agents, local or distant, concrete or abstract, who enable, support, teach and model as well as recruit, regulate, suppress, or withhold literacy—and gain advantage by it in some way." For Brandt, increasingly sophisticated uses of reading and writing must always be cultivated and supported by mentors, teachers, agencies, organizations, or social groups. Advances that any individual makes in literacy practices are thus shaped by the goals and self-interests of these sponsors. Literacy sponsors are not always beneficent, however. They sponsor with a particular attitude or agenda, and these preconceived or unexamined orientations can lead to obstructing some sorts of learning, just as they may encourage cognitive gains in other areas. The most common example might be the institutionalized sexism that long discouraged women and girls from studying math and science or the institutionalized racism that made higher education less accessible to African Americans students. Brandt's insights have been elaborated and debated by many other researchers since *Literacy in American Lives* was published in 2001 (see Duffy et al. 2014 for a wide-ranging discussion of the influence of that book). We take it as indisputable that the literacy health of any community depends in large part on effective and empowering literacy sponsorship for adults and children.

Another element of our understanding of networked sponsors comes from my earlier and differently oriented use of the term *sponsor*. In *'Round My Way* (1995, 25), I focus on "authority" as a quality developed by a writer through identification with more or less powerful social institutions: "a writer's authority in a society depends in large part upon the power and influence of the institution that sponsors that writer's authorship." An English major may learn about literature from an inspired and inspiring college teacher as a sponsor, but the influence and reputation of Literature as an object of study casts its institutional authority over the genres the student chooses to write within or the topics she chooses to write about. As English departments have fallen in prestige over the last fifteen or twenty years—reflected in the lack of academic jobs and the shrinking resources for publishing literary and critical works—the critic or novelist has become less visible as an influential intellectual figure in the American cultural mainstream. National and international prizes lend a certain juice to individual authors, but publishing in traditional genres such as poetry or fiction may not earn them much general respect, depending on the reputation of their publishing houses.

Certain authors write for sponsoring institutions rooted in dominant culture, such as literary presses or news agency websites or academic journals, but sponsoring institutions might also be rooted in nondominant cultures, such as storefront churches or neighborhood newsletters or comedy clubs in downtown bars. A writer gains *authority*, the ability to act as an author, through the backing of a more or less powerful sponsor (41). The poet laureate consultant for the Library of Congress may or may not be a "better" poet than one who publishes in a small South Jersey literary magazine, but the poet laureate draws on tradition, prestige, and access to media that a writer with more modest backing cannot match. Of course, institutional sponsorship isn't simple to analyze or easy to evaluate. The political ramifications of sponsorship become starker if we imagine an author publishing an editorial on the Black Lives Matter movement in a national venue such as the *Wall Street Journal*, a local online media site like the *Ferguson News*, or an African American–oriented news service like *The Root*. In each case, the relationship with larger and smaller audiences is crucial, as well as the perceived status and social agenda of the author. Influence can vary with the nature, history, and reach of the publication, but particularly in the relatively nonhierarchical environment of social media, a powerful message can spread without the blessings of the *New York Times* or an appearance on Fox News.

In short, where Brandt looks at the effects sponsors have on individuals at a particular moment in history, I emphasize the function and influence of social institutions themselves. Both individual and institutional orientations toward sponsorship enable us to see literacy learning as more than a matter of effective or ineffective instruction. Through these lenses we can see the dimensionality and connectivity involved in any person's growing facility with reading and writing, and we can recognize how much humans need trust, identity, and a sense of belonging to thrive as producers and interpreters of language. Unequal access to powerful sponsors and influential institutions leads to inequities in literacy broadly. Returning to our definition, those without the right sponsors or sponsoring institutions are often barred from the most crucial and politically effective *conversations* in society.

The shifting interplay between individual and institution provides a fascinating ground for investigation but also a rich base for organizing and educational activism. Both Philadelphia and Arkansas are places where access to quality education, public services, and housing are heavily affected by race and other social factors. The aggregates we call or imagine as *networks* intersect and intermingle at times, offering moments when individuals can cross barriers and groups can form new alliances.[4] For example, in chapter 7 I describe an African American church in far South Philly that leases a large plot of land nearly for free to a horticulture nonprofit that organizes urban farming for church members and immigrants from Africa and Asia who have moved into the neighborhood. Farmers at Growing Together Garden raise crops alongside one another and thus develop friendships or alliances that would otherwise never have formed. Networks can also coalesce around themes or special interests. A theater group in northwestern Arkansas that David discusses in Chapter 9 has developed fluency and public advocacy among Latinx youth while also entertaining, enlightening, and challenging white audiences about issues in the region they may not have recognized otherwise.

For the moment, I'll set aside the more official sponsors of literacy such as schools, colleges, and universities. These are obvious examples, but for reasons we will touch on later, the most recognizable literacy sponsors are not necessarily the most effective. In urban environments almost anywhere in the United States (and to some extent in rural regions as well), sponsors classified by the nature of their primary expertise or focus might include

- Language support for immigrants
- Language training for English speakers looking to travel outside the United States
- Central libraries and their branches, bookstores, and literary centers
- Out-of-school-time resources for children and youth
- Job training, adult basic education, degree completion support for adults
- Museums for adults and children, historical landmarks and plaques
- Prisons, jails, youth detention centers, courts
- Police, fire, license and inspection, public transportation, other services and utilities
- Day-care facilities for seniors
- Community arts organizations focused on special populations, neighborhoods, or particular media such as ceramics or mural painting
- Print, video, and multimedia production
- Churches, mosques, synagogues, and other religious institutions

---

4. Network theory involves a complex literature ranging from mathematics to sociology to computer science. Sponsors of literacy can be framed with this same approach, but we do not have the space or the inclination here to account for the intellectual connections. We leave it to readers who care to follow up on network theory (see Dorogovtsev and Mendes 2003).

- Grass roots political groups such as town watch organizations, party ward leadership, neighborhood and business associations
- Recreation centers and parks, arboreta and public gardens
- Hospitals, clinics, urgent-care centers, and health outreach facilities
- Food distribution, cooperatives and supermarkets, nutrition information outlets
- Sources of information on housing involving access, safety, affordability, and financing, such as realtors and homeowner associations
- Banks, credit unions, insurance agencies, check cashing shops, and other financial institutions
- Sources of information on transportation
- Sports facilities and training programs.

Agencies, organizations, institutions, and companies focusing on these themes may or may not be publicly recognized as fostering literacy. They may not include literacy in their mission statements. Nevertheless, in the broader (yet more specialized) sense of literacy found in Brandt's work, all these categories include crucial sponsorship for developing citizens' (and noncitizens') ability to address and advocate for their own needs as well as enhancing the mobility of individuals across activities, jobs, and career trajectories (see Wan's helpful work on literacy and citizenship [2014]). Institutions of all sizes and descriptions sponsor the authority of participants and learners to create artwork, construct gardens, design websites, or make decisions about their own health—in short, to be the authors of their own realities. Thus, interconnected literacy sponsors, or learning networks, may serve to enhance or restrict movement across barriers associated with class, race, and other socially constructed identities (see Horner and Bawarshi 2020).

No single researcher could track all of the above categories. In the chapters on resources in our respective regions, we consider examples of complex public, nonprofit, and private learning networks in a large city as well as a rural and semirural state. In Philadelphia, I focus on after-school literacy centers, community arts organizations, and urban farms. David discusses work he's done with a health system, theater groups, and a grassroots Latino youth organization. We're particularly interested in the power and problems associated with the blurring of formal and informal learning that takes place in sponsorships not directly associated with schools. As Shirley Brice Heath and Brian Street remark on the efficacy of this blurring: "We often forget, in the face of the dichotomy of *formal/informal*, how retrieval of random information collected through casual exposure is quickly activated by a current real need" (2008, 75). The urgency of "current real need" makes informal, non-school sponsorship more compelling in neighborhoods where civic sponsors such as schools or the police are regarded with wariness if not downright hostility. Official authorities—teachers, principals, police, and politicians—all too often seem to privilege the ways and needs of powerful people and institutions outside the local community.

To point toward one striking and complicated example, I'll discuss in chapter 5 a small nonprofit called Tree House Books. Tree House illustrates what we mean about the power and limitation of a single agency's literacy sponsorship within a stressed community. This little organization stands in the shadow of a much larger nonprofit, Temple University, and their difference in size and resources is not all to the disadvantage of Tree House. One major obstacle toward cooperative efforts between the people of North Philadelphia and the university is that Temple so profoundly represents established power and codified knowledge. Well-meaning college students who plant a garden with kids in a North Philadelphia recreation center through a horticulture class can make connections with neighbors, but local adults may be wary about whether the university has designs on that property even if no administrator is involved. The informal feel of a nonprofit program unaffiliated with official literacy authorities allows for a less guarded focus for participants. This is an instance in which the social power of a large institution does not necessarily make it the best sponsor for certain types of literacy authority. In a smaller organization more attuned to the lives of the participants, learners' immediate experience and overriding concerns motivate the activities, rather than what they "should" know according to a standardized test or qualifying exam.[5] At the same time, a small organization must always struggle for funding, program leadership, and other tangible and intangible resources. It's a major accomplishment even to survive and continue serving the target population each year. Tree House isn't a poster child or a cautionary tale for small-scale literacy sponsorship; few nonprofits are purely unalloyed successes or illuminating failures. It is, however, an organization I have learned a great deal from and still care a great deal about. The Tree House origin story on its own may have value for readers, and in a broader perspective its survival through more than fifteen years of existential crises have lessons for us about the value and promise of literacy sponsors in a learning network.

---

5. Jabari Mahiri has been publishing in this area since at least 1991. See for example his 1998 book, *Shooting for Excellence*, and his 2004 edited collection, *What They Don't Learn in School*. He has been especially strong on sports and urban youth.

3   Literacy Needs in Two Regions

Our times demand that teachers and researchers study, conceptualize, and act in as responsible a way as possible within human environments under severe economic and social stress. Our purpose here is not to explain or resolve issues that, after all, lie within the province of social science disciplines far more directly than our own.[1] We simply propose an approach to literacy we call "learning networks"—a way of identifying the interconnected regional array of literacy sponsors frequently related by theme or shared interests—within which our own small interventions make sense in the local landscape. With this approach, we believe nonprofit organizations, government agencies, schools, and other groups can work together to ensure greater

---

1. Recent trends in writing studies have led younger scholars to seek training in empirical research, cognitive psychology, and even neurological science. We applaud these developments, but we also see the need for a more capacious and nuanced macro-level context for literacy studies. We hope that some future scholars choose to pursue additional training in social science fields such as economics, regional planning, geography, and sociology. No problem facing human beings today can be addressed by solutions drawn from a single discipline.

and more positive social mobility for those who have the least access to goods and services in this economy. Following the LEARN approach, we move now to consider the needs of our two areas. To survey need, in our view, is not to highlight deficit. On the contrary, we see tremendous possibilities in the people of Philadelphia and Arkansas, and we undertake all our projects with possibility as the guiding star. But we would be remiss in ignoring the statistics so many educators, foundation officers, and politicians focus on as representative of literacy in a given place. We hope to take the rest of the book to move beyond any emphasis on need toward a committed exploration of promise and potential in our home regions.

Literacy Needs in Philadelphia   Eli

Literacy learning, for better and worse, saturates the streets and institutions of Philadelphia. One of the oldest and poorest of American cities, its history underlines the importance of literacy as a habit of the wealthy, a hope for the disenfranchised, and an arena for debates that shape civic life. Here Benjamin Franklin's printing press operated only blocks from the slave auctions at First and High (now Market) Streets. Here Franklin published the antislavery arguments of the self-proclaimed "illiterate" and public provocateur Benjamin Lay (Rediker 2017). Here Franklin established the first lending library in North American and one of the first American universities while also advocating for English-only education to weaken the influence of German immigrants. Here W. E. B. Du Bois wrote his groundbreaking study *The Philadelphia Negro*, tracking the social history of an enslaved people transforming themselves into free citizens within the constraints and affordances of their city. Here immigrants from Italy, Ireland, Eastern Europe, and Russia as well as Puerto Rico, India, Ethiopia, Somalia, Ecuador, and Mexico have gone to school and worked in factories and service industries, built battleships in war and manufactured lace in peace, learned American by listening to baseball on radio and later watching basketball and hockey and football on TV. Immigrants and poor people sought their rights here through public interest lawyers and nonprofit support groups. It's hardly a paradise of literacy education—our public schools today are notoriously underfunded and underperforming—but reading and writing, public speaking and civic debate through a variety of media have always mattered in Philadelphia.

In North Philadelphia—the corner of the world where I work—*education* takes on an ironic, tragic, or mocking connotation, even as it holds promise for many. This area contains some of the poorest zip codes and the most dysfunctional public schools in the city, but North Philly is also home to Temple University, a major research university, as well as churches, hospitals and clinics, nonprofit organizations, and a historically significant museum. Since the late 1950s, African American and eventually Latino communities have come to make up most of North Philadelphia residential areas. The median income of households in North Central Philadelphia (two zip codes, 19121 and 19132, immediately west and north of Temple) is $18,845, and about 4 percent of North Central Philadelphia's residents hold a bachelor's degree or higher ("North Central Neighborhood" n.d.). For a number of reasons, in recent years there has been significant movement in these neighborhoods. Although overall the city's African American population rose 3.3 percent between 1990–2010, African American residents are leaving North Philadelphia and other traditional neighborhoods for other, less gentrifying areas further northeast of downtown. Similarly, by 2010 every zip code in the city had seen a rise in Hispanic residents except the two areas in the traditional heart of Puerto Rican North Philadelphia, where housing and business development is focusing on wealthier and whiter populations ("A City Transformed"). These economic and demographic shifts make educational access and service improvement a continual challenge.

Temple University, located in the 19122 zip code bordering the long and wide boulevard called Broad Street, is a school of about thirty-eight thousand undergraduate and graduate students. The university completed a new science research center in 2014 and a high-tech library in 2019, among the school's other major construction projects. The board of trustees proposed a new football stadium on its forty-acre campus in North Philly, 1.9 miles from city hall. The neighborhood and the faculty oppose this plan, but the stadium idea represents to some on either side of the controversy the manifest destiny of a university with little regard for its surroundings. Temple rightly claims to be much more diverse than most American colleges, but it is still a predominantly white institution. Twenty percent of students at Temple are non-Asian people of African American, Hispanic, or multiracial origin (Fall 2015 Student Profile). Students come from a wide range of economic backgrounds; tuition is modest compared to private colleges and a bit less expensive than the two other Pennsylvania schools partially subsidized by the state, University of Pittsburgh and Penn State. The average salary in 2016 for an assistant professor was about $66,000. The faculty as a whole is 70 percent white and approximately 9 percent non-Asian people of color. Obviously, the concentration of advanced degrees on the Temple campus is orders of magnitude greater than in the housing project bordering the College of Liberal Arts. The huge nonprofit corporation in the midst of North Philly is a highly tuned mechanism for moving people through programs toward degree completion and employment in the city and beyond. The target population, however, does not necessarily include the people who come from the North Central Philadelphia neighborhood.

The contrast is stark indeed between a predominately white, resource-rich university and the economically marginalized black and brown neighborhoods around it. Temple thrives (at least in relative terms) only blocks from abandoned buildings, housing units going up or coming down, drug deals and gun battles, break-ins and muggings. Many schools in the neighborhood operate without basic supplies, adequate staffing, or watertight roofs. A research university, on the other hand, supports and enhances the movement of ideas, people, and funds; within its campuses and by virtue of its networks, most of the current definitions of mobility related to information, social class, and capital can unfold. And yet, meters away from the campus police call boxes and high-intensity lighting of the university, literacy-related mobility manifests itself more through the school-to-prison pipeline or the flow of paychecks from check cashing shop to corner store.

Imagine social and economic movement in North Philadelphia viewed from a space station, with populations color-coded by age, race, gender, and access to revenue circulating from school to college and jobs or from schools to street corners to prisons and cemeteries. Picture young adults arriving on Broad Street from outlying suburbs and farm communities and cities all over the world or shifting from one block to another and from one low-wage job to another. If we could see all this as a kind of grand dance—encompassing flow and interruption, continuity and abrupt stops—the larger public might understand more viscerally how literacy enforces and creates the physical manifestations of inequality. At the same time, *mobilizing* has another pertinent meaning: agents for literacy sponsorship can mobilize into learning networks that change the dance as it's currently choreographed and lead to new, more equitable and productive ways for all people gathered in North Philadelphia and elsewhere to mingle and flow (see Goldblatt 2020).

Temple, of course, is not the only postsecondary school in Philadelphia nor even the only research university. Beyond University of Pennsylvania and Drexel, the city offers an array of two- and four-year institutions of higher learning. Among the more than eighty postsecondary schools in the region, many have significant commitments to the neighborhoods around them. For example, Philadelphia Higher Education Network for Neighborhood Development, a consortium of more than thirty colleges and universities in the region, supports member schools in cooperative efforts "to revitalize local communities and schools and foster civic responsibility among the region's colleges and universities" ("Our Mission" n.d.), but the gap between worlds remains vast.

A statistical overview of literacy needs in the city won't be satisfying but may be an adequate starting point. According to the city's Office of Adult Education in 2019, an estimated 550,000 adults in Philadelphia—more than half the total population of adults between 18 and 65 in the city—"lack the educational tools, skills and credentials they need to fully enter into the workforce and strengthen the economy" ("FAQ" n.d. Office of Adult Education). According to the US Census for Philadelphia, approximately 82 percent of adults older than 25 in 2012–2016 had high school or more advanced credentials, with only 26 percent holding a BA or higher degree, but of course this statistic doesn't reflect what people in the city know and can do, particularly if we have questions about what a high school credential represents for literacy abilities. Philadelphia is divided by race and class but also by job-readiness and the ability to navigate systems that make life possible. The Center for Literacy, one of the city's largest adult literacy programs, puts the situation like this: "almost 40 percent of the adult population in Philadelphia struggles to fill out a job application, struggles to read doctors' instructions on their medicines and struggles to help with their children's homework" (CFL "The Problem").

These numbers say little about young people between sixteen and twenty-four in the city, especially those who are "disconnected"—neither working nor in school. According to a 2015 study by Measure of America, 13.8 percent of adults in the United States fall into this category; one in four black youth and one in five Hispanic youth were found to be disconnected under that organization's definition. Philadelphia fared somewhat better in this survey than some other metropolitan areas, coming in near the middle of ninety-eight ranked populated regions, but the city still recorded 14.3 percent of youth in the category, with black youth at 23.1 percent and Latinx youth at 22.6 percent of the total sixteen- to twenty-four-year-old population. Putting the most positive light on their efforts to address such stress among young people in the city, the Philadelphia Youth Network says in their its 2016–2017 annual report, *Blueprint for Success*: "We see the potential and talent in our young people and are committed to addressing the many barriers that impede their progress. When education and employment are well-coordinated and connected, young people have tools to build pathways out of poverty." The barriers are indeed real, but hope in the city is too.

I started to write this chapter about the schools in Philadelphia. Schools are where the kids are, where you can find shining examples of student achievement and teacher dedication as well as discriminatory practices and bad attitudes toward learning. I am fascinated by schools and have spent much time in them. And yet the Philadelphia school scene is such a patchwork of types and approaches—public, charter, Catholic, Friends, independent, alternative, and home—that they do not cohere as a civic story, seeming to have little commonality of purpose or overlapping conversation. The School District of Philadelphia (SDP) is the eighth largest district in the nation by population, even though Philly itself is the sixth-largest city in the United States. The differences between those two rankings may have to do with the striking number of private and parochial alternatives available to some Philadelphian families. Two main divisions within SDP are district schools and charter schools, distinct categories because of funding and regulations. According to SDP's 2015 "District Schools" chart, 218 schools—149 elementary, 16 middle, and 53 high schools—enroll a total of 134,538 children. Among these are 17 selective or magnet schools, such as venerable Central High School (founded in 1836) and Philadelphia High School for Girls (1848), or more recent schools, such as G. W. Carver High School for Engineering and Science (1979) and Science Leadership Academy (2006). The district uses terms such as *neighborhood*, *citywide*, *alternative*, *vocational*, *Renaissance*, and *virtual schools* to indicate particular orientations and demographics in the school.

The SDP "Charter School" chart from the same year indicates 83 charter schools that educate an additional 63,441 children in the city. Charter schools represent a range of approaches to discipline and pedagogy, curriculum and worldview, and their administrators are freer to fire and hire employees than principals in district schools. The charter schools were established by law in Philadelphia in 1997 as "independently operated public schools that are funded with federal, state and local tax dollars." They provide alternative education to families in schools run by boards of directors and administrators "free of many of the local and state requirements that apply to traditional public schools" ("Charter School Office"). Charter schools mostly are not unionized, and their teachers are generally paid less than other district teachers. All non-charter schools in the district employ teachers who are members of the Philadelphia Federation of Teachers union.

Much controversy centers around the way these two types of public schools have interacted, intersected, and clashed since charters were established in the city (Welk 2010). Supporters of charter schools say the district schools provide too little structure and too little support for students, and that charters offer more focused and directed instruction. Supporters of the district schools complain that charters are poorly supervised and managed, pay teachers lower salaries, and bleed away desperately needed public dollars from schools open to all students. Some reports suggest that students with learning disabilities and other issues tend to be suspended more in some charter schools (Windle 2016), though the disparities are difficult to tabulate. As one article attempting to compare the two systems notes in frustration: "Digging into what is really behind the bumper sticker sloganeering takes you down a rabbit hole lined with funhouse mirrors" (Shepelavy 2015). Shepelavy writes that on the one hand charters seem to do a better job educating low-income students in some studies, but on the other hand "every study shows that charter schools in general have fewer Special Ed students and fewer non-native speakers than District schools." Thus, a broad comparison is nearly impossible to make between the two. Suffice it to say that there are fierce partisans of schools on either side, but nearly two hundred thousand kids need a system that can work for all.

There are clearly well-run schools and poorly run schools in all categories. The collective results of public education in Philadelphia may be improving modestly. According to SDP's own public report in 2017, the district's overall four-year high school graduation rate, including alternative schools, improved over the previous year by 1 point to 67 percent, compared to a 2015–2016 Pennsylvania public school graduation rate of 86 percent according to the National Center for Education Statistics. However, the state Keystone achievement exam results, for their limited picture on literacy, indicate that Philadelphia still has a long way to go in overall school performance. In 2016–2017, only 47 percent of second graders were reading at grade level, and 43 percent of high school students were proficient or advanced in literature. Only 21 percent of high school test takers scored proficient or advanced on the Keystone Algebra I exam that year (School District of Philadelphia 2012).

The most egregious problems are probably caused by the overall lack of sustained and equitable funding from the state. According to Dale Mezzacappa, writing in 2015: "In 2012, Pennsylvania ranked 44th in the percentage share of education costs covered by the state. Its 36 percent contribution rate compares to a national average of 45 percent." The low percentage of state funding forces local districts to provide a large portion of school support, thus leaving poorer districts at a loss to make up the difference that wealthier districts can cover. This also exacerbates racial disparities in educational access, as Mezzacappa notes: "An analysis by the Center for American Progress found that on average black students in Pennsylvania receive 89 percent of the funding that white students receive, less than in any other state except Nebraska and New Hampshire; Hispanic students receive just 85 percent." Philadelphia schools face severe trials since the tax base of city residents is so much lower than in the surrounding suburbs; the per-pupil expenditures between city and suburban schools is nothing short of appalling. The funding situation may improve somewhat if the current Democratic governor in Pennsylvania wins a second term, but structural impediments will probably remain for a long time to come.

Literacy Needs in Arkansas   David

Viewed from the perspective of traditional testing, the literacy lay of the land in Arkansas can seem rocky and unpromising. According to the Arkansas Literacy Councils' data, almost 14 percent of adults aged sixteen and older lack basic literacy skills, presumably as measured by the National Assessment of Adult Literacy (Arkansas Literacy Councils 2017). Data from the US Census Bureau show that of the approximately 1.7 million adults twenty-five and older, just over 162,000, or 9.4 percent, have less than a ninth-grade education, and nearly 265,000, or 15.3 percent, have finished some level between ninth and twelfth grade but lack a high school diploma or its equivalent ("American Fact Finder" n.d.)

Test results from Arkansas schools are similarly discouraging. The state-mandated standardized test for reading, math, and science is the ACT Aspire exam, and in 2019 just 45 percent of students in grades three through ten who took that exam scored at the "ready" or "exceeding ready" level in reading ("Results of 2019 ACT Aspire Exams Released" 2019).

The problematic status of literacy in Arkansas resonates into a range of issues directly connected to the quality of life for its citizens. The *US News and World Report* ranks Arkansas in 45th place in its list of best states, followed only by New Mexico, West Virginia, Mississippi, Alabama, and Louisiana. In health care, an area that demands substantial critical reading on the part of consumers, Arkansas ranks 49th. In education, it ranks 42nd. In the economy, another field that calls for critical and careful reading abilities, it ranks 43rd. In infrastructure, it ranks 47th, in "opportunity" 32nd. In fiscal stability, it ranks 21st, but in crime and corrections, another category in which literacy is deeply imbricated (see the essay on "Performance" in chapter 9), it ranks 47th. In terms of "natural beauty," Arkansas ranks 19th ("Best States Ranking" 2019). I'll attest to that ranking. My new "home state" is stunningly beautiful.

Let me emphasize that phrase *home state*. Unlike Eli, who has lived in Philadelphia for more than thirty-five years, I'm a relative newcomer to Arkansas, having moved here in 2005. But now, with both of us retired, my wife and I are staying here, for many reasons, but among the most important is this: I have found in Arkansas a place where people from all walks of life enthusiastically rise to occasions that create and tap into learning networks, fostering and improving critical reading, effective writing, and bona-fide social action. In retrospect, I have come to realize how fortunate I was to land a position that was created specifically because someone in Arkansas acted to his deeply felt exigence about literacy.

I actually stumbled into community literacy work at my previous place of employment, DePaul University. A few years before I started working at DePaul, the university had revised its undergraduate curriculum so that students were required to do something in their junior year that counted as experiential education, and this curricular change was what motivated my "stumble." Every morning, I walked from the L station to my DePaul office on the same route, and I developed a hi-how-are-you relationship with a man in the neighborhood who sat on the local school council at Lane Technical High School, where his daughter attended. Knowing only that I was an English professor, he asked me one morning if I could do anything to help Lane Tech students learn to write more effectively. English teachers there had a daily load of more than 120 students, which meant that providing helpful feedback on their papers was a huge challenge. I took the bait. I organized an undergraduate class in which the students would spend two intensive weeks with me on campus, learning how to run one-on-one writing tutorials and lead four-person writing groups. Then we would go to Lane Tech—my students were required to find three hours a week in their schedules to do so—and set up what I called a "triage writing center." We would work with the Lane Tech students individually and in groups, giving them that extra set of eyes and extra dose of helpful feedback that their teachers were frankly too overwhelmed to provide. The project worked, and I recreated it once more at Lane Tech before extending it to another Chicago high school.

In the meantime, DePaul's experiential education requirement had gotten a boost from a local philanthropist, leading to the establishment of the Steans Center for Community-Based Service Learning, and of course I was immediately attracted to its mission. Local businesses, industries, not-for-profits, and government agencies came to Steans Center staff with projects they thought DePaul students might be able to help with, and the staff recruited and supported a faculty member willing to develop a class that would take up the project. The staff fielded an inquiry from a settlement house on the southwest side of the city, its leaders wondering whether a group of DePaul students could lead conversation groups with families whose first language was Spanish so that the families could help their children with their homework more effectively. I said yes, and we built what I still consider to be an innovative community literacy program: almost none of my DePaul students spoke any Spanish, so there was lots of co-teaching (the children in the families were mostly bilingual, while Mom, Dad, Tio, Tia, Abuelo, and Abuela were not) and abundant teaching-by-mime.

So after twenty years in the professoriate—working with rhetoric and composition, writing assessment, and writing program administration—I was digging my new corner of English studies, and I was finding out where the interesting action was in Chicago, a city (like Philadelphia) with abundant resources for folks who want to read, write, and solve problems in ways they never had before. I was learning about what we call earlier in this chapter the "agencies and urgencies" of literacy in the city.

Then in September 2004 I got a call from the University of Arkansas. They had a new endowed position called the Brown Chair in English Literacy—a faculty job in the English department for someone willing to "improve literacy in the state of Arkansas" in whatever way he or she defined the multivalent terms in that phrase. It was a tenured, full professor position with a $3 million permanent endowment. Half of the endowment came from the Brown Foundation, based in Houston but with deep family roots in southern Arkansas. The other half came from the Walton Family Charitable Gift to the University of Arkansas's capital campaign. The story I heard about the Brown Foundation's impetus to fund the chair went this way: One of the current generation of Browns, a wealthy and generous man who lived in Little Rock, owned a beer distributing company, and he had an employee, in his fifties, whom he wanted to promote. He told the employee that all he needed to do to secure the promotion was to get his chauffeur's driver's license. Sheepishly, he admitted to the company owner he could not read. The owner was surprised by that revelation—little did he know that according to the US Department of Education and the National Institute of Literacy, approximately 32 million adults in the United States can't read, and according to the Organization for Economic Cooperation and Development, 50 percent of US adults can't read a book written at an eighth-grade level (Strauss 2016). So he decided his funds would help endow a position that might do something that spoke to this state of affairs. The Brown Chair appointee would teach one course a semester and would have access to a substantial portion of the interest earned by the endowment to support his or her research, fund graduate students, and establish literacy-enrichment programs throughout the state in any way he or she saw fit. After a whirlwind of negotiations throughout the 2004–2005 academic year, I found myself the initial occupant of the Brown Chair. Yikes!

When I arrived to get down to business in August of 2005, I had been to Arkansas exactly three times in my life: once for an initial visit, once for the official campus visit, and once to buy a house. Unlike Chicago, where I had spent two decades getting to know who does what and how with literacy, Arkansas was completely terra nova, and I felt as though I needed to get on a fast-track learning curve. For starters, I put together a helpful kitchen cabinet of advisors: Marie Clinton Bruno, who was executive director of the Arkansas Literacy Councils (and, yes, her middle name is *that* Clinton family); Fitz Hill, then the president of Arkansas Baptist College, a small historically black college in Little Rock; and Patti Williford, an adult educator who had been instrumental in establishing a migrant workers' literacy center in Hope. These in-state insiders led me to a whole range of other literacy movers and shakers: Suzanne McCommon, the director of the Great River Educational Service Co-op in Helena, who was waging a noble battle to stabilize public education in the Arkansas Delta; Eugene Vent, then the superintendent of schools in Forrest City; Otto Loewer, the former dean of the University of Arkansas College of Engineering, who was building a community-development not-for-profit based in Wynne, a small city in the Delta near his hometown of Fair Oaks; Gibson "Sonny" Morris, a development officer and federal grant magnet working at Mid-South Community College in West Memphis; Gene McKissic, a lawyer in Pine Bluff, exactly my age, who in 1973–1974 had been the first African American student government president at the University of Arkansas; Janis Kearney, who had grown up as one of seventeen children of a sharecropper family in Jefferson County and who rose to become President Bill Clinton's scribe and diarist during his White House years.

Tapping into these folks' wisdom led me to take two important steps. First, I convened a town hall meeting of folks who worked with literacy—in all levels of education, plus in government, business, and industry—to help me assess the status of and discourse about literacy in the state, inviting Deborah Brandt as the keynote speaker and my sister, Judy Fox, who had built a successful career as an early literacy specialist in western Maryland, as a consultant. I knew I would have substantial resources, generated by the endowment that supported the Brown Chair, at my disposal, and I wanted to be a good steward of the funds. The document generated by that town hall guided my work for at least the first five years of the Brown Chair's initiatives. Second, as I describe in chapter 8, I got in my car and drove throughout the state regularly during my first year there, talking to folks in their home locales about their definitions and perceptions of literacy and their goals for improving it in the state.

As I grew into the Brown Chair and began to launch the initiatives described in later essays in this volume, I came to realize that anyone attempting to characterize literacy and assess literacy needs in Arkansas is going to bump up against an inescapable array of demographic, economic, and political factors, one of which I noted at the beginning of this section, namely that Arkansas ranks as the forty-eighth state in the percentage of adults older than twenty-five who have a college degree ("American Fact Finder" n.d.). Here I list four factors that are relevant in any consideration of how literacy is defined and acted upon in the state.

First, in terms of *educational attainment*, a 2011 study by the *Chronicle of Higher Education* showed that Arkansas had the fifth least formally educated legislature in the United States: 25 percent of its 135 legislators had no college experience at all. Just over 60 percent of the legislators had a college degree, but that put Arkansas in forty-sixth place in the ranking, ahead of New Mexico, Maine, Delaware, and New Hampshire. Nationwide, the college-degree rate among state legislators in 2011 was 75 percent (Smallwood and Richards 2011).

Second, in terms of *geography and economy*, Arkansas is (I'd argue) actually *five* regions: the central circle, which is dominated by Little Rock and the increasingly Republican state government; the Northwest Corner, anchored by the holy trinity (and job-creation power) of Tyson Foods, J. B. Hunt Intermodal Transportation, and Walmart, where the principal cities of Fayetteville, Springdale, Rogers, and Bentonville are growing rapidly and flourishing; the northern highlands, comprising mostly agricultural communities in the Ozark Mountains; the lumber belt, which stretches horizontally across the southern fifth of the state; and the Arkansas Delta, a seventeen-county region that hugs the Mississippi River on the state's eastern border and that used to be the economic breadbasket of the state but is now perennially struggling with a sagging economy accompanied by job and population losses.

When the public and media discourse turns to issues related to education and literacy, the focus usually centers on the Delta as the most problematic region. In six central counties in the region, according to Census Bureau data, the percentages of households where families live under the federal poverty level ($25,570 for a family of four in 2019) range from 23.9 to 33 percent—in other words, between a quarter and a third of the population lives in poverty. According to the Arkansas County Health Ranking and Roadmaps project, the percentage of residents older than sixteen in those counties who lack "basic prose literacy skills" range from 17.5 percent to 25.5 percent—in others words from nearly one-fifth to more than one-quarter ("2019 Report" 2019). As I have maintained elsewhere (Jolliffe et al. 2016), the economic prosperity of the Delta, once buoyed by the healthy agriculture of cotton, rice, soybeans, and milo, was vitiated in the middle to late twentieth century by a triple whammy: mechanization (it used to take one hundred people to run a farm; now it takes four), globalization (the cotton grown in the Delta used to be shipped directly to the textile mills in the Carolinas, but now the cotton has to compete with a similar crop grown in South America or Singapore, and there are few textile mills left in the United States), and, believe it or not, the interstate, which comes whizzing past the small towns in the Delta and pulls the local commerce from downtown areas "out to the highway," where it generally becomes commerce not owned by local folks and not dedicated to helping the local area flourish.

Third, according to state law enacted in 2004, any school district in which the total population of students in grades kindergarten through twelve slips under 350 for two consecutive years can be closed and its schools *consolidated* within another school district (Holley 2013). Anyone who has ever lived in small-town America knows how the schools—particularly the high school—serve as cultural and entertainment centers and how the closing of the schools could lead to psychic shock.

Fourth, the Arkansas Department of Education has been, at least since I moved here in 2005, inordinately attracted to *educational vendors selling "improve your students' literacy" packages*—packages that purport to foster the achievement of the much-vaunted AYP (Adequate Yearly Progress) in literacy. Early in my time in Arkansas, teachers were encouraged to receive Literacy Lab Smart Step training, a three-year regimen of preparation to teach phonological awareness, phonics, fluency, comprehension, and vocabulary. Next, Arkansas was an early adopter of the Common Core State Standards and user of one of the Common Core's preferred assessments, the Partnership for the Assessment of Readiness for College and Career text, developed by Pearson. When the Common Core came under fire from both the political right and the left, Arkansas developed its own set of standards, which look for all the world like the Common Core, and the state entered into an agreement with ACT to administer the ACT Aspire and the regular ACT examinations as their state tests. Now teachers are required to be trained for the Arkansas Reading Initiative for Student Excellence program, another initiative that focuses on teaching the "basics" and "building a culture of reading" throughout the state. Despite the cavalcade of initiatives and acronyms, these literacy-teaching programs uniformly strike me as well-meaning consecutive examples of decontextualized "basic skills" programs. In my career as a teacher in four states—West Virginia, Texas, Illinois, and Arkansas—I have yet to witness a professional development project that succeeds at leading students to take up authentic, genuine inquiries to read deeply and critically, write forcefully, and engage in literate conversations in learning networks.

In Arkansas not only do all of these factors influence how literacy is defined, operationalized, and supported, but most of them are accompanied by an aura of deep anxiety, if not panic. Leaders realize that in an economy in which the best jobs require at least some college, the low percentage of college-educated adults is bound to discourage the location of new businesses and industries in the state. In both 2003 and 2007, Toyota opted not to build new plants in Arkansas. Most commentators saw these decisions as motivated by the quality of the available workforce in Arkansas (DeMillo 2017).

In the three parts of the state that rely primarily on agriculture to drive the economy—the northern highlands, the lumber belt, and the Delta—there are three especially anxious concerns:

- The three forces of mechanization, globalization, and interstate highway commerce have diminished the dominance of American agriculture, hitting these regions particularly hard;
- the resulting population drain from these regions has left behind a workforce, both actual and potential, ill-equipped to meet the demands of a new economy; and
- the diminishing population will mean that schools in these regions not only might be unable to offer high-quality courses and teaching but also ultimately might have to close altogether.

Finally, without casting aspersions too liberally, let me posit that the Arkansas legislature, which might be less thoughtful and perceptive about education policy than other states' governing bodies, has generally seen the solutions to these worries as calling for more regulation of curriculums, more reliance on standardized test results to guide decisions about funding priorities, and more attraction to curricular packages, rather than teachers' own initiative, to help students achieve AYP.

So in Arkansas, more than any other state in which I've lived as an adult, literacy is what Michel Foucault (1972) calls a "discursive formation": a concept that draws together a range of disparate elements and unites them under a label, a word or phrase, that gains currency by how it is used in the discourse of a particular group or groups. Sitting at the center of this discursive formation in Arkansas is the notion of literacy as good old-fashioned readin' and writin'—decoding texts accurately and encoding texts clearly and correctly—and at its periphery are elements and concepts of government, media, and economics that impinge on the central definition.

I would certainly never wish to diminish the importance of plain and simple decoding and encoding when assessing literacy resources and needs in my new home state, but I do want to point out the limited scope of this formation. What seems missing in this worried-filled conceptualization of literacy are two related elements: a sense of literacy as *doing* that we described in earlier in this chapter as "an ongoing process of inquiry, advocacy, and collective identity"; and a sense of *exigency*—a notion of how being a responsible citizen, being an Arkansan, motivates people young and old to immerse themselves in meaningful reading and writing projects of their own choosing, projects that will help them to recognize clearly the roles that their own reading and writing play in the active construction of knowledge and that will help them grow, personally, artistically, professionally, and even spiritually. In short, what seems missing from the discursive formation called *literacy* in Arkansas is the sense that it is an ability, a practice, a habit of mind that *people other than professional educators and government officials care about*—that it is, in our words from earlier in this chapter, "the ability to engage in a conversation carried on, framed by, or enriched through written symbols."

Later in this book, I assay a range of projects developed under the aegis of the Brown Chair in English Literacy between 2005 and 2018. I should note from the outset that one of these projects, the Arkansas Delta Oral History Project, was school based. It was not, however, part of a teacher's regular curriculum; instead, it was presented as a set of optional projects that students were encouraged to complete if they chose to do so.

Let me admit that a strong sense of personal preference led me to initiate these projects. Having grown up in a small town in West Virginia and having a wonderful older sister who has devoted most of her professional life to providing mental health care in rural corners of that state, I was immediately attracted by the prospect of partnering with ARCare on the community literacy advocacy projects described in chapter 8, "Health." Having taken my first high school teaching job in 1976 and working diligently that year on a countywide oral history project involving ninth graders, I had seen firsthand how planning and completing an oral history like the Arkansas Delta Oral History Project instills a sense of the exigency, the inherent importance, of literacy among young people. Having been an enthusiastic actor and director in professional, academic, and community theaters from my teenage years onward, I had experienced the power of drama, of live theater akin to the projects described in chapter 9 to forge and tell stories that might otherwise go untold.

As Eli and I discussed the conceptualization of literacy and literacy needs that ideally unifies all the essays in this book, I realized that the Brown Chair projects clearly manifest the three characteristics that flesh out our definition of literacy. First, live and unfolding meanings emerge from a web of relationships. In the Arkansas Delta Oral History Project, a group of high school students in Marianna unravel the ignored history of an African American boycott of both the schools and the towns' businesses in the wake of a poorly executed school desegregation in 1972, a protest they discover to their surprise that many of their grandparents had participated in. In the Latinx Youth Theatre Project in Springdale, a group of teenagers write and perform poetic compositions that interrogate what it means to be *from* a family, a town, a region. In each of these instances, the participants experience the wonderful generativity of reading and writing: the more you dig into a project that means something to you, the more you learn and the more you realize you need to learn.

Second, multiple conversations, characterized by specific purposes and contexts, generate specific literacies. In the Arkansas Delta Oral History Project, participants propose a topic, do background research, conduct an interview with a person who has an informed perspective on their topic, transcribe the interview—and then get *literacy carte blanche*! They produce a final product in whatever form or genre they prefer: traditional academic essay, spoken-word poetry, radio essay, one-act play, brochure, website, even an interpretive dance. In the Prison Story Project's *On the Row*, inmates on Arkansas's death row compose in various modes, including formal poetry, letters, and rap, to present their written excursions into the paths their lives have taken to end up with their facing the death penalty. In these instances, participants tacitly or explicitly address the questions, "What do I *need* to read and write? Who needs to read or hear what I've written? What will be the most effective way for me to meet my personal goals and my audience's needs and expectations?"

Finally, oral and interior utterances may be "literate" if they draw on knowledge or orientations associated with written texts. A student from Newport draws on the scholarship about alienation and deprivation in *The Tempest*, taught by her mentors, while she contributes to the devised theater piece, *The Tempest Tossed*, that she and her mates write and perform as part of the Team Shakespeare Project. A student from Crossett taps into the history and theology of African American Church of Christ congregations as she writes and performs her slam poetry about her home church and its checkered relationship with the all-white congregation that "sponsored" it.

But while the Brown Chair projects speak to my personal preferences and experience and while they generally represent the three features of literacy as conversation, the most vital reason for sponsoring them is that each of them offers participants a rich opportunity to engage in conversations "carried on, framed by, or enriched through written symbols," a chance to participate in real, exigent literacy experiences that ideally mean something to all involved: teachers, students, writers, readers.

Not Yet Ready to Knit the Whole Together

Better-qualified people than us have written about urban and rural schools, trying to intervene with varying success. What makes us most hopeful as researchers in community literacy are out-of-school programs for children and adults, small institutions that have no grades, standardized tests, or vice principals for discipline. For this reason, we highlight in succeeding chapters programs that stand after, outside, or apart from schools and colleges. The terms David and I have chosen—*conversation* and *learning networks*—can be intensified and maximized in small nonprofit programs rooted in neighborhoods. They may not reach as many people as city school systems or land grant universities, but smaller organizations or agencies have the potential to make enormous gains in individual lives with targeted programs and tactical outreach efforts. They also have the potential to address the particular needs of communities, attacking racial or ethnic oppression with positive cultural activities, book collections, speakers and artists and leaders who understand the distinctive talents and predicaments individuals from a specific group might face. Large-scale reforms can originate in networks of experimental and creative projects, promoting conversation among people in smaller numbers to overcome racism or sexism or discrimination based on other social stigmas through more intensive care.

We have chosen to leave a more detailed discussion of the comparisons and contrasts between our two regions until the last chapter. This is a book of stories and conversations, and we felt we each needed to lay out literacy projects in all their messy web-embedded nature before we tried to knit the whole together. As David said in chapter 1 and we echo in the conclusion, we chose these two sites not because they represent some facile contrast between country and city that we might dispassionately investigate. Rather, Philadelphia and Arkansas have simply been our respective homes for so long that we thought we could make some useful observations rooted in familiarity and love. The parallels and contrasts in our two places have been a consistent part of our conversation as friends and colleagues over the years, which is how we came to collaborate on a book.

Before we begin to sift through each environment, we do want to highlight one similarity that shapes and shadows all other characteristics. That similarity is segregation, due primarily to race and class. So much else flows from this perennial and heinous characteristic of American life: the poor—defined and despised because of their skin color, their accents, their ethnic associations or religious affiliations—are less likely to receive the benefits of education, civic standing, or other public goods that their wealthier fellow citizens take for granted. Race oppression in this country is dependent on the habit of othering, disqualifying some people as worthy of concern or recognition while a dominant portion is privileged to count as true Americans. Class, less well recognized but certainly as much a part of the complex mix of oppression in US history, amplifies discriminatory practices based on race. We saw that strikingly in the aftermath of Hurricane Maria, when the federal government responded inadequately to the disaster, and President Donald Trump denied the credible reports of nearly three thousand deaths in the 2017 storm (Klein and Vazquez 2018). In Philadelphia African Americans have lived under stressful and nearly invisible conditions since before the Revolution, as writers such as W. E. B. Du Bois, Ralph Ellison, Lorene Cary, John Edgar Wideman, and Elijah Anderson have duly noted. In Arkansas the KKK enforced "sundown town" rules where black folks couldn't be out after dark, and separate-but-hardly-equal higher education persists to this day. These are the present-day conditions and historical context for the learning environment in out two regions, affecting white, Hispanic, Asian, Pacific Islanders, Native, and African Americans of all ages and classes.

Despite this hateful legacy, we have witnessed over the last decades a persistent effort in our hometowns to construct hope for young and old residents, even in the poorest neighborhoods. This common commitment in our communities arises in response to segregation and injustice. People who have not gotten a fair deal in the past do not give up. Our experience shows that there are always allies within neighborhoods who are willing to show up for meetings, attend performances, participate in art projects, weed gardens, and reimagine their situation in a way that leads to positive change. We are acutely aware of discouraging statistics, environmental degradation, woefully underfunded schools, and persistent unemployment in Philadelphia and Arkansas, but we have chosen to highlight what people have done about the bad news around them, how they have drawn on the gifts they have or the gifts they intend to shape for themselves. This is the story we choose to tell.

Conversation on Attitudes

David: We're offering this conversation as a transition from the opening section of our book into the section of essays about our actual community literacy projects. I think we need to talk about positionality first—how our own identities have influenced our work.

Eli: That's a good start. What does it mean for two older white heterosexual men to be writing about literacy in multicultural and multiracial communities?

D: We've talked about this for years: We are who we are. We cannot change who we are. We can't change where we live. We don't really want to change our intention of working with communities that have been ignored and voiceless in discussions of literacy and to help them find a way to assert identity and voice. I try to make this clear when I meet potential community partners. I'm not just an older middle-aged white professor from the University of Arkansas coming to their community to do *my* projects. I'm coming into the community to get to know the people, establish a common base with them. One thing I've been able to count on is the fact that I grew up in a small town on a river in West Virginia. So when I go to the small town on a river in Augusta, I know how small towns on rivers work. Finding allies in the community means we're doing this work together. So I say to folks, "Let's use our pooled talents in ways that will really benefit the people we are working with." It's not like I'm constantly building a facade, but I'm genuinely going to people and saying, "Here's who I am and here's what *we* want to do. How can we do this together?"

E: I think I would put it, in my own life, a little differently. I grew up feeling more like an outsider. When I was in college, I started hitchhiking. This was in the very early seventies, during the Vietnam War protests, the counterculture years. One thing I learned from hitchhiking was that you should shut up and listen. People pick you up because they have stories they want to tell and they want to stay awake while they're driving. If you give them enough space, they will tell you all kinds of cool stories that you couldn't hear if you got in the car and started talking. So I've found that the first move in a community I don't know is to listen, find out what people are thinking and what people want to do. I'm just not that damn important compared to everybody else.

D: Right.

E: The way you draw on your experience in West Virginia, I draw on my experience growing up with a parent in the US Army, moving all the time and always having to learn a new place and a new set of people. I never felt like I could be the expert or the boss of things because I was too busy learning what was happening. I've tried to learn as much as I can about African American literature and history, traveled in Latin America and can converse in Spanish, but always with a sense that I need to learn more to work in African American and Latinx communities. I come to a new community—or even a community I've worked with a long time—with wonder and hope rather than a conviction that I know how get things done. Does that make sense?

D: Yeah, it sure does.

E: We'd better clarify for readers how we deal with our own privilege. I think that has changed for me over time. When I first started being a college professor, especially when I worked in places like prisons or communities that didn't have many resources, I didn't hide where I was from, but I tried not to make very much of my position. I think what I've come to realize—after being scolded a couple times about this—is that people want me to represent honestly. "Look, it's ok for you to have the position you have," they might say, "but you have a responsibility to use your privilege to help people the way they want to be helped." Hiding your degrees or even demeaning the university is just a different kind of dishonesty. So when I go to a neighborhood, I don't try to dress down the way I did when I first started teaching high school. I try to dress more or less the way I would if I were teaching a college class, out of respect for the people I'm meeting. I'm just trying not to be overbearing about who I am or what I represent.

D: I'm on the same page in a number of ways. I've been so fortunate to have someone like Joy Lynn Bowen to work with me on everything I did in Augusta from day one. I talk about Joy Lynn in the essay on "Health" (chapter 8). She not only knows everyone in the community and everyone knows her, but she knows who their mama and their daddy were. And so, she can say to people who know her very well: "Here is David Jolliffe from the University of Arkansas." Joy Lynn has been my entrée into these communities. But she makes it clear, as I do, that while I have this professorship, my dad sold insurance and my mother was a second-grade teacher. I'm just a kid from West Virginia. That's who I am, just like you're an army brat—it's a persona but it's who we are.

E: Right.

D: I think sometimes when people look at college professors they have in mind some multigenerational elitist from Harvard or Yale or something like that. We've got to help people understand who we are.

If we're working with high school kids or college kids, then the most important thing to stress is not what I want do but what do *they* want to do? I ask them, "Here's what we're going to sponsor but what do you want to do with this? And how are you going to build on this?" When Steve Boss, who leads the University of Arkansas sustainability program, and I went down to Brinkley High School to introduce the Students Involved in Sustaining Their Arkansas (SISTA) project there—I talk about SISTA in the concluding chapter of this book—I said to them, "We are here to help you become famous. You students are going to do these projects, and fifty years from now, someone's going to take a look back and say, 'Whose idea was this healthy eating clinic? Whose idea was this music school named after Louis Jordan?' And folks fifty years from now are not going to think about David Jolliffe. They're going to look back at these kids who were juniors and seniors in high school who can say, 'This was MY idea that got things started!'"

E: At the same time, we should state explicitly that you and I have also really benefited from writing about our work. We don't make any money from academic publishing, but we've been hired and promoted for what we do and write. We've published books and articles about organizing writing projects outside university campuses. That's just true, and I don't think either of us apologizes for it. In fact I guess we're both proud for helping to make it safe for younger scholars to do research and teaching in the area of community-based literacy. I think that's our point: certain conversations bring about positive action. Our job is to listen to what people want to do and try to play it back for them, encourage them to act on their own vision. And yeah, we've been very, very lucky to carve out a professional life. All we can do is make the best of it for other people.

D: Yeah, we've been lucky. But we've also been the people who've said yes to a lot of things.

E: Right. [chuckle] I've said yes a lot over the years, including to a few chores I wish I'd never said yes to. We both have. We've served on many committees and directed programs inside our universities as well, partly because we've felt the need to be citizens inside as well as outside, and partly because that's how we built academic constituencies for connections outside. I don't know that we deserve a medal for all those yeses, but I think there's no other way to do this kind of work. You've got to be willing—as I've seen you do—to go across the state and show up at a library to meet with a bunch of people who were thinking about a project and just say, "Okay, I can help you with this and this and this. Let me call this person." I spend a lot of my time, even now that I'm retired, meeting with former students or people in government and nonprofits, connecting people to other people. I think promoting networks is part of our responsibility for having had the privileges we've had in our own lives. That's why learning networks are such an important part of this book.

D: Absolutely—networking is crucial to what we've done. Before we move on, do we want to say a bit about how issues and attitudes involving race have figured in our work?

E: Yeah. In my case, class—in the form of military hierarchy—was always the big social frame in the army. You learn about class early because you learn about rank: insignias on uniforms not only indicate what soldiers earn but where they and their families live. Military kids grow up with the simultaneous and contradictory truths that everybody goes to the same stores and has the same access to base facilities (if you're a kid) even while people of different ranks obviously get different housing privileges. My father was a doctor at middle rank before he died, so we lived in modest officers' housing. I knew some black kids who were in enlisted housing and some in officers' housing. I played on racially diverse baseball teams when we were posted in Germany. I knew fewer Jews than African Americans growing up, and my parents were unofficially punished once for taking the side of a black family in a dispute at my sister's nursery school. In Georgia, the largest post we lived in, there were perhaps a dozen or so families and fewer than twenty GIs at the little makeshift synagogue we attended at Fort Benning. My mother had a master's degree in sociology and wrote her thesis on what they then called "race relations" in a small town outside Chicago, so my parents were quite liberal in their opinions during the civil rights movement of the early sixties. In fact, when we were stationed in Georgia in 1964–1965, they joined the NAACP, though they probably didn't make much of it to their neighbors. Social justice was always a central principle in my home and, even today in my extended family, progressive politics is an assumed, if somewhat unexamined, orientation.

D: Growing up in a small town in West Virginia, I had a very different experience from yours, Eli. Both my hometown and the schools I attended were 100 percent white. The closest thing we had to diversity was the Cuban man who lived twenty miles away and who drove the bread delivery truck. I can remember the first time I saw an African American person—in Wheeling, the "big city" that was an hour's drive from my hometown. My undergraduate college had a very small minority population, and when I taught high school in Wheeling, I had few African American students. It really wasn't until I moved to Chicago in 1984 that I lived in a truly diverse location. But, oh, what a glorious time for a young liberal, who had for years longed to have a local cause for racial equality to support, to live in Chicago. I was there when Harold Washington assembled the coalition that enabled him to become the first African American mayor of the city. I was there when the Latinx population coalesced into a bona-fide voting block and began to elect brown politicians. People who know me well know that I've always had a "fight for the underdog" mentality. The rise of equality in Chicago, rough and tumble as it often was, spoke to my heart. Now, after fourteen years in Arkansas, I find myself fighting for the same rights of recognition and treatment for black and brown populations as I witnessed in Chicago.

E: David, why don't we move to a new but related subject—the attitudes that we've carried into our work and how we've tried to proceed in the various projects we've pursued and supported. Or how do we think about organizing for literacy projects?

D: Let me come at this with three points to get started. First, I have found it very interesting that people around the state of Arkansas often cannot believe that I'm coming from the university and that I actually want to work with them. As far as I can tell, and I'm trying to say this as graciously as possible, I have not discovered much evidence of previous efforts by my university to get ourselves off "the hill" in northwest Arkansas and out into the state. When I grew up in West Virginia, at the little school I attended, which was eighty miles from the state university, we would have choral clinicians come from WVU and direct our choir for a long weekend. When I was in musicals in high school, we had a choreographer from the university come do choreography for us. As I was becoming editor of the school newspaper, I went to Morgantown to participate in a journalism camp. In short, there was a strong sense of the university going out into the state and the state coming into the university. That doesn't seem to be the case here in Arkansas. I think this may be so because we're primarily such an agricultural state and every county has an extension office affiliated with the College of Agriculture at the university. But that's primarily there to help the farmers grow more and better crops. So it can be a challenge to kindle the notion that I'm here from university, with university support, and I really want to work on real, active literacy-oriented projects within these small communities.

Second, on occasion I've encountered resistance from other universities in cities where I want to initiate a project. In one city that housed a smaller state university, I met some teachers who were eager to work with the Arkansas Delta Oral History Project. The university folks basically said to me, "Go away. That's our high school and you're not allowed to work there." I've tried to make friends with these people, but they clearly didn't want to have me anywhere near their territory. I've gotten the same kind of wariness from school boards and from city governments. City governments have rarely understood what I'm trying to do, and I've occasionally encountered relatively strong push back from city government. When I wanted to sponsor a student's project in the Arkansas Delta Oral History Project or later in SISTA—a project that required some interfacing with a government agency—I would get the red tape excuse, "Oh you can't do that because you're not going to follow the bureaucratic process." So those situations required, quite frankly, some politicking. We eventually succeeded in most cases, but I had to sell the projects as good for the communities.

But then third, what has superseded those two bits of pushback is just the genuine enthusiasm I find in communities when I have gone and said, "I hear what you'd like to do. Here's a vehicle we might use to accomplish your goals. We'd like to work with the community on this. Join in." I talk a lot about Augusta in the essay called "Health," but another place I fell in love with was McGehee, Arkansas. McGehee was the hometown of my right-hand person at the university, Anne Raines, so she served as my entrée in that town. McGehee was part of the Arkansas Delta Oral History Project from the beginning. The high school students there caught the oral history bug and on their own conducted a series of interviews with Billy Siemens, a ninety-four-year-old photographer who had been taking beautiful pictures of the Delta for six decades. We published a little book about his work, with his photos and interview transcripts and essays by the students. When we first started working in McGehee, the townspeople were so enthusiastic to get the community and the high school involved together that they had a little tea party for us in the town. They rented out the town museum and served refreshments. They brought people in and said, "Come meet this guy from the University of Arkansas.

Come meet these kids from McGehee High School who are going to be working with him."

So the pushback was there, but what superseded it was finding really enthusiastic communities that said, "We realized that this is something that was going to make life richer and better in our community."

E: There's certainly always a lot of pushback from people—in the university or in government or other institutional settings—who just want to do things the way they've always done them. They don't really want to try anything new because they're more comfortable in control of what's currently going on. Like you, I've been asked to leave school buildings, presumably because I was bringing in ideas the principal couldn't control. I've had executive directors refuse to speak with me because I was working with other organizations they saw as enemies. Whether a project is valuable or not may not matter to people who want to be in charge.

When I meet with a group, I'm not looking for what's wrong. I'm looking for what's right. What do they have going for them? What are their strengths? What are their enthusiasms? I think you and I share this attitude of supporting good ideas and supporting hope. I start by searching for the virtues not only of the community but of individual people, the way you appreciated Joy Lynn from the beginning, the way you connected with the people she knew.

My principle in working with schools or neighborhood centers is always to do projects with people I like. Now, maybe that's the wrong way to put it, but in my experience the people I like are usually trying to do something for more than themselves. That's what I like about them. And so it's not that I like them because they like me—at first sometimes they do and sometimes they don't—but they have something they're trying to accomplish. And what they're trying to accomplish is not just their own self-aggrandizement, you know? I think that the virtue I most appreciate is generosity—of spirit, of conception—and a willingness to appreciate other people. When you find leaders like that, they can make a lot of good things happen.

D: For sure. I think of the inclusiveness of the populations I've worked with. A case in point is the home literacy workshops we offered in Augusta. We thought we'd offer them primarily for young parents and caregivers. We did have some very young parents show up, and we thought they were going to be our primary clientele. But grandparents showed up. Sunday school teachers showed up, and so did people from down the street whose kids were grown and gone but who knew the kids in the neighborhood. There was one young woman who was on the custodial staff at the ARCare health clinic, and her kids were all grown and gone and she didn't have any childcare responsibilities at all, but she said, "I just want to learn from what you're doing."

One thing that the Delta may have in common with North Philly is that statewide an awful lot of people have written off these poorer communities. Their schools are not really great, the population is dwindling, and the economy has soured. People might say, "Well, let's move to other parts of the state that are more prosperous." But people in these communities are starved for opportunities to learn, to act, to grow, just like anywhere else. The work speaks to them so strongly that you just have to say, "Yes, this is for everybody—come on in!"

E: Right, right. I think it's worth saying directly that more often than not the communities being written off are black or Hispanic or hail from other countries. Maybe it's old-fashioned to say this, but I don't think either one of us can stand to see communities being written off. We both think it's flat-out wrong. It misses the richness that's hidden by a bad reputation about a neighborhood, a school, even a region.

D: I'm thinking about a "come-to-Jesus" meeting that Joy Lynn and I had with the kids at Augusta—I talk about this meeting in the essay called "Health." This was the year that forty-eight students graduated from the high school, but only twenty-two took the ACT, and only five went to college. We brought them into the school library and shut the doors and said, "Okay guys, let's talk about this." They said, "Oh, you know, we're from a small town, we're kinda dumb. We'd get lost in college. We're not as good as kids from the big city." So that attitude they had learned from the town became a self-fulfilling prophecy. I challenged the kids to take issue with this attitude. I'd tell them, only slightly tongue-in-cheek, that there are a lot of people in Arkansas who wish the Delta would just shrivel up, fall into the Mississippi River, and float away. "The state would be better off without them," these folks would say. But I'd say to the students, "This is where you're from, where your parents and grandparents are from! These were vibrant, rich towns once upon a time. We may not be able to bring new industries back in, we may not be able to build new schools, but we can invigorate the spirit of living here."

E: At a moment in American history—and maybe there have been a lot of moments like this—when the public discourse can be so poisonous and so dismissive of people of color, of people without money, that things sometimes get turned on their head. Politicians address white people without much money: "You see you've been neglected because of these other people. You need to rise up against them." That to me is criminal, driving division between people who really should be natural allies. I think outrage is one thing that has always drawn us together, you and me.

D: There's a politics of division going on right now, orchestrated by the current occupant of 1600 Pennsylvania Avenue. As my friend Gary Kappel says, "What Trump is doing is merely the latest rash in the underlying disease that's been in American history a long time." The idea of sharing resources, accepting that we're all in this together, is periodically a very foreign idea in US history and it certainly is right now.

E: Let's end this conversation by considering what's coming in the next chapters. In the rest of the book, we try to apply the attitudes we've talked about in particular situations and tell stories about how people gained power and a sense of what they want to do by coming together around projects and pursuing action nurtured through learning networks of literacy sponsorship.

D: I'll start. I think what I'm discovering is how much, over the past fourteen years, I've been surprised by what I've learned. This feeling of surprise, I hope, is coming through in both of my essays, one on "Health" and the other on "Performance." I might have started out to write an essay about the connection between health and literacy in Arkansas, but that's not what the chapter is really about. The chapter ends up being about these questions: What do we mean by the health of a community? How do these projects help people understand that the health of a community is more than just its physical health? It's also personal, professional, spiritual, emotional health. Health is something to make life less stressful here, more productive. I've experienced genuine surprise as I write about health.

E: Right.

D: Then there's a real surprise to me as I write about performance because my experience with performance has always been scripted, planned performance. In all three of the performance experiences I write about, there emerges a serendipity of unusual performance. There's the curtain-raiser that the Team Shakespeare kids did in *The Tempest Tossed*, which I talk about in "Performance." There's also serendipity of the LatinX Theatre Project and its devised theater productions. There's the major surprise of finding outstanding, deeply soulful writers on death row in Arkansas.

Here's what I've learned: once you give people the opportunity to craft a vision of the world through their work with dramatic performance, it becomes something very different from what a traditional view of performance is all about.

E: That's great. What I found in writing my chapters is that I chose projects I thought would be fun to do. The greatest privilege in my job over the last thirty to thirty-five years has been choosing projects that were profoundly, seriously fun. One good example is in the "Community Arts" chapter, talking ideas with my friend Grimaldi Baez. When Grimaldi and I get together, we talk for long stretches—once for six hours straight.

D: Wow.

E: We just have a lot to say to each other. What does "community arts" mean in places where people need livable housing and meaningful employment? How do you make art after Hurricane Maria? What does "art thinking" add to the quality of a life? Grimaldi grew up in a Puerto Rican neighborhood of Boston. He could relate to working in an African American neighborhood in Philadelphia.

On almost every project I've done—even when it was really hard and I didn't know where to turn next—what kept me going was a sense of joy at working with people who were just outstanding human beings.

D: Yeah, I like that. We've got these three themes for the work we do: outrage, surprise, and joy. I hope this encourages people to read on in the book.

PART II

Learning Networks in Philadelphia

5 Out-of-School Literacy Centers

Philadelphia is blessed with a burgeoning class of nonprofit and non-school organizations aimed at promoting and enhancing literacy learning. In this chapter I survey the range of nonprofits directly concerned with enhancing literacy among underserved populations from school age to adult. I would not argue that this array of agencies is a learning network as we've defined it earlier, but informal links and alliances occur enough that I have hopes a more organized network could form and function. At the end of this chapter I return to the idea of a learning network formed from organizations that explicitly name literacy as an element of their mission. I don't think anyone in an out-of-school-time agency or group wants to see grand overarching bureaucracy for literacy in the city, but greater cooperation and connection would have significant advantages for organizations, large and small.

I start this chapter with an account of Tree House Books, a small nonprofit that I have worked with intimately from 2005 until the present 2019. Tree House is not necessarily a model for informal literacy learning or even the most effective out-of-school program in the city, but its history and struggles to survive do represent the challenges nonprofit centers face if they devote their mission to literacy education in an urban setting.

Tree House Books

I have written elsewhere about Tree House Books, a small nonprofit literacy center located a few blocks from the Temple campus in North Central Philadelphia (Luetzow et al. 2014; Goldblatt 2007). As I write this in the summer of 2019, Tree House has been serving about 25–30 children from ages 6 to 13 in after-school activities during the school year steadily for fourteen years. The program also involves anywhere between 8 and 15 college students in various volunteer positions over the course of any one year. In the summer, Tree House offers a camp that goes from morning to afternoon for six to eight weeks, depending on funding and staff availability. Since its founding in 2005, the operation has gone from a single executive director tending a long, narrow one-room used bookstore into a two-storefront facility for after-school activities run by a paid staff of four and four to eight volunteers each day. The bookstore idea remains, but now all books can be given away or returned (donations gladly accepted). The majority of books the organization offers are written for children and categorized by reading level and subject. THB also features a large African American collection, but on the shelves you can still find the odd Aeschylus play or a copy of *Middlemarch* or a book about conspiracies to kill JFK. With all the books Tree House gives away (seventy-one thousand in 2018–2019), the staff still recognizes that a book by itself is no magic talisman to change lives. As the website proclaims: "Having books available is just the beginning! We also promote a life with books through our Literacy Programming." The history of the organization bears out this commitment to a socially engaged literacy alongside access to books.

In 2003 a community development council sponsored by North Central Philadelphia's Church of the Advocate did an economic study of the two blocks of Susquehanna Avenue west of Broad Street, a corridor that once had been a thriving business district but at that moment looked vacant and forbidding even on a bright spring afternoon. The report suggested various possible small businesses, such as a hair salon and a discount dry goods store—both of which opened and have done well—but the authors also suggested a used bookstore. A local developer named Jon Weiss was looking at a property on that stretch of Susquehanna, and he was taken with the idea of selling books on the street that neighbors still refer to as The Ave, in reference to the avenue's once thriving business district. The building he bought had a storefront at the street level and apartments upstairs. It was a wreck inside; the roof leaked so profusely that an ailanthus tree had taken root in the first-floor store area. Jon asked his crew, after renovating the upper floors, to fit out the storefront with bookshelves on both long walls and install a counter area for a cash register midway down the eastern side. The lead author of the report, a white woman named Joanne Jackson, decided she'd had enough planning for other people and asked Jon if she could run the bookstore. He agreed, and they settled on the name Tree House Books, in homage to the uprooted ailanthus and the loft his crew had built for kids above an alcove of books.

Soon after Joanne opened Tree House for business in spring 2005, one of my students walked by the store, which is about five blocks from my office across the campus. My student came back and told me I had to see this new addition to the neighborhood. So I walked over one afternoon and met Joanne. We talked about potential readings and activities for neighbors in the shop, and she suggested I speak to Jon about his vision for Tree House. Joanne wanted the store to remain a business and felt she could make enough money selling books to pay herself and cover rent and utilities; Jon wanted THB to become a nonprofit promoting literacy in the neighborhood. She had her doubts about that direction, but he was forming a board and would need members. Meanwhile, I returned to my department and asked the director of creative writing if one student with a graduate assistantship could devote half her or his teaching time to Tree House, and the director agreed. I put out a call to the grads with assistantships, and an African American fiction writer named Mecca Jamillah Sullivan volunteered. She had grown up in Harlem and had done a little work with kids in the past; she was extremely interested in contributing to the lives of people in North Philadelphia. Mecca started in the fall semester of 2005 and met with kids regularly at THB until she graduated in spring 2006.

Jon and I got along immediately, and he asked me to join him in creating the organization. At the time, I was involved with another nonprofit literacy program in the Latino section of North Philadelphia about fifteen blocks from Temple's main campus, but my little institute, New City Writing, had nothing significant happening at the time in the African American neighborhood immediately bordering Temple. I decided I'd like to take a chance and work with another nonprofit in North Philly, and so I agreed to join the board, which didn't meet officially until December 2005.

Tree House opened without a defined mission to provide programming to the community, but that changed quickly with Mecca working there every week. Joanne was committed to the well-being of the neighborhood, but she wasn't a teacher or a particularly extroverted person. She didn't dislike children, but she didn't quite know what to do with the kids who started to troop into her shop after school. They wanted to read the books and ask a lot of questions. Mecca was ready to work with them, and she brought enthusiasm for writing into her interactions with the kids. According to a report she wrote at the end of the 2005–2006 school year (Sullivan 2006), she and some volunteers developed and taught two workshops called the Young Writers Program that year. The fall 2005 workshop was offered three days a week for four weeks, with the following units:

- *Week 1—My Life:* Writing exercises prompted students to write about and discuss their families, their favorite sports and activities, and their likes and dislikes.
- *Week 2—Making the News*: Writing exercises prompted students to serve as reporters on their communities and write down what they would like to see on the daily news and in the newspaper.
- *Week 3—If I Ruled the World*: Writing exercises prompted students to describe what changes they would make (both practical and imaginative) if they were in charge of things.
- *Week 3—Wrap up:* Revising and assembling handmade books and preparation for final reading.

Mecca involved her friend, another African American fiction student named Natacha Leonard, and also recruited a Temple graduate art education student named Martina Arnal to work with the kids on drawings and Styrofoam printmaking to accompany their poems and stories. They had planned to recruit a dozen fifth graders for the workshop, but they ended up with fewer fifth graders and more younger siblings and school friends. Mecca noted in her report, for example, that one of the outstanding participants was a second grader whose confidence grew throughout the year, as well as a third grader who was one of the most "original" and "prolific" contributors.

In addition to encouraging writing, Mecca and her colleagues also read the children poems by Langston Hughes and stories by Jamaica Kincaid. The workshop featured prints by African American artist Elizabeth Catlett. In short, their philosophy was to involve reading, writing, speaking, and listening as well as art making and viewing, with an emphasis on African American creators. They wanted the children of North Philadelphia to see that authors and artists who looked like them had produced world-defining work and been recognized for their accomplishments, but they also wanted the children to see themselves as producers in their own world. Mecca and I talked extensively about projects supported by the New York–based organization Teachers and Writers Collaborative, the group that developed the Poets in the Schools approach based on Kenneth Koch's famous 1970 book about teaching poetry to children, *Wishes, Lies, and Dreams*. The final reading that first semester brought in dozens of children and their parents as well as the friends of Mecca and her colleagues. The Temple student newspaper covered the event, and four of the poems the kids wrote were printed on bookmarks and inserted into the Temple Creative Writing Program's annual publication *In/Vision*.

In the spring the workshop focused on a single exercise borrowed from *Don't Forget to Write*, a 2005 book published by 826 Valencia, a well-known children's literacy program that had started in 2002 at a storefront in San Francisco's Mission District. The exercise was called "King or Queen of My Own Country," and kids drew national maps and flags, made up national poems or songs, described founding myths or discoveries, and otherwise characterized their own countries. They gave their fantasy-land names like Royala, Pink and Red Land, Zevonia, and Kaylearian. Five of the ten regular participants that spring prepared a poster presentation and gave a talk about their creations. One of the most impressive was a fluid reading from a kid who had come to Tree House earlier that year claiming she could not read at all. This time Mecca was accompanied by a white creative writing grad student named Darcy Sebright (later Luetzow and now Staddon) and white grad art education student Rachel Shaffaran. Creative and ambitious projects that engaged the whole child within an African American context became the expected norm at Tree House.

A number of the persistent challenges for the organization emerged that year as well. Financial stability was a problem from the outset. Even though all the staff in the after-school program were volunteers, lack of money meant every board meeting was about how to increase revenue. The founding board was composed of seven members, four of whom were black (including two who had been Black Panthers in the sixties). Two members lived in the neighborhood, a third was principal of a neighborhood school, and a fourth was a public librarian. This gave us some strength in the neighborhood but didn't promise a large donor pool. With the exception of Jon Weiss, the board chair, none of us were businesspeople with contacts in the financial world. Thus, the board wasn't in the position to raise much money through personal donations or colleagues with disposable wealth. My little institute, New City Writing, had a small endowment that contributed about $550 for supplies that year. Admittedly, this budget far exceeded the zero dollars available to the art teacher at Duckrey Elementary School around the corner, but THB couldn't yet publish or exhibit student work effectively, especially since some of the meager budget went to fees for volunteers' state clearance and background checks.

Recruiting children in time to fill the program became a double-edged sword: too few kids meant the workshop couldn't get started on time, but too many might overwhelm the staff. Behavior issues sometime disrupted activities on any given day, and the young staff wasn't trained to handle elementary school children. However, the most difficult challenge to the organization was the growing tension between the new board, intent on forming a nonprofit organization, and Executive Director Joanne, who resisted applying for the nonprofit 501(c)(3) status and saw no reason to apply for grants. THB sold few books in the first year, and it was clear we were not going to balance the budget on book sales. The tension finally became too much in the late summer of 2006, and Joanne was asked to resign that September.

By the time Joanne was preparing to go, Mecca had left for a PhD program and Natacha had taken the part-time assistantship at Tree House. Darcy, who had graduated with Mecca in the spring, was still actively involved with Tree House and had no full-time job. Jon and another founding board member, Walter Jordan Davis—who worked at Temple with five local schools the university was managing at the time—and I served as the committee to handle the transition. We thought Darcy was committed enough to work with the kids, imaginative enough to develop new programming, and energetic enough to learn what it took to take over as director, at least in the short run. Joanne herself agreed, and she wrote a gracious letter supporting Darcy's appointment. However, she pointed out two crucial aspects of the job that Darcy was going to have to grow into. The first was managing finances. For Joanne, this meant keeping the accounts as well as developing an online presence to sell books, but board members all knew that fundraising was the real challenge for the future director. The second was community relations, and Joanne was so eloquent on this point that I quote a full paragraph from her email:

> Even more important is the need to introduce Darcy to the community and to gain community support for her new role. We are all indebted to Barbara [a founding board member and an activist in the neighborhood] for helping the store gain acceptance and support at a neighborhood level during the past year. Because Barbara is recognized as a longtime community resident, her presence at the store has given us all a level of credibility and respect that would not have been forthcoming for a store operated by outsiders, no matter how well-intended. In light of my past experience with Advocate Community Development Corporation, I have a (much lower) degree of recognition among community members as well. Darcy can also gain acceptance and recognition in the community; but no one should assume that community support will be granted automatically in a neighborhood with a history of mistrust of Temple University. (September 2006)

Taking Joanne's advice into consideration, along with the recognition that Darcy was young and inexperienced, we asked Darcy if she was willing to try anyway, and once she agreed, the full board approved her appointment.

Darcy went on to lead Tree House for the next six years, only stepping down to take a new job in the late summer of 2012. I will not trace the many highs and lows of a nonprofit on the edge, but suffice it to say that we celebrated when grants came in and cried, literally cried, at times when it looked like we would not be able to pay the director or open the doors the next year. Somehow the organization survived. At one point, a professor couple in the Temple College of Education, Wanda Brooks and Will Jordan, facilitated a big gift to Tree House from their church philanthropy, and this check alone saved the organization for more than a year. I was able to pay a user fee from my endowment each year to defray the cost of training and supervising so many Temple undergraduates each semester. The program remained loosely defined and improvisatory at times, leaning sometimes toward the arts, music, and performance and sometimes toward homework help and childcare, but it was led by Darcy's philosophy that love and personal attention would sustain the children and nourish the staff. In the essay Darcy and I wrote with staff member Lauren Macaluso (now Macaluso Popp), Darcy put her core belief this way: "Tree House has strong programs, but the programs would disappear tomorrow if the relationships stopped. We could have purposeful programs all day long every day, but without building trust and relationships, the kids still would not stay. And the other side of the reality is this: If we didn't have the relationships, the adult volunteers would not stay, either" (Luetzow 2014, 31–32). Although I found the program a little light on pedagogical principles and hazy about literacy development, elementary school students continued to produce surprising works and college student tutors continued to come back to me transformed by the experience at Tree House. We had precious little measurement of improvement beyond impressions and the writing published in *The Ave*, an occasional magazine Tree House produced. But Darcy's grant writing improved with help from board members and friends, and funders continued to give us small grants of a few thousand dollars and some larger multiyear grants of twenty to forty thousand dollars.

One of the greatest gifts that Darcy gave Tree House was three young people she recruited and encouraged within the organization. The first was Lauren Macaluso, a white journalism undergraduate who lived near Tree House and wandered in one day in 2008. She hoped to pick up some part-time work at the bookstore and didn't leave till 2016. She started as a volunteer, then got paid a small amount to help other college students develop the kind of respect for the neighborhood that she had learned by experience. In 2011 a couple who had been giving New City Writing money for a summer writing academy I ran at Temple agreed to shift their support to Tree House when the academy closed. The gift from Sue and Bob Wieseneck of Chicago (Sue had graduated from Temple's College of Liberal Arts years before) allowed THB to hire Lauren as a volunteer coordinator, and she continued in that capacity, adding further responsibilities for program development, until she left for the next stage of her life.

In our 2014 article "Garden from a Vacant Lot," Lauren tells a story about a realization she had about Tree House as a sanctuary for kids like James, a former Tree House regular:

> James rode his bike up to the fence of our garden and seeing he had my attention said, "Hey Ms. Lauren!" I replied by asking him if he wanted to try a carrot. I handed it to him through the metal fence and as he grabbed it, our attention was drawn to the left where some Temple students were throwing a party. . . . As the carrot was exchanged through the fence, we heard the crash of a 40 oz. glass beer bottle that was thrown over the fence and into the empty lot by one of the students. My eyes wandered back to James. He saw the same thing I had but thought nothing of the act and continued to tell me about his new school and why he hadn't been at Tree House lately. (41)

From the outpost of Tree House Books, Lauren could see her peers and the narrow life so many college students accept as their world. She grew from a tentative but enthusiastic college kid to a mature married woman and mother in her eight years at Tree House, wise about kids and local politics and the trials of small nonprofits, still committed to the mission in North Philadelphia.

After Darcy left, the board hired a new director named Vashti DuBois, who was herself a writer but soon recognized the way participating children struggled with reading. She gave greater emphasis to reading instruction and organized the Tree House library significantly, but she clashed with the board and left after less than year. Mike Reid was named interim director in summer of 2013 and soon after became executive director, a position he held until 2016. Mike was a friend of Darcy who decided to volunteer at Tree House after she told him about the excitement and challenge there; he was added to the organization as a paid employee in 2008. An African American man with a BA in theater from a nearby art college, Mike grew up in suburban Virginia and California. He brought a passion for the arts and African American history and culture to his work with the neighborhood. He also made a strong effort to connect with black middle- and upper-class professionals in Philadelphia, going to social functions and representing us in places Tree House had never been mentioned before. He added new African American members to the board and often invited people he met socially to Tree House. I joked with him that he was the only black Republican Tree House kids would ever know, but whatever his affiliation really was, he brought a seriousness and insight to the program that I came to treasure.

Mike instituted a weekly VIP visit from African Americans professional and businesspeople, and he led the organization to prioritize the African American content of the program, as we had begun to do in 2005–2006. Under Mike's leadership, Tree House strengthened the focus on reading by adding Words on Wheels, a program to deliver books to children's homes by bike courier in the summertime. Tree House had already been giving away books regularly; according to the annual report of 2009, the bookstore gave away 2,500 books that year. Words on Wheels not only addressed the "summer slide" too many children experience during the long break from school, but it also gave Tree House concrete numbers to cite and exceed: in 2014 Tree House gave away over 12,700 books. Mike and Lauren developed a small paid and volunteer staff that shared the vision of an active African American literary and literacy center in the community.

The third person who came in under Darcy's directorship is a young African American man from the North Philadelphia neighborhood named Nyseem Smith. At the time I met Nyseem, he was a thirteen-year-old student at Duckrey School. He happened to be standing by the door when Lauren walked in to ask for a job at Tree House. Bright and gregarious, aware of but undaunted by the violence and instability in his neighborhood, Nyseem found a home at Tree House and grew to identify deeply with the college student tutors he met there. He was only sixteen when we included him in a discussion on Tree House for our article, but he spoke much more like a staff member when I asked him what he most appreciated about his years at Tree House: "I've seen the growth of kids, which is my favorite part. Getting a chance to talk to them, seeing them change from not knowing how to express themselves to then getting them to a place where they can trust in us, talk to us, and even read with us. When I was a kid, reading was always easy for me but not for the kids around me. They would always cry or find different ways to act out" (33). The last comment indicates to me something I suspected about Nyseem from the beginning: that Tree House was a refuge for him as a place he could safely be "school smart" and invested in learning without being teased or rejected by his peers. In 2016 he finished an associate's degree at Pierce College and worked as a part-time staffer running many of the after-school activities at Tree House. He said then that he wanted to go into business or media production for a career. The children loved him and would try almost any book, art project, or writing assignment he suggested. Since leaving Tree

House, Nyseem has gone on to work effectively as a community outreach coordinator with another organization in the neighborhood, Philadelphia Urban Creators, which I discuss in chapter 7.

Because of funding and personality differences, 2016 became a moment of considerable transition. Mike and Lauren left over the course of six months. The organization and board searched for a new strategic plan to sustain funding and direction. Later that year the board named as interim director June Bretz, a white woman in her forties with a master's degree and experience in nonprofit management and a background working with her mother's church, based in a traditionally African American community. She brought a passion for language and literature, and a commitment to make this small nonprofit thrive. In her first months on the job, she fell in love with the kids, the organization, and the North Philadelphia community. Nyseem and a few other volunteers remained to run daily programs but left soon after. June consolidated the organization, hired a new program director, established a consistent educational program, and articulated clear identity for the organization in the cultural community of the city. She started a spring celebration called Philadelphia Literacy Day, held in Fairmount Park, the celebration attracted more than five hundred kids and parents to receive free books, hear music, and receive a personal greeting from Mayor Jim Kenney. The board worked with June and her development assistant, Karen Maloy, to ensure her success, but funding continues to be a major struggle for the organization. In the fall of 2018, both June and Karen left, in large part because both had families; Tree House hours were long and the pay minimal. The program in 2018 was run by three young people—Arthi Selvan, Emma Goldstein, and Leonard Chester—who took on, respectively, the after-school programming, book distribution, and community outreach. In 2019 the board hired a new executive director, Michael Brix, a white man who has a long history of organizing in low-income communities throughout Philadelphia and, like Mike Reid, a background in theater. The annual gifts from the Wiesenecks became a sustaining part of the funding plan, and I worked with them each year to make sure they continued to feel comfortable supporting the little organization. In 2018–2019, they renewed their commitment of sixty-three thousand dollars, enough to solidify the budget for another school year.

The history of Tree House is, in many ways, the history of ongoing attempts to put the literacy learning of kids and their parents in relationship with a larger community. Joanne believed the books themselves would somehow sustain the organization, but even she recognized, in her letter about Darcy, that a relationship with the neighborhood would be crucial to the survival of the fledgling nonprofit. Mecca saw her own childhood in the children of North Philadelphia, but she also saw—as a writer—how important it would be to link Tree House programming with established creative pedagogical efforts developed by writers and teachers elsewhere. Darcy emphasized reading and writing in the context of a loving partnership of support for the kids, and she often had public readings where even the littlest kid got to read a poem or a statement into the mic in front of an audience. Vashti connected us with education faculty who could institute reading assessments. She organized reading material for children in grade appropriate categories and reinforce the Afrocentric connections Mecca had begun. Mike built on Vashti's Afrocentric focus and concern for assessment while adding the VIP program to connect successful black businesspeople and professionals with Tree House, both for the sake of the kids' perspective on literacy and for possible new funding sources. Lauren succeeded in spreading the word about Tree House throughout Temple, at sororities and student groups, in classrooms and her own journalism program. June brought greater notoriety for Tree House through an annual festival that included the mayor, and Michael hopes to foster more alliances with socially engaged nonprofits throughout other stressed neighborhoods in Philadelphia. The Words on Wheels effort, started one summer with Temple students on bicycles traveling to neighborhood blocks and giving books away, is perhaps most effective not simply for getting books into families' hands but for figuring literacy as a gift outside of schools and testing and grades. Tree House models reading and writing in the context of a "life with books," and that means people reading, writing, and thinking together.

Before I leave the particulars of Tree House, I want to describe the growth and formation of the board. Every nonprofit needs a board, and the way the board relates to the staff is not only an indication of the organization's health but one possible model of how a given population can relate to the larger society surrounding it. Some populations served by nonprofits are "at risk" or "marginalized" or demonstrate "special needs," but in a larger sense no dominant group can function in a democracy without mechanisms to address the needs of minority or disadvantaged groups, whether they are defined by geographical location like North Philadelphia, disability like blindness, or special interests like youth basketball. The relationship between board and organizational program reflects a sustained interaction between privileged citizens and the population specifically identified for assistance or aid. In short, nonprofit boards must develop a plan to address racism and historical oppression in a substantive way.

As I said earlier, the small board that founded the organization was composed of three black members and three white members. All had at least a college degree, one was a principal of the school a block from Tree House, two worked for Temple and one for Community College of Philadelphia, and one worked for the Free Library of Philadelphia. Jon, our chair, developed and rented properties in North Philadelphia and elsewhere in the city. All worked within twenty blocks of Fifteenth Street and Susquehanna Avenues, and most of us worked within ten blocks of Tree House. But a major purpose of boards is to raise money for the organizations they oversee, and other fiduciary and supervisory functions also pointed to a need for accountants, lawyers, business and government professionals. Nonprofits need people who understand the mission intimately, but they also need people who can write checks or get their friends to write checks.

Without going into specifics, I would say the board was fortunate to add people with the means to contribute generously and to invite well-to-do friends to the fundraising event Tree House began to hold once a year soon after Darcy took over. Under succeeding board presidents Ted Swanson and Cass Bailey, the members demonstrated a desire to help the neighborhood and improve the literacy lives of the kids and parents who attended Tree House. Over time, however, the board became whiter and more populated by businesspeople who worked in Center City and lived in neighborhoods outside North Philadelphia. Even new board members of color were not people who lived near Tree House. We lost our last board member from the community in 2015. The folks who remain have shown great loyalty and commitment to the organization during times of financial and staff stress, but the ability to formulate a viable strategic plan becomes compromised when board members aren't steeped in the life of families who use the program every day. The board also had too few members who knew enough about literacy education to sustain a considered discussion about the pedagogical direction of the organization.

Lessons from Tree House

In a very large city, Tree House is a tiny organization dwarfed by a research university and a district elementary school right around the corner from its doors. And yet, even this little nonprofit has a history and internal culture too complicated to encompass in a few pages. I want to consider now what others outside Tree House, or North Philadelphia, or even the urban East Coast might gain from the story of this little literacy sponsor in an area of need and potential.

Once Tree House opened its doors, actors from all sides responded out of a desire for mutually satisfying literacy experiences. Young people came in after school, parents inquired about activities their children could sign up for, college students wanted to volunteer, and staff fell in love with the possibilities for meaningful reading and writing events in a place that few might expect to find them. Board members gladly gave their mornings for monthly meetings and local funders soon found a reason to approve grants. A church not even in North Philly gave Tree House a huge gift, and for seven years a couple from Chicago gave more than fifty thousand dollars each year to support Temple volunteer tutor training and supervision. As difficult as it is to sustain a program like Tree House, so many people want it to succeed. Setting aside test scores and testimonials, for me the experience of the open mics at Tree House was enough to bring me back. A seven-year-old read his "griot story" about the place: "A bee stung you in a space ship. You were taking pictures of monsters on the moon when the bee stung you. You let the bee in the castle where you live. The bee had magic powers. It became invisible. You left the bee in the moon. You planted a tree on the moon, and it grew into Tree House Books" (Reid 2009, 8). An early teen read from his "sound journal" about what kids hear in a day: "Birds singing. I woke up and got breakfast then went outside. We went to the park where the sounds of people fighting echoed. I didn't want to get in the middle. I went home. My brother and sister are loud. I had a tough day" (Mancinelli 2009, 8). Not deathless prose nor angry polemic, the writing and reading at Tree House is about response and relationship, discovery and connection. When I read the above texts, I'm reminded of James Britton's (1994, 149) brilliant phrase "shaping at the point of utterance," which he glosses this way: "I want to associate spontaneous shaping, whether in speech or writing, with the moment by moment interpretive process by which we make sense of what is happening around us. . . . But the intention to share, inherent in the spontaneous utterance, sets up a demand for further shaping." The children who come to Tree House Books get precious little time to invent and share freely about what they read or what they see in their lives. It's not that they don't have folks who love them or care about them; it's that reading and writing as communicative and playful acts are not regular parts of their lives. School is so much about meeting standards and getting through material, and home is so much about finding safe places in a hostile outside world. As Britton emphasizes, unfettered and engaged talk *about* reading and writing is the crucial link between how one makes sense of the world (which all humans do under any circumstance) and how one interacts with others to establish a shared sense of the world through written symbols. Tree House affords a space for "shaping" that involves composing and interpreting, speaking and listening in the company of others. Conversation, both written and oral, means something to everyone involved and draws people together in mutually respectful relationships. Or, as the Tree House mission says, "to grow and sustain a community of readers, writers, and thinkers in Philadelphia."

Over the years, easily a hundred college students interacted with Tree House children and parents, plus hundreds of others the organization touches through its book distribution system. I personally know dozens of undergraduates who volunteered at Tree House and came back changed and charged to work in communities like North Philadelphia. I sometimes think—not without a bit of sadness—that the largest beneficiaries of Tree House are the undergraduates who visit, tutor, and then become transformed through their experience there. One outstanding student in my 2009 literacy class, Danielle Mancinelli, did her community project at Tree House, stayed when she received a university honors grant to direct their summer program, and wrote an honors thesis the following year about her work there. She started out adamant that she would *not* become a teacher like her mother. A year after she visited Tree House, she was applying to Teach for America in New Orleans, and three years later she came back from Louisiana to earn a master's degree in literacy at Saint Joseph's University. She has been a classroom teacher, then a literacy coach for teachers, and—as this chapter is being drafted—she's a vice principal in the school district. She wrote me about the experience at Tree House: "It was the stark opposite of my own educational experience and background, yet a safe space for me to flesh out my own bias and privilege. At Tree House Books, I was free to explore, create, and soak everything in—it allowed for unrestricted inventiveness. Because of my experience, I entered teaching having critically examined my individual identity within power structures while cultivating empathy. My experience at THB has led me into a life of advocacy, and a critical lens to examine the world" (2016). She valued this opportunity to cultivate empathy and recognize the worth of students who lived in different circumstances from her upbringing in a white suburban community outside Philadelphia. Thus the influence of Tree House ripples out to the classrooms and teachers Danielle continues to affect today.

In the same way, I could tell stories of elementary or middle school youngsters who attended Tree House and grew to take their studies more seriously through high school and, sometimes, into college. The staff has few solid statistics on the long-term outcomes, but the organization's 2017–2018 annual report says that 310 children were served on site, involving 6,122 volunteer hours overall and 39 home visits. That year 67,665 books were distributed to families. The numbers at Tree House are minimal compared to the 202,538 total students in the 2017–2018 Philadelphia School District, not to mention the additional 50,000-plus in private, parochial, and independent schools in the area. The statistics about violence, low incomes, and incarceration rates in the North Central neighborhood can seem to overshadow small instances of hope and joy on Susquehanna Avenue. Numbers matter, but numbers don't tell why we do such things. Relationships are built slowly, but they have a tendency to reach in unpredictable and branching directions. Certainly I don't think numbers keep me coming back to Tree House, but relationships do.

My account would be incomplete if I didn't register board-staff and board-neighborhood connections as crucial pressure points in the health of the organization. This is not to say the Tree House board didn't taken significant steps to preserve the organization's fiscal well-being and strengthen its administrative structures, but, as in any nonprofit in an area that has little access to resources, the need to bring in money can overwhelm the need to maintain a vibrant connection to the neighborhood Tree House serves. As the organization worked toward a sustainable business model that supports a consistent pedagogical practice, the staff also had to deepen connections to the schools, churches, neighborhood organizations and parents in North Central Philadelphia. At the time I am writing this, the board is nearly all white, and no board member lives within ten blocks of Tree House. One of the most pressing needs for the organization is to bring the board back into alignment with the neighborhood, and that includes having at least half of its membership African American, preferably with at least two representatives from the community Tree House serves. As of the fall of 2018, two of the three staff members are not white, and the board realizes that having a person of color as executive director must be a priority. Resolving divisions caused by race, class, and gender is an ongoing challenge in any organization, but one that a small nonprofit must keep at the forefront of both its long-term vision and its daily operations.

Literacy Resources in Philadelphia

Other enrichment programs survive and sometimes thrive in Philadelphia. Looking strictly at those that have an explicit mission aimed at literacy development for K-12 children, I have placed student tutors in at least four of these programs. One of the most successful, from the standpoint of learners served and funds raised, is Philadelphia Futures. Marciene Mattleman, a legendary leader in public education in the city, started Futures in 1989. The organization linked a few students to mentors who helped them make educational and life decisions and also contributed some financial support. Over the years their Sponsor-a-Scholar program developed a mentoring and enrichment orientation, following more than fifty students in each grade from ninth to twelfth, helping them find places at appropriate colleges, keeping up with them through college, and often assisting them in their job search after college graduation. In 2011 Futures merged with the White Williams Scholarship Fund. White Williams, an outgrowth of one of the oldest charitable organizations in America—the Magdalene Society, founded in 1800—has been offering financial incentives for low-income Philadelphia high school students since the early 1920s. The merger formed Future's College Connection program (Philadelphia Futures 2018b). This program gives educational support similar to Sponsor-a-Scholar but does not supply the intensive mentoring.

Altogether, according to their website, Philadelphia Futures programs "annually serve nearly 600 high school and college students with academic enrichment services, personalized college guidance, placement and retention services and financial resources" (Philadelphia Futures 2018a). The organization's 2016–2017 annual report says that 100 percent of its senior class that year graduated on time, and all of them were accepted into one or more colleges. As of 2017, 639 of their Futures scholars have graduated from college. Again, this is not a number that will turn around the district, but Futures has grown significantly in coverage and reputation, making an impact both on families across the city and on the ten or more partner colleges and universities that regularly enroll their students. I also admired the way Futures has made a concerted effort over many years to hire a diverse staff. Currently, the staff is a remarkable 50 percent people of color, especially African American and Hispanic. One program that was started more than ten years ago by an outstanding African American staffer named Gabriel Bryant is called the Young Men's Initiative, and it has been a valuable support to African American, Latino, and Asian male students in facing the daunting challenges of the Philadelphia streets. The success of that initiative could really only have come from the leadership of a wise man with the deep personal experience Gabe brought to the job. The program demonstrates the importance of staff that understand intimately what their students need.

In 2003 I joined a new Futures effort now called the College Admissions Marathon. In collaboration with eight writing coaches and an array of staffers, I lead writing sessions for about one hundred rising seniors associated with Futures in a three-day residential program held in the last few years at Haverford College. Two of my former grad students join me in lecture-discussions that cajole, challenge, surprise, and amuse students about the flexibility and investigative power of writing, and then we visit small groups to lead peer reviews of student essays. Each summer I am impressed again by the commitment of students and staff toward writing not only as a ticket to college admission but also as a means of sustainable personal growth and inquiry.

Futures' approach has always been to help students find compelling stories from their own lives to share, ones that reflect the quality and nature of their personal struggles but that figure the student as an agent rather than a victim. For instance, in 2008 a student I'll call Abdul wrote an essay about losing his stepfather, the only paternal figure he had in his life, early in high school. This was a subject Abdul only came to near the end of an initial draft of an essay mostly devoted to getting away from a neighborhood dominated by drug dealers. Abdul was able to write about his stepfather and basketball, suggest that the neighborhood he came from was difficult, and demonstrate that the loss of this important man in his life was motivating him further: "I had not lost just a father; I had lost my coach, my best friend, my father figure and my hero. I promised myself that I would do my best to keep my mother happy by doing great in school and being successful in life. I no longer play on the basketball team, but I am still working hard in school and earning high grades in order to go to college to keep this promise alive" (2008). Abdul enrolled in community college but soon left school. Although he was one of a small number of Futures alumni who did not finish his four-year degree, the change *in him* during the process of writing and rewriting (students typically go through six to eight drafts of an essay in the course of the three days' residence at a local college) was both compelling for all of us around him and typical of the transformation Futures students undergo at the Marathon. The Marathon emphasis is on revising for audience and purpose, on asking probing questions, and listening in supportive ways to others. Young people find an element of themselves that they can present to others as genuine, worthy of recognition, and the basis of persistent effort they will need to make it through college. The Marathon is a very expensive program to run, but Futures has been brilliant at raising money and getting its name out to funders and educators over the years. I come away from the Marathon every year tired, refreshed, and hopeful.

Another organization that has grown and flourished in the city is Mighty Writers. Probably the closest in spirit to 826 Valencia programs in other cities, Mighty Writers provides after-school writing seminars for children between seven and seventeen years of age. According to its website, the organization has more than three hundred mentor-tutors working with more than two thousand kids annually. It began in 2009 with one site south of Philadelphia's downtown, Center City, but it has now reached out to many neighborhoods with four sites—El Futuro, North, South, and East Mighty Writers—including a small branch (North) only a few blocks from Tree House. Its site in South Philly, historically an area associated with Italians and Jews but now heavily Mexican and Southeast Asian, focuses on Spanish-speaking children, many from undocumented families. All branches offer classes for kids younger than twelve and groups for teens up to seventeen, as well as an academy at least once a week, an after-school program for twenty-five to thirty-five participants from 3:00 to 6:00 each weekday that reserves an hour for homework and then has focused activities for writing. The program also takes writing workshops to schools, libraries, and centers where youth congregate. I have visited its South site, and I have had students work with the organization over the last few years in other sites. It lives up to its excited descriptions online, with careful attention to young writers and inventive workshop themes.

Mighty Writers has been highly successful with its website and regular email updates in gaining a citywide presence. A person on the mailing list can expect a colorful and upbeat newsletter-type message at least once a week. The organization's donor list is impressive, and it has received considerable grants from both local and national foundations. Tim Whitaker, the founder and executive director, started his career as a teacher but then had an extensive career as a journalist and professional writer. Like Dave Eggers, the founder of 826 Valencia, Whitaker has reached out to fellow writers and former colleagues for support, and this has been an excellent approach to establishing the organization's reputation and financial solidity. Rachel Loeper, the education director, has been with Mighty Writers since the beginning and has brought both a consistent pedagogical vision and a commitment to appealing and generative workshop ideas for children and youth. Loeper and Whitaker are both white, but of the other eight staff members in 2017, four were African American and one was Latina.

Other organizations with an explicit program in literacy include Puentes de Salud and Philadelphia Spells Writing Lab. Puentes de Salud is a health clinic designed to serve the Latino, primarily Mexican, population in South Philadelphia. However, the cofounder and executive director—Steve Larson, a faculty member of the University of Pennsylvania Medical School—has always insisted that a crucial part of the mission is literacy for the community the organization serves. It has a very active program for Spanish-speaking children and their families, with a great emphasis on English as a second language. Puentes seems to be successful in fundraising like Futures and Mighty Writers, but in addition it has access to government and insurance funds for health and additional patient support. Spells Writing Lab, on the other hand, is an entirely volunteer organization focused on writing workshops offered to public school classes. Founded in 2009, the same year as Mighty Writers, Spells Writing Lab does not have a brick-and-mortar home at the time I'm writing, holding most of its workshops in schools and occasionally in community centers. It has been in talks both with Tree House and a North Philadelphia community arts group called the Village of Arts and Humanities to develop a closer working relationship with an organization that can form a working home for its programs.

I could multiply the list many times by including adult literacy, family literacy, and high school or college completion programs in the city. As long as I've been engaged with nonprofit literacy organizations in the city, I'm still finding new ones I'd never heard about. I could name at least twenty other projects, including (in no particular order) the South East Asian Mutual Assistance Association Coalition, Nationalities Service Center, the Welcoming Center for New Pennsylvanians, the Philadelphia Senior Center Coffee Cup Branch for Chinese elders, East Kensington Community Center at Visitation, Providence Center in Latino North Philadelphia, Children's Literacy Initiative, and many more. This list doesn't include all the exciting projects the Philadelphia Free Library has started in recent years, such as the Culinary Literacy Center located in the main Center City library on Logan Circle or the specialized library branch at the Community Health and Literacy Center in South Philadelphia.

As a way to understand city literacy efforts more comprehensively, I have been working with Philadelphia's Office of Adult Education, the former Mayor's Commission on Literacy, to develop some networked projects and place Temple students in internships. In cooperation with the Center for Literacy, the largest provider of adult literacy instruction in the city, the Office of Adult Education has developed an online means called myPLACE for recruiting prospective adult students and then placing them in more than eighty literacy and workforce development programs for classes. As I indicate in the next two chapters, many organizations in Philadelphia, like Puentes de Salud or the Village of Arts and Humanities, focus primarily on health, the arts, or other life-giving concerns while recognizing literacy as a vital component of their mission. I want to conclude this chapter with some thoughts on the networking potential of literacy sponsors in an urban center because that, in my view, is probably the most pressing next step for a nonprofit sector with so many components.

Learning Network for Literacy Sponsorship

Philadelphia is a big city with classic urban problems. One problem we don't have is a lack of nonprofits addressing the needs of the communities they serve. Still, nonprofits typically compete with other nonprofits for funding from foundations, government agencies, corporations, and donors. A year that Tree House receives a five-thousand-dollar grant from one foundation may be the year that the same foundation doesn't give a grant to another worthy group. The competition leads programs to hone their message and make their work distinctive by geographic location, program specialties, or target population. This can be good for programs that are diffuse or poorly organized, but it can also encourage mission constriction or, alternatively, mission creep. The money sometimes drives the message and even the whole institution. Tree House started off as an inventive writing program, but staff and volunteers soon realized they needed to enrich reading abilities in their students to make a big difference. Reading and writing should, of course, grow together, but under the circumstances of competition and marketing, reading began to overshadow writing at Tree House because Mighty Writers was having such success in writing and our message needed to stay sharp and distinctive. Words on Wheels offered impressive increases in numbers of books delivered. It's much harder to tell a nuanced story in a grant proposal or even a news article, so small organizations become needlessly specialized.

I see no reason for all the literacy-related nonprofits in Philadelphia to merge into one large mega-organization. In fact, I can think of many reasons to avoid such a consolidation of services and staffs. The rich tapestry of small organizations can be excellent for the specific needs of neighborhoods and populations. But at the same time, an alliance between and among similar groups can make them all stronger. Already I have met a number of aspiring young teachers or researchers who have worked at Tree House, Mighty Writers, and at least one center for adult basic education. Imagine the power of a pool of volunteers and staffers who have deep experience in writing and reading pedagogy and a growing sense of the differences and similarities in neighborhoods and ages and reading levels. What if foundations or government agencies began encouraging cooperative efforts across the city rather than setting organizations off against one another? I used the word *mobility* in an earlier chapter, and I think a *call to mobilize* into learning networks in order to sponsor literacy describes an effort to set programs in coordinated motion for the good of Philadelphia's many communities.

We return to this question later, but I am struck with one peculiar likeness between rural and urban literacy settings. David has had success working with a health-care group that recognizes the link between literacy and health. Funders in the state also recognize the way literacy plays into the greater economic success for an entire area. His struggle was to get the local public school to cooperate with the health-related nonprofit. In Philadelphia, schools are so large and so troubled that they hardly notice organizations beyond their walls. Tree House is five hundred yards from the school most of its kids attend, but there is little interaction between the two except when a staffer at Tree House makes an exceptional effort to reach out to a particular teacher. We have nonprofits to address all sorts of populations, but centers and agencies can't work together sufficiently to address the total need in an urban population. Instances of greatest progress come when staff, boards, administrators, and funders can hold in their minds both the particulars of a type of instruction or support—reading children's books or instruction manuals, writing college applications or stories about the neighborhood—while still comprehending the larger forces and greater promise that comes with a population that can frame its own destiny and advocate for itself. To my mind, a branching and constantly extending network rather than a closed institutionalized system best fits the multifarious purposes of urban literacy conversations.

6 Community Arts

Philadelphia is rich in community-oriented arts programs, with more than forty organizations dedicated to grassroots arts education throughout the city. Two have been in operation for more than a hundred years. Samuel Fleisher started the Graphic Sketch Club in 1898 as a place where low-income immigrant boys could take art lessons for free but grew into a school offering classes for adults and children of any race or nationality in a noncompetitive environment. People could come to study art, but they could also meditate and hold family gatherings in a deconsecrated Episcopal church near the classrooms known as the Sanctuary. The Graphic Sketch Club was renamed the Samuel S. Fleisher Art Memorial on his death in 1944, and it remains an excellent place to take quality art classes for modest tuition. Similarly, the Settlement Music School was founded in 1908 as a part of a settlement house for immigrants in the same neighborhood of South Philadelphia. Settlement now has six locations throughout the Philadelphia area, offering lessons from highly trained musicians at modest fees. Settlement's accomplished alumni include not only famous singers and instrumentalists in classical, jazz, and popular traditions but also writers, scientists, professors, and businesspeople.

Fleisher Art Memorial and Settlement Music are two examples of an older neighborhood arts model. Both organizations offer classes and individual lessons oriented toward classical technique and traditional art forms. Although now both have incorporated more recent art styles and outreach to schools and neighborhoods, they remain essentially conservatory programs designed "to provide access to the arts for everyone, regardless of economic means, background, or artistic experience" (Fleisher Art Memorial 2015b). Fleisher has a long-standing relationship with the Philadelphia Museum of Art; Settlement served as the precursor for the world-renowned Curtis School of Music (Settlement Music School 2010) and continues to employ Philadelphia Orchestra members to teach advanced students in their program. Contemporary arts nonprofits are less tied to mainstream arts establishment and tend to focus on interactive and developmental relationships, not only with learners but also with communities. Let me offer two examples of this more collective orientation.

Asian Arts Initiative, founded in 1993, states on its website that it "create[s] community through the power of art." Based in Philadelphia's Chinatown neighborhood, north of the Center City business district, AAI offers programs "connecting cultural expression to social change." As the website puts it, the organization's artists and teachers use "art as a vehicle to explore the experiences of Asian Americans and the diverse communities of which we are a part" (Asian Arts Initiative 2018). Among its other efforts in and around their physical location, AAI has sponsored an ambitious and multiyear campaign called the Pearl Street Project. Starting in 2011, AAI received a grant that sponsored California architect Walter Hood to develop plans for Alley Galleries and "base level" improvements in lighting and street features in the four-block alley called Pearl Street that runs beside their center, linking "the homeless shelter from one end of our block to the luxury loft apartments and condos on the other, and the wealth of artists, immigrants, and community members interspersed throughout" (Asian Arts Initiative 2014). Since that time, they have sponsored block parties, outdoor dinners, interactive video documentaries, pop-up art shows, micro-events, and larger showcases to involved artists, residents, homeless people at the Sunday Breakfast Mission, and visitors from outside the neighborhood to meet, create, and talk about the state of the surrounding community.

Spiral Q, located in West Philadelphia, began in 1996 as a politically engaged street performance puppet troupe in the tradition of Vermont's famous Bread and Puppet Theater or Minneapolis's In the Heart of the Beast Puppet and Mask Theater. Their early work focused on ACT UP–style HIV/AIDS queer activism, and the organization still represents the power of LGBTQ+

perspectives in arts and social justice action. In recent years Spiral Q sponsors workshops and community-based shows and pageants reflecting the concerns of adults and children in the underserved neighborhood of Mantua, where its center stands. Their mission reads: "Spiral Q builds strong and equitable communities characterized by creativity, joy, can-do attitudes, and the courage to act on their convictions" ("Company Overview" n.d.). Much of their funded programming takes place in five public elementary and middle schools in West Philadelphia, culminating in the Be the SPARQ parade for kids in mid-May. Open to all is their annual Peoplehood Parade in late October, when a hundred or more people of all ages make their way 1.2 miles from the Paul Robeson House to Clark Park in West Philadelphia and then join in on "participatory art-making" activities at the park through the afternoon.

These are examples of nonprofit organizations sponsoring art-making and performances within Philadelphia neighborhoods. Each has its donors and supporters, and each contributes in distinctive ways to the cultural life of Philadelphia as a whole. The model of access to fine arts instruction represented by nineteenth- and early twentieth-century education for immigrants and poor populations has been challenged and broadened today by programs devoted to community well-being and self-definition. Maryo Gard Ewell (2011), an influential community arts advocate, wrote that "'community arts' does not merely mean 'access,'" as the founders of Fleisher and Settlement framed their original mission. She went on to offer this definition: "Community art is of and by the people of a place and culture, often facilitated by a professional artist. It reflects the values, concerns, and meaning of living in that place or culture." Beth Feldman Brandt, executive director of the Stockton Rush Bartol Foundation, which funds many small community arts organizations in Philadelphia, concurred with this view when I interviewed her in 2016. To her, such programs offer "arts experiences that define themselves as being relevant to a particular community, usually a marginalized or underserved community" (Elizabeth Feldman Brandt, personal communication, December 31, 2016). Thus, the emphasis in community arts tends to be on particular groups of people—distinguished by geography or common identity such as country of origin or race or social category—rather than the quality or prestige of the artwork presented to a given audience.

Programming in community arts sites functions both individually and collectively. For individuals, the message is that all people can be creative and have valuable experiences from which art making grows. For example, teen writers can use their own communication styles to shape poetry rooted in their families and neighborhoods, the violence they may have witnessed, but also the hopes they may never have spoken aloud. At the same time, participants can come to think of themselves as part of a larger social unit that has the power to organize, advocate, and affirm. People on a block can gather together with an artist-facilitator to generate ideas for a mural on a blank wall in their midst, then participate in bringing their collective image to life in that mural. A group can advocate for itself and define itself through joining voices in the act of making visual art, poetry and fiction, music, dance, video, or some other art form.

One example of this process of building individual abilities and group solidarity through the arts is a project sponsored by Philly's LiveConnections at the Henry H. Houston School in the Mt. Airy section of Northwest Philadelphia. From November 2015 to June 2016, thirty-five fourth to eighth graders at Houston worked with musician Andrew Lipke, writer and director David Bradley, and other artists to compose, shape, and record sixteen songs for a CD called *A Day in My Life*. On a given song, the group brainstormed as a whole, broke into small groups to draft lyrics for single stanzas, and worked with musicians to perfect harmonies, rhymes, and chords. They went on field trips to other parts of the city, interacted with another elementary school in South Philadelphia, and worked with professionals to record their CD. They explored styles from hip hop and gospel to smooth crooning, and they worked with devoted Houston School music teacher Ezechial Thurman as well as other studio musicians to layer the drumming and instrumentation. The words are occasionally predictable—about catching a touchdown pass and wanting to achieve dreams—but more often the songs are fanciful and surprising, fresh and even shocking. One song tells the story of a young girl shot dead by a stray bullet on the street, the cop who comes to investigate, and the mother who receives a call about the shooting while she's hanging up decorations for her daughter's birthday. The chorus goes:

> I have a dream we're playing, just flying on the swings
> Then there are shots and then there are screams.
> I hear the school bell ring, and know that it's all real
> I want to know what can be done
> To stop the fear I feel, to stop the fear I feel.

But this isn't a mournful chant. Their refrain, "One life taken / One life spared / Is this right? / Is this right?," sustains a call to action with a searching and determined beat. The music videos representing this and other tunes on the CD show young people having fun, exuding confidence, and—as they sing on another number—dancing "like no one's watching."

Houston School presents a mixed picture that could improve considerably with more attention and financial support. Houston kids come from a neighborhood very near my own home. West Mt. Airy isn't dangerous, with violent crime ranked fifty-second and property crime ranked fifty-first out of fifty-five city neighborhoods, according to *Philadelphia Inquirer* data in 2018 ("Crime in Philadelphia" 2018). The average West Mt. Airy family income that year was above $92,000, and yet 100 percent of the students at Houston qualify for free meals during school hours. Many of the children of folks with higher incomes, black or white, go to private or parochial schools. Of the student body at Houston, 86.6 percent is African American, with an additional 10.8 percent of nonwhite racial background. Over the three-year period 2013–2016, student attendance remained relatively stable at over 90 percent, teacher attendance (a measure of morale in the school) rose to the district average, and suspensions were roughly half what they are in elementary schools located in more economically stressed neighborhoods. However, during that period, reading and math scores for students at every grade level were at or slightly below school district averages on state standardized tests. This is a school ripe for innovative programs that motivate and inspire students not only to take their studies seriously but also to enjoy the experience of learning. That's what well-designed community arts programs can do.

This chapter considers community arts organizations as literacy sponsors in urban settings. This doesn't mean that community arts programs are the same as community literacy programs. Rather, they work toward much the same results but by different means. Both cultivate abilities, attitudes, and motivations crucial for the richest participation possible in a democratic society among individuals as well as groups. In my view, Asian Arts Initiative, Spiral Q, and many other large- or small-scale community arts organizations in Philadelphia are practicing forms of literacy sponsorship. They engender habits of mind and engagement—indeed valuable conversations—with the world very like the habits developed in programs like Tree House Books, Mighty Writers, Center for Literacy, Puentes de Salud, or any of the other literacy based nonprofits discussed in the previous chapter.

I'm tempted to invent a term parallel to *literacy sponsorship* to reflect that art and literacy are not the same, that some ways of thinking and being cultivated in painting or dance studios differ considerably from habits of mind fostered in college analytical writing or adult basic education classes. Certainly each can learn from differences with the other. Yet—and here I ask my friends in the arts to forgive me—I'm going to stick with the frame of literacy for this discussion because I want to widen the term's reach rather than narrow its focus. A literate person, especially in the contemporary global economy, must be flexible enough to account for data and intuitions that challenge traditional explanations for the world while also being inventive enough to adjust to new genres, novel modes, unfamiliar audiences, and unexpected purposes. A person who makes art comes to recognize that the work must be motivated from within and must connect with an audience in some central way. Both literate and artistic people recognize that whatever contributions they make to the culture must inevitably be embedded in what has come before. Writing for the *New York Times* or painting on a cave wall, writers and artists produce work that hosts and deepens a conversation between makers and receivers, creators and the crowd outside the studio. This dialectic of invention and reception links literacy and the arts intimately.

Before I return to consider the array of community arts in contemporary Philadelphia, I want to focus on an example of community writing that reflects and elaborates this point of connection between art and literacy. Hal Adams—an educator in the tradition of Paulo Freire, Antonio Gramsci, and C. L. R. James—founded the Neighborhood Writing Alliance and later the Community Writing Project to foster independent and experience-based writing among working-class and poor adults in Chicago. His publications, the *Journal of Ordinary Thought* and later *Real Conditions*, exemplify an attitude toward writing that rhymes and resonates with the projects, performances, and exhibitions sponsored by community arts nonprofit organizations that have grown in Philadelphia since the early 1990s.

Every Person Is a Philosopher

Hal Adams was an education professor at the University of Iowa and later at the University of Illinois–Chicago (UIC). He is little known among writing studies or community literacy scholars associated with English departments, but he is better known in progressive education circles. Hal was a visionary organizer of writing projects in low-income African American and Latinx communities for more than thirty years. After twenty years of teaching counselor education at Iowa, he gave up tenure there in 1987, moved to Seattle, and began teaching homeless children and their parents. He moved to Chicago in 1991 to pursue popular education and locally focused publishing. He organized his last writing groups in the Minneapolis assisted living facility where he died in 2011 (Ayers et al. 8). What he accomplished was not radically different from what others in community literacy have done, but his approach was perhaps the most purely tuned to community needs, the least influenced by university agendas, and the most similar to arts-based empowerment projects carried on by nonprofits in local neighborhoods. David and I both knew Hal and admired his work, and we feel his version of popular education resonates with the out-of-school approaches to literacy that have most attracted our attention.

I first interacted with Hal in 1997 through emails, phone calls, and finally a visit. My colleague Steve Parks and I had just founded New City Writing, the outreach component of the writing program at Temple (Parks and Goldblatt 2000), and we were casting about for models of publishing efforts that connected directly with neighborhood writers. My friend Bill Lamme in Chicago said I should read the *Journal of Ordinary Thought*, a magazine Hal began publishing in 1992 in collaboration with a welfare-to-work program associated with UIC (where David was teaching at the time). It featured writing by groups in specific neighborhoods, often parents meeting in local elementary schools or men and women (usually in separate groups) at housing project community centers. As Hal's biographical sketch recounts, when Hal started working with women in Seattle homeless shelters, he put their stories alongside the latest educational journals and decided that the Seattle women offered "more compelling insights about personal struggles and social change" (Ayers et al 2016, 8). He decided he needed to publish a magazine that made those insights available to more readers.

Hal developed a highly tuned understanding of the writing group both as a ground for building the rhetorical abilities and self-confidence of individuals as well as a source of power for group members to advocate for themselves. He formed the Neighborhood Writing Alliance as a nonprofit to support *Journal of Ordinary Thought*, which headed each issue with a simple but profound statement: "Every Person is a Philosopher." When he felt that organization wasn't adequately meeting the needs of the local writers, Hal formed a second group through UIC called Community Writing Project, which published its own journal called *Real Conditions*, announcing in its mission statement that "every person is a thinker and an artist." In the process, he worked with Janise Hurtig, among other colleagues, to establish writing groups and foster writers in housing projects and community centers throughout the city. Hurtig and Adams described the dynamic results of their work in a 2010 essay: "Through the sharing of stories, workshop members come to celebrate the unique contribution each participant makes to the group, while respecting the value of the workshop group as a community of writers. In this way the writing workshop seeks to strike the kind of balance between individual and community that are fundamental to democracy" (19). This link between individual growth and community solidarity is one common theme I recognize between Adams's writing groups and many community arts projects in Philadelphia. Both community writing and arts projects grow out of a desire for and a commitment to a vibrant democracy rooted in the lives of "people who do not ordinarily consider themselves writers or artists," as they put it in a 2002 article (Adams and Hurtig, 147).

Adams had written as early as 1995 about this dynamic—the way writing becomes valuable for each writer while collectively strengthening an entire group—in a compelling essay called "A Grassroots Think Tank" (Ayers et al. 2016, 9–22). In that piece he emphasizes two other aspects of writing groups as well: the vital contribution that people can make to their social well-being by drawing on the evidence of their experience and the power such "self-activity" can have in transforming concepts into political action. He tells a number of stories about women and men who learn through writing and discussion to recognize the wisdom and knowledge they've attained by experience. Even though they've taken their tacit knowledge for granted and assumed no one wanted to hear from them, the warm response they receive from their peers and their readers helps them embrace the power to speak. Summing up one section about a group of women who met after school in a Chicago neighborhood, he observes: "The stories rolled on, about family life, raising children, relations between the sexes, living amid violence, finding affordable housing, dealing with the public aid system, and surviving as women. The mothers first came to the writing group because they wanted to learn how to help their children with schoolwork. They returned for the chance to explore the meaning they had gleaned from lives lived under stress of poverty and because it was comforting to make explicit to each other the common struggle they shared" (13). His account of the group work is informed by a theoretical orientation toward popular education, especially Gramsci's understanding of "ordinary" people who emerge from the control of dominant cultural norms by examining and coming to value their own ideas alongside others in similar circumstances (10). Yet Adams's prose remains free of political terms that imply judgments. He simply reports with a quiet admiration the subtle and profound changes people undergo in the groups he organizes.

Adams and his coauthor Hurtig refer specifically to the Trinidadian theorist C. L. R. James on a point relevant to this chapter. They note that "James thought the artistic expression of ordinary people contained truths essential for social change" (Adams and Hurtig 2002, 154; see also Ayers et al. 2016, 10). This isn't the place for a discussion of James's version of artistic expression, which is rooted in an early twentieth-century notion of great or important literature even as it demonstrates his commitment to the growth of artistic writing in the Caribbean. I want instead to consider what "artistic expression of ordinary people" means on the streets of Philadelphia at the moment I am writing this chapter. Furthermore, I want to allow the complexities of art practices in diverse and urban communities to widen, critique, and redefine what "literacy" can mean to educators, policy makers, and everyday citizens. Adams and his collaborators focused largely on written stories, observations, and opinions as the product of their group work. There were also some examples of photography in the two journals, but the main thrust of their work was with writing rather than visual art, music, dance, or other expressive media. However, they treated writing as an art in itself rather than as a preparatory tool for further achievement, as literacy is too often regarded. Their groups focused on acts of reading and writing expressly to foster conversation and action about the eponymous *real conditions* in their lives. Community arts groups often operate along similar lines.

Academic Literacy and Literacy in Arts

In 2009 a group of organizations associated with the teaching of writing in schools and colleges published a document called "Framework for Success in Postsecondary Writing." This statement was an attempt by professors of composition and rhetoric and directors of college writing programs to articulate for teachers and the general public the ways of thinking, composing, and presenting that characterize college writers who excel in their classes across many fields of study. It's a broad statement of abilities—not limited to sounding out words or spelling correctly or speaking with textbook English grammar—and it represents literacy capacities as construed by thoughtful academic educators. Here are the eight habits of mind they identify:

- Curiosity—the desire to know more about the world.
- Openness—the willingness to consider new ways of being and thinking in the world.
- Engagement—a sense of investment and involvement in learning.
- Creativity—the ability to use novel approaches for generating, investigating, and representing ideas.
- Persistence–the ability to sustain interest in and attention to short-and long-term projects.
- Responsibility—the ability to take ownership of one's actions and understand the consequences of those actions for oneself and others.
- Flexibility—the ability to adapt to situations, expectations, or demands.
- Metacognition—the ability to reflect on one's own thinking as well as on the individual and cultural processes used to structure knowledge.

"Framework for Success in Postsecondary Writing" has been challenged lately within writing studies, especially because the original group that drafted the list was almost entirely white. My purpose in sharing the findings of the "Framework" proponents here is not to assert the primacy of any specific list but to emphasize that contemporary scholars strive to look beyond correctness and standard usage and aim for creative attitudes and intellectual openness as goals for academic literacy education.

As we discussed in the opening chapter, learning networks of literacy sponsors can focus on activating capacities rather than fulfilling minimum standardized requirements. These capacities can be tapped and strengthened not only through reading and writing in classroom settings. Informal and even unsanctioned activities like Adams's writing groups, online fan fiction, and satirical plays can foster such habits, as can practices the public doesn't normally connect with writing like drawing, giant puppet construction, free movement, or video production. They all foster both a rich conversation among participants in a community setting and a wider conversation between participants and the world—hostile, indifferent, or potentially useful—that surrounds their community.

At the same time, literacy learning in non-school settings can encourage and develop other sorts of habits of mind than the ones writing faculty in universities invoke. Take for example the description of "Our Process" posted on the website of the Mural Arts program, one of Philadelphia's best-known community arts organizations. MAP has sponsored and produced murals all over the city and calls itself "the nation's largest public art program, dedicated to the belief that art ignites change" (Mural Arts Philadelphia 2015a). I'm certain their organizers and artists hope to develop "habits of mind" along the lines of the ones named by "Framework" in the youth and adults who participate. Yet MAP's description of the process of producing a mural differs strikingly from the rhetoric of habits of mind, even though we can find all the elements of the academic list within MAP's more collective orientation toward their work:

Look: See the Big Picture

Change starts by looking beyond the surface. Our work starts with a genuine curiosity about what makes Philadelphia tick. We look for the issues that drive and make our city, and we look for the problems Philadelphia and its residents are grappling with daily.

Listen: Active Listening is Powerful

Listening as part of change is about learning and understanding. Each project begins active listening: we ask questions, and foster dialogue among disparate groups. This is the listening that makes sure that everyone is heard, the listening that amplifies voices that have been muted.

Connect: Build Bridges of Dialogue

Connections begin when people picture themselves in each other's shoes. Once we have found our inspiration, we mobilize our partners and build a team of individuals—artists, participants, residents, nonprofit leaders, funders, policymakers—anyone who wants to help us make change happen. We connect people and institutions who normally do not talk to each other, and build bridges of dialogue over long-standing chasms of misunderstanding, distrust, or ignorance. The connections are not always comfortable or convenient. But they result in important conversations that spark change—in attitudes, in understanding, and in hearts and minds.

Celebrate: Both the Journey and Each Other

The art is simply the most visible part as the end product of a long and complicated process of collaboration—which in itself leads to substantive change. We create resources and opportunity. We create moments for reflection and celebration. We create hope and optimism about a different future. Our process of collaborative art making becomes a powerful vehicle for inspiring these other creative forces. The bonus is that through this process, we also create a lot of beauty along the way.

MAP's community approach recasts habits such as "engagement," "creativity," and "persistence" in terms of the group, the collective effort, the community from which the artwork and the participants emerge. The group characterizes "listening" in more active language than "Framework" describes "openness," and MAP's explicit commitment to "change" contrasts with the more neutral call for "responsibility." In addition, we see new goals articulated, such as "collaboration," "celebration," "beauty," and "hope."

The MAP process is cast in directly emotional and democratic language. Of course, an organization focused on disenfranchised people in neighborhoods needing more services and economic relief will be freer to articulate their goals in an emotive and political key than will representatives of dominant culture and higher education, but the contrast is instructive. The two public documents illustrate the differences in literacy sponsorship—what is at stake for each, what purposes and audiences they serve, how they earn their money and public support—between two widely disparate institutional settings. Where "Framework" addresses literacy in the context of the ladder of academic achievement and must use the school-oriented language of individual progress and "success," the MAP description can simultaneously take individual growth and group cohesion into account.

To explore the potential for literacy learning in a community arts setting, I turn my attention now to one particular example of a community arts project in formation. During the fall of 2016 and into the spring of 2017, I met regularly with Grimaldi Baez, an artist in residence at a deeply rooted community arts organization in North Philadelphia called the Village of Arts and Humanities. During his employment with the Village, we talked widely about arts and literacy, about politics and organizing, about mainstream galleries and collaborative object-making with people who have no training in the arts. In the following pages, I share some ideas and strategies that Grimaldi used to prepare for and elaborate his residency project, not as a study in creativity or an exemplar of arts practice. The story is more about the challenges and complexities involved in approaching art as a community-building project, a means of identifying and intensifying human resources in a neighborhood long demeaned and dismissed for its economic failures and violence. By rejecting the image of art as primarily the precinct of the wealthy and educated elite, Grimaldi and other community artists imagine art with new audiences and purposes. As with the work in Hal Adams's community-based writing groups, valuable lessons for literacy learning follow from this reconception.

Material Memory into *System Zero*

Lily Yeh founded the Village of Arts and Humanities in 1986 when she gathered neighbors in North Philadelphia to rebuild a vacant lot into a garden of mosaics and performance space. She developed a working friendship with a man named Joseph (JoJo) Williams, a talented drummer who was squatting in a nearby abandoned house, and soon they met James (Big Man) Maxton, a six-foot-eight former addict who became the Village's operations director and an accomplished mosaic artist under Yeh's mentorship. Many other adults joined in, especially once children started making colorful painting and sculpture that became public monuments. Yeh said in a 2014 interview: "My role as an artist is to share with people my experience of how creating together can change our surroundings and ourselves. I often term my work 'urban alchemy,' transforming chaos and abandonment into order and deep connection. It began with the personal quest for authenticity and centeredness and it continues to surprise me that my work would have impact on others. Some people call it changing the world from inside out" (Whittaker 2014). She focused on the joy of making with people who lived in stressful environments, and the community-building aspect of their work together transformed both individuals and the group.

The spot on Germantown Avenue had already been a place for art making long before Yeh arrived. The acclaimed African American dancer Arthur L. Hall housed his Black Humanitarian Center and from 1969 to 1988 trained his dance troupe Ile Ife where the Village now offers its main programming. Arthur emphasized arts and literacy connected to music, movement, and African pride (Burgee et al. 2008). In a 1968 *Philadelphia Inquirer* article, Hall said about his decision to focus on African dance: "After all, there are 20 million black people here, and I think we must know something of our culture. Our people are not aware of their culture and heritage. I saw in the dances a chance to bring grandeur back into blackness" (Webster). Lily turned the focus out of doors and recruited kids and then adults to create angel murals in an alley, undulating sacred mosaic walls along the street, and the Tree of Life sculpture in the middle of Meditation Park, where once the wind blew through vacant buildings, junkies shot up, and empty lots captured Acme bags in the weeds. She still drew on African iconography, but her influences ranged more widely, and the final products reflected what the neighborhood artists wanted to create. Lily had a great commitment to a particular area in North Philadelphia, and she reasoned that bringing beauty to a place would build community identity and pride.

At the time Grimaldi and I were meeting regularly, the Village had twelve full- and part-time employees (half the staff are African American or Hispanic), programming for youth and adults, and an active artist-in-residence program called SPACES. The organization's overall mission sounds like that of many other community arts nonprofits: "Our mission is to amplify the voices and aspirations of the community by providing opportunities for artistic expression and personal success that engage youth and their families, revitalize physical space and preserve black heritage. We value the power of creativity as our most powerful and effective tool for catalyzing healthy and sustainable change—with, for and as neighbors to our community" ("The Village of Arts and Humanities" 2018). Within the broad rhetorical strokes, however, a reader can detect the roots of the organization. The call for "artistic expression" as a way of amplifying already existing voices and involving families is a common thread for both Yeh and Hall, while "revitalize physical space" references Lily's outdoor projects and "preserve black heritage" nods to Hall's early Afrocentrism. Here creativity is portrayed as a tool for health, change, and collective solidarity. The Village announces itself as a place where art isn't defined by an individual's career or a growing curriculum vita of commissions and gallery shows, even though any given artist or student passing through will have a trajectory to follow and a reputation to make. In this public document, art as a commodity merits no mention at all.

But the world is more complicated than mission statements make it out to be. Artistic process becomes artistic accomplishment in the world's eye, and an individual artist sometimes gains recognition even if she does not seek it.

In fact, recognition leads to further work, and the most selfless artist wants to keep working. Over the course of years, the Village received various awards from city, state, and federal government agencies as well as national foundations for its community development work, reinvigorating lots into gardens and shells into habitable buildings, employing people in the community along the way. With awards came money to keep the nonprofit afloat and growing. Yeh herself received a Pew Arts grant, a Lila Wallace fellowship, and a Ford Foundation award, among other honors, for her work in North Philadelphia and, increasingly, internationally. By 2004 she had left North Philadelphia—where she had lived since she arrived for graduate school from her home in Taiwan in 1963—to pursue projects in places such as Ecuador, Ghana, Kenya, China, and Rwanda through a new nonprofit called Barefoot Artists.

The Village went on without Lily Yeh, but it struggled financially and organizationally, as is often the case when a charismatic leader leaves an institution she has founded. Big Man died in 2005; JoJo stopped working for the organization soon after and died in 2014. Individual leadership and vision matter, even in the context of the most collectively conceived projects. But the Village survived. Today it doesn't have the reach or the recognition and means that the nonprofit had in 2004, but it has maintained a commitment to drive local development through the arts, drawing on the capacities of neighbors and enhancing the physical environment for all. At the same time, Lily's vision proved to need more than beautification and collaboration to bring investment and prosperity back into the neighborhood. Yeh was among the early community artists trying to address urban ills, and foundations responded enthusiastically to her approach, but the neighborhood itself did not appreciably improve over the twenty-five years since the Village began. The 19133 zip code remains one of the poorest residential areas of the city, with an average adjusted gross income in 2012 of $20,744 (compared to $61,434 for Pennsylvania) and estimated median home prices at less than a third of the state average. Today the challenge both to the individual artist and the neighborhood participants is even greater than Lily Yeh had imagined.

Every project the Village undertakes now, therefore, must widen and elaborate that original vision in a way that addresses stubborn contemporary challenges like inadequate housing, underfunded schools, food desert conditions, elevated levels of violence, and chronic unemployment for people in North Philadelphia. Creative approaches and, indeed, arts-based efforts remain promising modes to improve life in this area, but what has attracted attention and funds in the past will not compel residents or funders there today. Thus, the organization is caught in a bind: the legacy mission is one of social uplift and art as a grassroots movement, but continued funding depends on renewed artistic visibility and inventive approaches that will update the vision of Lily Yeh. They can't remain a relic of a previous revolutionary age, but truly fresh approaches are hard to come by.

The present story starts in 2015, when the Village received a grant to fund two African artists—Olanrewaju (Lanre) Tejuoso of Nigeria and Kwasi Ohene-Ayeh from Ghana—who would live and create at the center for six months during 2015–2016. Although the story of both artists' projects is quite pertinent to my discussion of community arts and literacy, I'll focus on Lanre's work because his residency served most as an instructive prelude to the project Grimaldi developed at the Village when I met with him there.

Lanre arrived in North Philadelphia from Lagos, where he had made a successful international career exploring environmental issues and climate change through installations, often using waste or unwanted materials in aesthetically intriguing and conceptually surprising ways ("Olanrewaju Tejuoso" 2018; Fallon 2016). The Village blog for July 26, 2016, says: "Lanre plans to explore issues of loss and trauma through the stories of abandoned/discarded sites and objects. By treating trash as a precious art supply and focusing on the unspoken needs of the community, Lanre hopes to offer an alternative to the damaging ways humans treat the environment and their space, both physically and emotionally" ("Olanrewaju Tejuoso Begins Work with Discarded Materials"). Inspirational gallery language, to be sure, but the words do not reflect the process or even the result during the fall of 2016 in the Village building.

The rhetoric here represents a compromised mixture of Lanre's intent and work style combined with the idea in the grant, written by Village administrators, to sponsor an arts project commemorating the traumas and losses of people in the community (Fallon 2016; Melamed). I began to learn about the process just as Lanre was putting up the final show, so most of my understanding of his approach comes from Grimaldi, who worked as a kind of crew chief with community people hired to help construct the artwork Lanre designed. In the end, the exhibit called *Material Memory* that Lanre mounted was in many ways an artistic success (see photos and the description as "incredible" in "Go See the Village" 2017). However, differences between the artist's conception and the organization's grant commitments seemed to lead to significant tensions in the process of creation and even more significant tensions with the neighbors who participated in the project. Grimaldi, too, admired the final pieces but reported that few of the people he worked with on *Material Memory* felt they had been intimate contributors to a process that emphasized "art" more than "community."

I do not mean to suggest that this mixed outcome is any particular person's fault, especially not Lanre's. He came into North Philadelphia with his methodology and artistic history, but the grant and institutional exigencies reframed his work with expectations that he could not have met. His "local" was Nigerian and his artistic orientation was international. He was not explicitly briefed on Lily Yeh's historical commitments, the grant's call for attention to the "unspoken needs of the [North Philadelphia] community," and the Village's mission to "catalyzing healthy and sustainable change." Nor could he have quickly adapted his practice to meet such homegrown understandings of art-as-community-building among people he did not know and had no time to learn about. At the same time, the Village was putting more emphasis on "trauma-informed pedagogy," led by a compassionate African American educator named Michael O'Brien. The organization, it seems, needed a strong artistic expression to bring visibility for their long-term commitment to address the pain in the neighborhood. Lanre's international stature made a good match on paper, but the implementation was harder than perhaps anyone recognized at the time.

Lanre indeed used discarded objects in his Village exhibit, and he was not insensitive to the losses a neighborhood like North Philadelphia suffers, but he knew little about local circumstances before he arrived. Lanre knew no one there nor anything about the way black and Latino residents thought about the deaths or disappearances of loved ones. He knew how people in Nigeria live and work, celebrate and mourn, but he had no informants in Philadelphia except the assistant they hired for him: Grimaldi, a Puerto Rican artist in his early thirties who grew up in Boston and had lived in Philadelphia about four years. Perhaps more telling, Lanre had no experience working with community members as equal contributors in a project, seeing the neighbors as paid workers who would lend their hands to form and construct the material elements of his conception. He didn't see the effort as community building or as an experiment in democratic process; for him this was a venue to showcase his work and challenge himself in a new environment. An African artist was a real draw here, and his work with found and discarded objects seemed in tune with the Lily Yeh's historical orientation to making beautiful objects cheaply and with common materials. But the luster of an outside artist cannot make up for a mismatch in purpose or audience in a large-scale undertaking like this residency. Not that a more egalitarian attitude toward art making is exclusively American or even common among American artists, but at the Village this attitude is more taken for granted even if it isn't fully realized with each initiative.

Grimaldi was a promising choice to help Lanre realize his design plans during the residency. Recently graduated from Temple with an MFA in printmaking, Grimaldi brought to the project a range of skills in three-dimensional construction and two-dimensional design, an inquisitive mind, and a vivid and politically oriented imagination. More important, because of his background and personal story, he easily connected with people in North Philadelphia. He grew up in a neighborhood of Boston that had a mix of Puerto Rican, African American, and working-class white families. School didn't seem to offer him much, nor did he see a place for himself in the American economy of the time. He managed to graduate high school—when others he knew were dropping out or going to prison—and someone offered him a job waving the flag on a highway construction crew. Highway work paid well, and so he told his father that's what he thought he'd do rather than go to college. But his father asked Grimaldi what waving the flag would lead to. Did other guys go on to do better jobs from that position? He'd noticed Grimaldi spent a lot of time drawing comics. With little experience in the arts—Grimaldi's father had trained as an accountant in Puerto Rico but worked in factories in Boston—he judged his son's drawing was pretty good. If he wanted to go to art school, well, that was okay. But whatever he chose to study, Grimaldi needed to go beyond a high school diploma.

Grimaldi worked his way through community college in a nearby town, living in a rooming house with troubled military veterans. He finished a BFA at the Massachusetts College of Art in Boston, meanwhile picking up experience and wisdom in machine shops and print studios and pursuing his own reading agenda in philosophy, politics, and art history. I met him in 2013, when he was starting the Temple MFA program in Rome; my wife and I were teaching at Temple's undergraduate program there that semester. We bonded over the visual overload and cultural angst that came with living in the historically ornate and politically confounding Eternal City during the last days of Prime Minister Silvio Berlusconi. Grimaldi and a few other grad students had Thanksgiving dinner at our little apartment that year. Once Grimaldi graduated, he and I decided to talk more regularly about community arts.

When Lanre's residency came to an end, Grimaldi showed me around the final exhibition, and in the succeeding months he shared with me developing plans for his own work at the Village as the next artist in residence. The grant had given Lanre a small budget to employ a group of community men to help him assemble his artwork. Grimaldi functioned as the work group leader, assembling the workers into a "sewing circle" and setting up expectations for their contribution. They fabricated elements of the final installation as Lanre wished, but under Grimaldi's leadership, the group also talked about what was going on in the world around them and what they thought they were doing with their own lives. Lanre had the men binding and sewing up long pieces of fabric scraps, tying knots in materials he provided them, but the handwork also became a meditative way to calm people down and focus the conversation. Soon Grimaldi and the others had gotten to know each other well. For them, the outcome of the art exhibit was secondary to the quality of the talk—joking, serious, outrageous, or light—even as the collective craftsmanship improved in efficiency and finish.

Following the theme of commemorating loss in the original grant, the Village staff decided to hire a woman whose specialty was trauma rehabilitation and healing as an addition to Grimaldi's community work. Lanre was neither involved with her hiring nor associated with her contribution to the project. She had definite ideas about how discussions should go and what she wanted the men in the "sewing circle" to confront in their lives, even though they signed up to work for a few months at an hourly wage on an "art" project. Suddenly they found themselves not only unwitting subjects of the art itself but directly confronted about sexism and other highly personal issues. The healer urged the group to talk about their feelings for friends who had been killed or arrested, plunging them into a therapeutic environment they had not expected. In addition, she wanted to know why only men were recruited for this group, and she recruited a parallel group of women to work on similar projects. She became angry that the men were getting paid but the women were not. Men started to object to the way she spoke to them; some quit, and others stayed away or became silent. Grimaldi felt the whole project spinning out of control. Lanre was little help—the healer confronted him too, and so he simply absented himself from the fabrication process, occupying himself with designing the installation and conveying to Grimaldi what he needed from those working on the various components.

Grimaldi felt caught between all the players, but he managed to keep the "sewing circle" together by ending their meetings with the therapist. The final exhibit garnered attention in the *Philadelphia Inquirer* (Melamed) and a sizable visitor turnout in a part of the city not known for galleries or art shows. Lanre left on good terms with the Village though with little real regret from the men who had worked for him. Grimaldi had earned the respect and gratitude of the staff for helping to realize the project, and his diplomatic debriefing pointed the way to art projects that more equitably and reciprocally drew on the strengths of the neighborhood. In February 2017, once Lanre's show had closed, the Village asked Grimaldi to serve as the next artist in residence.

Starting his residency in April 2017, Grimaldi proposed a project he called Zero System. The Village had, among its properties, an unoccupied house that could be used for artists from out of town. Grimaldi worked with all the "sewing circle" crew who wished to continue, as well as some of the women who worked for Lanre and other artists. They stripped the house down to its shell. Together they decided what a communally useful house should contain, what activities it would support, and what art-related objects it might produce. Grimaldi equipped one room with a printing press for making lithographs, wood and linoleum cuts, and handset type, simply because printing was a craft he knew and the replication of images were attractive for others to learn. He found a supply of hand tools in the Village basement, and he added these to the inventory of the house. He had wanted another room to contain sewing machines, and yet another to be devoted to digital design on computers the Village had stored away from a previous grant project, but those elements in the end didn't materialize. The point was not to establish a profit-making industry for the participants—he wanted to maintain a commitment to art making without an emphasis on commodification—but to use the focus on craft and imaginative thinking to foster art and literacy-related habits of mind and hand (see Fallon 2017). In this way, Grimaldi was reaching back to Hall and Yeh but without a predetermined art form or design plan.

Although he had multiple influences for his thinking about community arts and his work at the Village, Grimaldi was particularly influenced by a book that offers an ingenious synthesis for artists in this field. Pablo Helguera's *Education for Socially Engaged Art* (2011) runs just short of ninety pages, but it efficiently covers a wide range of approaches and challenges for any artist who wants to address and, ultimately, improve life in a stressed community.[1] Helguera acknowledges that "the prevailing cult of the individual artists is problematic for those whose goal is to work with others," but he asserts that the "uncomfortable position of socially engaged art . . . is exactly the position it should inhabit" (4). His is a particular version of the wider field of "community arts," but because his language is so precise and so applicable to literacy sponsorship of the type Hal Adams proposed, I think it worthwhile to consider Helguera's ideas in some detail.

Artists can resist and challenge their roles in the conventional gallery-based economy while still carrying on activities they call art. Art thinking can reconfigure contemporary situations within a strange and ambiguous territory where taken-for-granted power relations and assumed values are critiqued and new social possibilities imagined. Helguera's vision for socially engaged art reminds me of Marianne Moore's famous line in the 1924 version

---

1. Helguera does not deemphasize art making for the sake of economic development or social justice, as does Arlene Goldbard in her *New Creative Community* (2010). Goldbard prefers the term "community cultural development" because she wants to draw on "the more generous concept of culture (rather than, more narrowly, art)" (21). She links the work to activities not normally associated with art, such as activist organizing, oral history, and social media, for economic and political ends.

of her poem "Poetry": "imaginary gardens with real toads in them." Invented gardens afford us a rare glimpse of actual creatures we overlook and underestimate so easily in everyday life.

Helguera's account of socially engaged art (SEA) strikes me as resonant with Adams's practices and attitudes in his Chicago neighborhood writing groups. Helguera's insights detail his vision of SEA building and enriching both communities and individuals, but they also suggest a view of informal and non-school-related literacy learning—reimagined through the arts—as a living and fulfilling practice beyond standardized tests and graded assignments. Like Adams, Helguera highlights participation as a hallmark of community engagement. The traditional version of participation in art galleries or museums is that a viewer must cultivate heightened perceptions of color, shape, foreground and background, spatial placement, and other formal compositional elements in order to appreciate the work on display. As Helguera notes, SEA raises questions about what he calls "multi-layered participatory structures." He recognizes four ways a person who is not the artist can participate in artworks: nominal, directed, creative, and collaborative (14). The first requires not only heightened compositional perception but also perhaps reflection to see ways an art object implicates the viewer him or herself in social injustice or ecological damage. The second asks participants to take a prescribed action, such as filling out a Post-It note to stick on an artifact the artist has made or choosing elements in a digital array presented on a screen. The third asks for independent action by participants but within prescribed parameters, as when randomly selected players in a musical performance are asked to make sounds or say words or phrases within a certain time frame. The fourth invites participants to join the artist in thinking about and making an object or a performance or an action. At each layer, participants must invest more time, attention, and inventiveness to make the work come alive. With each layer, the artist becomes less a master or individual creator and more a leader, facilitator, and eventually one among many makers.

We can see a contrast in participation between Lanre's project and Grimaldi's Zero System. Lanre's art could not help but respond to conditions in his homeland more than in North Philadelphia; he knew little about the United States and made no space for the Americans he encountered to collaborate in the design and planning phase of the work. Lanre asserted his guiding vision for the installation as primary. Grimaldi's "sewing circle" was paid above minimum hourly wage to fabricate objects for the installation to Lanre's specifications, with little creative freedom to act themselves. Lanre wanted to draw on materials readily available in North Philadelphia, such as plastic twist ties and trashed aluminum lawn chairs, but more often than not he brought the form and the referents for his materials from Nigeria. In a piece of the installation, for instance, he displayed on one wall a bank of elastic fabric rings like those women in Nigeria use to carry heavy weights on their heads. The piece itself was visually stunning, and neighborhood people helped fabricate it, but its look and feel were not rooted in North Philadelphia.

Grimaldi brought a different vision of participation to his residency at the Village. In Grimaldi's plan for Zero System, he provided both a print shop for others to make their own inventions and a space in which participants could invent and build their own workshops. This is a freer system, less dominated by the originating artist, but much harder to envision or bring to productive completion. Grimaldi didn't deny that, as the artist, he was motivating and shaping the overall project, but his conception put much higher expectations on all participants to work collaboratively.

Grimaldi's Zero System had mixed results, though for very different reasons than did Lanre's exhibition. Most of the original crew eventually left the project, in large part because they needed to earn more money for themselves and their families doing other work. The wage was better than a person could get at an entry-level service job, but work on Zero System was part time and offered no benefits, nor could the Village promise long-term employment once Grimaldi's residency was over. As one participant said to Grimaldi as they were stitching one day, "Everybody sees things in terms of a hustle." Grimaldi himself presented his work as a hustle of a different type, but that concept just didn't capture what he or they were doing in the house. They did make some cool objects, including a giant fabric balloon that stretched down to the street from the second-floor window and a set of drawings done in response to walks through the neighborhood, but the most characteristic and valuable outcomes were frank and often painful conversations about what members of the crew were dealing with every day. In the end, Lanre produced a final show that garnered positive attention from art critics while Zero System did not. Grimaldi didn't care to hold a final show, even though he did have work he could have displayed to good effect. A final show wasn't in Grimaldi's vision of the overall project.

Although the last members of the crew had a strong relationship with Grimaldi, one after another split from him because they didn't see what art had to do with their immediate needs. Perhaps Zero System was too open for them to invest their own dreams into the work. During that time, Grimaldi tried to shift and accommodate the work toward what the young men wanted to do, but no matter how much he talked to them, reinvented the project, or railed against conditions in the neighborhood, he had no persuasive reason for them to stay. At times, he told me, he questioned what art really *did* have to do with people who needed to pay for food, childcare, and housing, people who had no training or family connections to assure them of paychecks in the future. Fast money on the street called one crewmember away, another was jailed after a fight, a third managed to piss everybody else off before he walked away. The violence and pressures of the neighborhood tore at the fabric they were trying to sew together.

At one moment, police shot a low-level drug dealer around the corner from the Zero System house during a block party. This sent shock through the local community. The event challenged the Village to take a stand, to bring a peaceful vision to the situation, but the organization wasn't able to respond meaningfully. Grimaldi, again, felt caught in the middle of events and factions, and the Zero System house lost standing among the neighbors. Grimaldi was nearly ready to close up shop and walk away from the last stage of his residency, much as he needed the final paychecks. Then at a local gathering he met a young African American man in his early twenties I'll call Foster. Foster visited the house and loved the printing materials. He had an entrepreneurial energy coupled with a vision of advocacy, and he immediately recognized the value of neighborhood connections Grimaldi had developed. In the final weeks of Grimaldi's residency, Foster used the shop to produce posters, plan out meetings and actions, and talk about ideas with Grimaldi and others. Although the Village would have liked a final show or some other production reporters could write about and photographers could document—Village administrators were the ones writing the grants and under pressure to demonstrate effectiveness for funders—perhaps one of Grimaldi's proudest moments in a six-month residency was a meeting of about thirty people Foster organized for neighbors to address violence and crime reduction. This wasn't art, but it was a promising outcome of Zero System.

SEA Applied to Literacy Learning

Huelguera's analysis of participation maps onto conditions both for reading and writing in school and home settings. At the nominal level of school activities, students read what they are assigned and write what they're told, simply filling in the blanks of worksheets or running their eyes over passages in a textbook. This rote version of literacy can be found in some homes, too, not only when homework is completed in a rush but also any time literacy is linked with duty rather than pleasure or invention. But the analogy goes further than this caricature. A more engaged level of "nominal" participation can admit creative perception and need not be limited to perfunctory or dutiful response. Just as a visitor to a gallery may undergo a truly valuable internalized experience of the art on the walls or pedestals, a parent reading a bedtime story for the sheer enjoyment of the bonding event might ask for no active response from the child. The next levels, however, require more investment in the work. Writers or readers directly involved in creating new work for an audience must formulate a position or a stance that can feel heady, dangerous, or tricky. The richer the possibilities for participation, the more crucial the reflective ability of the teacher or parent to provide a safe and supportive environment for active literacy engagement. Even if a writer is working independently, with no parent or mentor or supervisor overseeing the process, the success of any project depends on the writer's ability to make his or her own "zero system," relatively free of unspoken fears and doubts that might hold back or deform the work. Truly "independent" projects must be deeply connected to potential audiences or they will have little effect on anyone outside of the writer him- or herself.

Helguera concedes that many artists and curators "have expressed wariness about the notion of a preconceived audience" (24) because it can limit and trivialize the outcome. However, he notes that no one really creates only for him- or herself because any working version of self is partially based on a tacit understanding of the social environment from which the artist comes. Helguera remarks: "to speak to one's self is more than a solipsistic exercise—it is, rather, a silent way of speaking to the portion of civilization that is summarized in our minds" (25). Artists who create without examining their sense of audience can often create work that excludes or even affronts people who do not have a place in the artist's default "civilization," thus incorporating racist or sexist images when the goal was "universal" truths.

Lanre's sense of audience limited his work in the Village setting. His early problems started with the staff's chosen theme of "commemoration": he was understandably unprepared to comprehend either what needed commemorating or what constituted commemoration in the context of North Philadelphia. From conversations Grimaldi reported to me, Lanre quickly realized that because he imagined himself as the source of any originating vision of the project, the theme wasn't workable for him. He might have been able to make a commemorative piece had he treated the participants more fully as collaborators, but that wasn't his orientation, nor was there time built into the residency for him to get to know the neighborhood enough to weave it into the fabric of his vision. Quite frankly, despite the public language of community building and response to trauma, the grant budget placed the power of conception firmly in Lanre's hands. The Village called for participation, but the grant framed the project as artist centered rather than collaborative from the start.

In a sense, Grimaldi faced the opposite problem. Having established a principle of wider and deeper participation, and resisting the need to have gallery-ready products emerge from Zero System, Grimaldi framed the question of audience as diffuse and ambiguous, almost inappropriate. Is audience simply another name for a marketplace where participants can sell fabricated objects to their North Philadelphia neighbors? Is there a wider public audience for Zero System as an alternative system? If so, whom should the documentation address? Perhaps Grimaldi and his cohorts could have mounted an exhibit in City Hall or given a lecture at the Philadelphia Museum of Art, but what would be the point for them or for a middle-class audience? Who would buy the T-shirts? What "hustle" would it appropriate?

His residency didn't produce tangible results in conventional art-world terms, but it did teach Grimaldi a great deal about the tremendous commitment required to work with people in a stressed neighborhood. It touched a number of lives among those who passed through or stayed till the end, and Grimaldi feels certain that at least now and then the "sewing circle" came together in solidarity and trust. Grimaldi has gone on to do intensive reconstruction work in Puerto Rico after Hurricane Maria and tend the ceremonial fires at the Pine Ridge Reservation in South Dakota, always drawn to moments of high emotional investment among a small but determined group. Yet much of what he's done among groups since the Village he wouldn't call "art"; he maintains an art-making practice in his home studio but hasn't found a way to connect outward and inward gestures. At the final weeks of the residency, Foster taught Grimaldi to be more careful that participants develop a personal stake in the art making, or at least in the power of arts as an organizing tool for improving the lives of actual people. His Village residency demonstrates that community art must attend to institutional sponsorship, the role of maker and audience, and the purpose of art as a task in itself. In a conception of art that rejects traditional venues and verities, the "uncomfortable position of socially engaged art" requires hard thinking about context, method, power relationships, and the needs of specific communities.

Here art mirrors literacy. Rhetoric has always been centrally concerned with audience. How are listeners persuaded or outraged or terrified? How can factual evidence, credible speaking style, or emotional appeal convince readers in a given situation? According to the Western rhetorical tradition long before Aristotle, neither readers nor writers can develop any sophistication in their craft without a highly developed ability to imagine and test the reactions of the appropriate audience. The frustrating problem for literacy learning is that school tends to undermine the sense of audience for writers: students write primarily for their teachers as the ultimate judge of correct and appropriate performance. All too often, the teacher cares more about certain mechanical aspects of a text (punctuation, grammar, accurately reported information) and less about meaning, excitement, or investment. Without the petty expectations of conventional usage, words in an informal and social context can cultivate an audience of peers or interested participants without reference to correctness. Clearly there may be judgments in any communicative act, but—given a supportive and collaborative environment—decisions about what's appropriate, surprising, or disgusting are grounded in standards both readers and writers develop together every day among themselves.

Again like Adams, Helguera pays special attention to dialogue in neighborhood projects. Dialogue happens only within a safe and interactive social setting. Conversation cannot seem scripted, policed, or disregarded if the exchange of words or images is to feel productive to all participants. And if the goal of SEA is to build a community into a high functioning and egalitarian social unit, dialogue provides the ground for that growth. Helguera connects the role of the artist in creating a rich and revealing dialogue to theorists like John Dewey, Jürgen Habermas, Richard Rorty, and Paulo Freire, a list Adams might well appreciate. Helguera sees all these philosopher-teachers point to an emancipating pedagogy that opens space for conversation not limited by formality but also not so undirected as to feel purposeless. He seeks a "convivial environment" (43) within which participants can "arrive at mutual understanding and learning without losing the balance between interlocutors" (46). For this reason, Helguera urges artists to study effective teaching, not so much to convey information as to foster satisfying exchanges among those who enter the world of an art piece.

As nearly every writing teacher will attest, the enemy of good writing instruction is the institutional demand for content coverage. Most American universities these days have programs for teaching writing across the curriculum or in the disciplines—an approach that started in the mid-1970s—to involve professors from many departments in the effort to teach students writing beyond their first freshman courses. Too often, however, writing-intensive courses sink under the weight of material in the major, overwhelming the students' joy or curiosity in composing. Writing simply becomes another test of knowledge rather than a tool for discovery if there is no sense of dialogue built into the writing tasks a teacher sets. Especially in a community setting, writing takes time to learn and attention to teach because dialogue needs time and attention to foster in a "convivial environment." Dialogue can't be prescribed or mandated in writing any more than in art.

A Learning Network in Community Arts

In the early spring of 2017, Beth Feldman Brandt, the executive director of the Stockton Rush Bartol Foundation, asked me to offer a workshop called Arts Plus Literacy for teaching artists and writing instructors based on the thinking I had been doing for this chapter. Beth had been one of the first people I called when I started the chapter because she has come to know almost every organization and teaching artist working in the city over the last two decades. Bartol is a small foundation that made twenty-four grants in 2016, mostly for five thousand dollars each, to Philadelphian community arts organizations such as Asian Arts Initiative, the Village of Arts and Humanities, and Taller Puertorriqueño. Beth and I planned together over a few months and in April the workshop attracted nearly forty participants. We began with a warmup from Bartol board member Jeannine Osayande, executive director and founder of an African dance company in town. She taught the group three movements and rhythms which she combined into a brief dance, and then she set small groups to produce an original haiku on the theme of home accompanied with movements, which each group performed accompanied by her company's drummer, Ira Bond. I worried that the dance introduction might take too much of our workshop time, but Jeannine so completely demonstrated the link between dance movements and language—even without the haiku—that the group moved readily into lively discussion about literacy and the arts after the exercise.

We held the workshop at the South Philadelphia branch of the Settlement Music School, one of the city's oldest continually operating neighborhood arts organizations. The participants included artists, art teachers, or community arts administrators as well as writing teachers associated with colleges, high schools, or after-school literacy programs. Some of the literacy attendees found out about the event through the Philadelphia Writing Project, a well-developed local network of schoolteachers based at University of Pennsylvania and associated with the National Writing Project. Others came through my connections at Temple and the local Writing Program Administrators organization. The arts participants came primarily through Bartol contacts and grantees. Ira and Jeannine stayed for my portion of the workshop, since Jeannine regularly teaches K-12 and college students, and Ira works in an Afrocentric high school in the city. I stressed from the beginning of the session that participants should meet each other and leave with the beginnings of a new relationship, an unfolding project, or at least an expanded perspective on common goals.

I started my part of the evening by asking people to jot down every daily task they could think of that involved reading and writing. In small groups and later as a whole, I asked them to discuss what mental and emotional abilities were needed to accomplish these tasks. We talked about cooking and driving, keeping a journal and scrawling a grocery list, intuiting emotion beneath cryptic text messages, and feeling pleasure from reading a novel. I have led conversations like this many times in classes and visiting seminars, but people that evening were particularly perceptive on the topic and highly responsive to each other. One person observed that she needed to read and write carefully to "sort and discern" the relative value of information she was receiving all the time. I was struck by this remark because *sorting* sounded so mechanical while *discerning* traditionally refers to religious introspection for purposes of a life decision. Both the mundane and the profound dwell in the daily rituals of literacy, and this mixed economy of perception and production works within art practice as well. I urged participants not to accept the popular definition of literacy as a skill measured by minimum standards but as a constantly developing constellation of emotional and intellectual capacities. Our list of abilities associated with reading and writing illustrated that no easy definition would do. In short, the group seemed to embrace the recognition that, whatever *literacy* means, the term touches on the most perfunctory as well as the most momentous decisions we make every day.

I gave a little talk after our discussion, starting with my usual working definition of literacy: "the ability to engage in a conversation carried on through written symbols." I told them that in the context of arts practice, "written symbols" was too limiting a medium; it didn't adequately name the dance Jeannine taught us, the rhythms Ira played on the djembe drum, or the visual images at an art opening. Once again, I emphasized that in this context literacy should be characterized by capacities rather than minimum skill, and in this context I introduced the eight habits of mind from the "Framework for Success in Postsecondary Writing" along with the four principles of art growth described by Mural Arts. I invited the artists in the group to consider ways they practice and teach these habits in their own work, and then I touched on Helguera's analysis of SEA. I used examples of arts practice common in Philadelphia: murals at an urban farm that *widen participation* in a community, an intimate concert among musicians that deepens *audience awareness*, and a particularly effective collaborative pop-up book project at Asian Arts Initiative that *fosters dialogue* between an artist and a group of previously homeless men. I closed with a suggestion that organizations assessing their work should resist the demand to justify their success through scores or reading levels, but instead they should collect as many stories of interaction and investment as possible. A few stories can be dismissed as anecdotal evidence, but many stories become data that carry both validity and persuasive value.

Beth ended the workshop on a hopeful note. She had not expected such a turnout of writing people—usually their workshops brought in twelve to fifteen teaching artists and administrators—so she wanted to find a way to continue the collaborative spirit the discussion had sparked. She talked about the mission of the foundation to do more than give grants to organizations; the workshop series reflects Bartol's mission to support arts organizations with educational and developmental events as well as money. She invited everyone back to Bartol workshops next year, but in addition she promised to help foster arts and literacy collaborations across nonprofits in the city. As they filtered out, various people told me that they had met prospective collaborators and were considering new partnerships already.

Beth's closing words gave me a great lift. Bartol doesn't have a huge endowment, but its programming and funding effectively reflect and shape what is happening in the neighborhoods and classrooms of the city. My wife, Wendy Osterweil, is an artist and art educator who served six years on the Bartol board, three as chair. Long before either one was associated with Bartol, Wendy and Beth worked together in Philadelphia community arts. I haven't done another workshop like that for Bartol, but in retrospect I see Bartol as a foundation that fosters exactly the sort of learning network of literacy sponsors David and I are imagining. The organizations and artists supported by Bartol through workshops and grants focus on art making that involves children and adults in immersive and empowering activities. Organizations need not work together in some kind of gigantic art megalopolis to be a learning network; the interchange and dialogue Bartol encourages with all its investments are key to refreshing and deepening art education practices that map directly on the "literacy as conversation" model we embrace. At the time of my "Arts Plus Literacy" workshop, I thought that presenting the habits of mind alongside MAP art principles would be useful to make the links between literacy and art teaching and assessment. Perhaps it was—especially for those in search of language about assessment for future grants—but I think I presented too much and left too little time for discussion and relationship building. In retrospect, the most important element of that workshop might simply have been getting those various players in the room to talk to each other. We can all use more of that.

Grimaldi attended the workshop that evening. Wendy and I went out afterward with him to a South Philly bar called The Dive. He was his amused, skeptical self—didn't like the dancing haiku because it delayed discussion, hated New Age remarks by people who thought that just having students look at pictures was enough to qualify as arts-based literacy, and judged we hadn't adequately defined "art" in relation to literacy. Complaints aside, Grimaldi was remarkably enthusiastic about the possibilities for dialogue between art and literacy practitioners. Wendy applied the exercise on literacy abilities to artwork, saying that she is constantly making choices, creating and responding to relationships, when she draws or makes prints. We felt the connections were palpable in the April evening, even if the institutions that sponsor arts and literacy education habitually separate the two. Grimaldi told us about the sweat lodge he was building with friends in an obscure corner of the Philadelphia's Fairmount Park, near a place where homeless folks take shelter. He had lent his tools to their makeshift encampment, and they in turn accepted the sweat lodge as another part of the landscape. That accidental partnership ought to produce lively conversation about literacy and art in the next few years.

7

Urban Farms

In 1878 an impressive list of civic business leaders such as John Wanamaker, W. Atlee Burpee, and Governor James Pollock established the Sunday Breakfast Association at the edge of Center City Philadelphia. The association provided food, shelter, and religious support to homeless men, in response to the unemployment and dislocation of the so-called Long Depression that affected the United States and Europe from 1873 to 1878.[1] As of 2017 the Sunday Breakfast Rescue Mission was the largest emergency shelter for homeless people in the city, serving four hundred meals a day, three free meals per person for every day of the year. In order to supplement the food it buys, the mission raises fruits and vegetables on its own farm. Members of its small long-term residence program, the Overcomers, helped design and build the farm in 2015 under the guidance of urban farmer Meei Ling Ng with the help of a grant held by a neighboring arts organization, Asian Arts Initiative (see previous chapter). The farm is a marvel of design, economically using a limited area between a cinder block wall and a parking lot, beautifying an ugly

---

1. It's estimated that during this depression, one-third of Pennsylvanian workers were unemployed for extended periods of time (Barga 2013).

space on a busy commercial avenue while also producing in 2016 more than a thousand pounds of raspberries, blueberries, zucchini, tomatoes, string beans, and much more for the mission kitchen.

When I met her to talk about the mission farm, Meei Ling explained she had come to this project through a long journey that involved both art and farming. She was raised on her mother's orchid farm in Singapore, trading fruits and vegetables with their neighbors to make meals in a place where there were no grocery stores. Then, in her teens, the military evicted her village to make way for military expansion. She found herself in an urban apartment, far from open ground for planting. As a child, she had always drawn—often in the dirt while she was playing outside because they had little paper at home. Once she settled with her family in the city, she pursued art as a natural extension of her response to the nature she had known. She went to art school and worked as a graphic designer for many years. Eventually she grew bored with commercial art and decided, with two friends, to apply for art school in America. New York was too expensive; Philadelphia was close to the mythical city and cheaper. Meei Ling filled out all the forms and received a scholarship to the Philadelphia Art Institute, but when it came time to go, her friends admitted they had never applied. Still, she'd gotten the offer, so she packed up and left by herself.

After studying 3-D modeling and animation technology, Meei Ling intended to return to Singapore, but she was hired by a multimedia company on the spot at her senior show. She learned web design, coding, and video production and then was promoted to art director of a design unit, but eventually she'd had enough sitting at a computer all day. She freelanced for another few years but also developed her own fine arts practice as a painter and sculptor. Married to an American from outside Philadelphia, she began commuting from nearer her husband's family home, where farmers sold produce on the weekend at a small market. She helped these farmers develop graphic materials to promote the market. During this time, she began raising crops herself near the market on some unused land. Soon after, she also started farming at Elkins Estate, forty-two acres in Montgomery County once owned by nineteenth-century railroad magnate William L. Elkins but later taken over by the Dominican Sisters for a spiritual retreat. Working the ground at Elkins Estate revived her love of farming and natural settings, and she threw herself into raising food for her family, neighbors, and the community served by the market. The farm became part of her art, and her art became part of farming.

Meei Ling's story exemplifies her lifelong literacy learning, driven by a need to survive and a fierce desire to create independently. Her father, a professional truck driver, had developed a family business on the side, recycling construction materials he was hired to haul to the city dump. Meei Ling recalls hours in her family's apartment, stripping insulation off copper wires or taking apart old electronic equipment for the valuable bits. The work was grueling and probably unhealthy, but she learned that a resourceful family could make money from other people's trash. At the same time, she also learned how valuable the bartering economy had been in her family's original village, how tied it was to the nurturing culture among family and friends who made their way together to the city, how fragile the home community was when transplanted to a high-rise apartment in an overcrowded city. In both Singapore and Philadelphia, Meei Ling learned technical skills, design principles, and creative practices that earned her a living but also satisfied her longing for the natural patterns and images of her childhood. She remembers her mother making toys from pieces of wood and shells, musical instruments from coconut leaves. Her literacy remains vibrant and inventive, oriented toward ecology and community, because her imagination is fed by her past and present surroundings.

The project at the mission was a logical and joyful extension of all Meei Ling had been doing, and she found working with the Overcomers a particularly exciting addition to the mix of farming and art. At the mission, the Overcomers also have a crucial literacy story. Depending on the time of year, the mission feeds between 150 and 400 emergency guests in a day—the staff will serve anyone who hasn't violated house rules against violence and drugs in the building—but the mission community includes a population of men who join in a more sustained way. The Overcomers are men who have committed themselves to pass a monthlong "blackout" period, during which they make no contact with anyone outside the facility and do not partake in any drugs or alcohol. If they make it through that stage successfully, the men can stay at the mission for up to eighteen months, taking life skills courses and helping to provide services to other clients. The mission is also a nondenominational Christian community, so the Overcomers participate in religious prayer and study, though Muslims and nonbelievers can also be participating members. When a man graduates, he must have a full-time job, or the equivalent in part-time work, and he must have a place to live, requirements that the mission staff helps fulfill.

As Meei Ling was busily preparing the garden for planting, Overcomers began to take notice of her developing project. One Overcomer named Greg, interviewed for a documentary video about the garden (Meei Ling 2017), talked about starting with the garden: "It drawed me to come out here. I used to look in the window upstairs and I could see it out of the window and I said 'Wow. That thing is real nice.' And I started hanging around, you know what I mean? It's like the old saying goes: 'You hang around the barber shop long enough, you get a haircut.' I came out here and I've been out here every day." He went on to say that the garden brought out his attention and care for plants, the need to weed and protect new growth from being crowded out or strangled, and then he turned to his struggle with addiction. Caring for the garden became a metaphor for his own process:

> It's like planting something and there's a bunch of weeds in there, too. And sometimes you can't get the weed out of there from choking the plant because you'll pull the whole plant out and then now you have no growth. And then once it gets strong enough, then you can pull the weeds out from around it. It's just like us, you know what I mean, you get rid of some bad stuff in your life, get rid of some stuff that's not helping you grow, and later down the line it turns into something of beauty, it turns into something that somebody else can get something from.

Recovery is a notoriously difficult path to follow. The language of recovery can seem overly sentimental or reductive or impermanent. While Greg speaks in the video, his fingers release a single green bean from a tendril wrapped around its middle. The tenderness of his action reinforces the urgency in his voice. Whether or not the garden, or the mission itself, could "save" Greg from long-term addiction, the experience of raising food for the mission tables brought him to equate a moment of vegetal growth and a moment of personal release. That moment of tenderness represents for me the connection between knowledge and action, experience and yearning, cooperation and individual striving, that an urban farm can foster for its participants. This tenderness in action can apply as much to literacy as it does to agriculture.

I tell the story of the mission farm, Meei Ling, and the Overcomers not merely because it's an excellent transition from the community arts focus in the last chapter to urban farming in this one. The farm is small, but it represents both the history of socially committed food distribution and production as well as the complex reasons why urban farms have grown so vibrant today. Planners, architects, activists, and ordinary people have sought to establish farms and gardens in urban environments for reasons that range from economic and political to aesthetic and spiritual. In the twentieth century, architects such as Frank Lloyd Wright and Ludwig Hilberseimer proposed rather fanciful designs to bring the agrarian and the urban together and thereby convert vertical, dense cities into horizontal landscapes that incorporated farming, manufacture, and living spaces in extended suburban utopias (Waldheim 2010). Jac Smit, described in his 2009 obituary as the "father of urban agriculture" (Nasr 2009), analyzed the many trends worldwide leading to increased urban farming. In addition to the pressing need for food security driving this development, Smit and his coauthors (2001) note that globally, "food buyers from the lowest to the highest income are increasingly asking and insisting on knowing where food was produced and preferring locally-grown produce over other products" (7) and that "consumers, particularly in wealthier countries, are demanding to *see the farmer's face* on their food" (8). Thus, raising crops in cities not only serves to feed people without access to cheap and healthy food but also fulfills a deep cultural desire to know the sources of nutrition beyond the boxes and plastic packages on supermarket shelves.

Philadelphia's urban farmers offer a bracing array of reasons for their efforts. Greensgrow, a relatively large farm founded in 1997, emphasizes sustainability and recycling on its website and in its operation. Mentioning the farm's green roof, composting toilet, voracious farm pig Milkshake, and offices made of reclaimed building materials, it says:

> Rethinking land, abandoned space, ideas, oil barrels, PVC, tools and trash is what we do. Veggie waste composts into fertilizer, a shipping container grew into a garden shop and rain gutters find a life as a farm. Many things we own, from our 6000 square foot greenhouse to our mobile market trucks, have come from a previous owner. Because we don't over capitalize on equipment we have been free to change things up. Everything we buy goes through a stringent cost benefit analysis to prove that it can be used at an optimal level. Some people call this cheap, we call it smart. (GREENandSAVE Staff 2017)

Greensgrow's economical approach appears rooted in the do-it-yourself American tradition—from Thoreau's Walden Pond and the arts and crafts movement of the late nineteenth century to *Popular Mechanics* and the countercultural *Whole Earth Catalog* of the twentieth century, to the Internet-based DIY networks and instructional websites of the twenty-first.

At the same time, many urban farmers take ecological action as fundamental to both spiritual and physical health for individuals as well as the human collective. Philadelphia's Jewish Farm School, formed in 2006, says about its project: "We are driven by traditions of using food and agriculture as tools for social justice and spiritual mindfulness. Through our programs, we address the injustices embedded in today's mainstream food systems and work to create greater access to sustainably grown foods, produced from a consciousness of both ecological and social well being" (Jewish Farm School 2014). Many farms in the Philadelphia area, like the Jewish Farm School, place education as a crucial part of their mission. Mill Creek Farm and Bartram Garden's Community Farm and Resource Center are two of the many examples of functioning agricultural operations that devote considerable energies to activities, programs, and camps for school children as well as horticultural and culinary workshops for adults. Some of the farms—including Grow Philly, Growing Home, and Growing Together—focus on displaced immigrant populations from Southeast Asia, Africa, and Latin America who want to be able to grow food they know, using techniques (and sometimes seeds) they have brought with them through their long journeys to the United States.

In preparation for writing this chapter in 2016–2017, I compiled a list of twenty-one farms within Philadelphia city limits, but that number doesn't include many independent neighborhood plots, some of them quite sizable, and gardens associated with Philadelphia Parks and Recreation's Farm Philly Program. The Pennsylvania Horticultural Society also oversees farm sites not on my list, including two in city prison facilities. In addition to the farms themselves, large organizations like Philabundance and the Food Trust provide educational support, outreach, and food distribution in the area and beyond, for the sake of nutritional justice and economic alternatives to the US mainstream commercial food system.

Literacy Learning in a "Community of Practice"

Learning in an urban farm brings people together through a truly "grounded" literacy. At every stage of the process, from designing the garden layout to preparing the soil, seeding the beds, watering and weeding, all the way until harvest and closing up for winter, the actions farmers take are purposeful and consequential, communal and personal. A little child learns what a seed can be; an elder remembers the okra she used to pick and cook with her grandmother. Every step is part of a greater sequence, and every sequence is keyed to earth and sky as well as the particular eating traditions of the people at work and the market where produce will go. A person can work wordlessly in the field all day even as the sustained practice of farming is framed by spoken and written language associated with scientific knowledge, folk customs, economic calculations, fairy tales, and weather predictions. A farmer is an author planting in rows rather than writing in lines.

One striking element of the urban farm scene is the way new participants are always being ushered into the collective, historical, and technical experience of growing food. Education is an element of nearly every farm operation in Philadelphia. As with almost any nonprofit operation that depends in part on grants or donations, education becomes a part of an urban farm's mission because funders so often want to see an ongoing connection to marginalized or developing populations. Even the few for-profit farms—such as an intensive hydroponic operation I tried (and failed) to visit in an industrial part of

South Philly, a green factory in a rehabbed warehouse—offer specific training sessions about their techniques to selected visitors who do not represent a competitive threat to their business. But in nearly all cases, the educational element of urban farms is informal, inclusive, and physically demanding work. We can understand the learning in such settings as an "open apprenticeship": not delimited by a specified contract as in more formal trade apprenticeships but still framed within a hierarchical master-journeyman-initiate relationship and embedded in what has been called a "community of practice."

Sociologists Jean Lave and Etienne Wenger (1997, 30) described learning within a wide variety of apprenticeships as "legitimate peripheral participation in communities of practice."[2] New learners are *peripheral* in the sense that they aren't yet capable of fully performing the tasks of a more adept participant. However, those entering a trade or a skilled occupation are still *legitimate* members of a community defined by a specific knowledge base and an established practice with a history and social function. This would be as true for medical interns at a city hospital as it would for initiates into a street gang in Los Angeles. Lave and Wenger discuss the examples of Mexican Yucatec midwives, Liberian Vai and Gola tailors, and American naval quartermasters, union meat cutters, and non-drinking alcoholics in Alcoholics Anonymous meetings (59–88). In each of these cases, and many more one can imagine, the transfer of knowledge and skill is embedded in an extended socialization process, a disciplined induction into behaviors and attitudes accepted by the larger group over time. The authors point out that apprenticeship does not always take the well-being of the inductee into account. For example, American meat-cutter apprentices are sometimes inadequately trained on a range of butchering skills because the supermarkets need them to do one repetitive task rapidly in order to keep their costs low (76–79). In such circumstances, apprentices become full participants quickly but within a limited segment of the community of practice.

Etienne Wenger, with his wife and coauthor Beverly Wenger-Traynor, define community of practice in a 2015 piece, and their definition suits the urban farm particularly well: "Communities of practice are groups of people who share a concern or a passion for something they do and learn how to do it better as they interact regularly." This definition touches on three characteristics that distinguish a community of practice from most social clubs, book groups, or casual assembly of friends. First, it requires commitment from the mem-

---

2. Scholars have recognized the value of Lave and Wenger's work for the field of writing studies. See especially references to the concept of "communities of practice" in Adler-Kassner and Wardle's *Naming What We Know* (2015). Here I am interested in emphasizing their understanding of "apprenticeships."

bers to a specific domain of interest, often one focused on building knowledge, skill, and experientially learned expertise. Members may differ in their mastery of this domain, but all wish to deepen their abilities by drawing on shared activities. A group that gets together monthly to eat and discuss a chosen literary work may not qualify, but a group that meets for three months to learn about Costa Rican coffee cooperatives before traveling to Costa Rica together could be called a community of practice. A group that picks up local produce every two weeks over the summer from a community-supported agriculture buying club might not fit the definition, but a group that meets in a different garden each week to see what's thriving and how general agricultural principles apply in specific cases certainly would. Second, the community must meet together regularly to exchange information about the domain practices and learn from one another. This characteristic wouldn't apply to the totality of visitors to Rodale's Organic Gardening website, but it might describe participating members of an online chat group regularly discussing organic pest control. Third, everyone in the community must engage in certain practices and draw on what Wenger and Wenger-Traynor (2015) call "a shared repertoire of resources," which might include commonly consulted books and websites but also commonly recognized solutions to challenges like reclaiming soil in abandoned city lots or addressing vandalism in a high-crime neighborhood.

By this definition, school seldom qualifies as a community of practice unless the institution or classroom is expressly organized to foster such an environment. Even a class designated as English or writing too often orients itself around a curriculum independent of student concerns and aimed at increasing students' performance on state or national tests. This is not to say that students can't learn a great deal in school, but I find the power of learning through participation in a community of practice extremely compelling. Philadelphia has an agricultural school called W. B. Saul High School, where students tend to crops and livestock at a working farm (McCorry 2013). One project involves the collecting, tending, and distribution of compost, a large-scale venture developed in collaboration with Weavers Way Co-op. As the developer of this project, Scott Blunk, remarked about the collaborative project, which earns money for both partners: "Vegetables and cow poop turn to gold. But really the best part about it is the kids—getting them involved in the process" (Blackmer 2013). This is a rare example of a community of practice in a school, especially in a time when few resources are going to vocational or hands-on programs in a cash strapped school district.[3]

---

3. Sports teams, school newspapers, and other after-school activities could qualify as communities of practice. Sadly, too often school districts cancel these activities early in cost-cutting times.

In Lave and Wenger's study (1997), perhaps the most surprising example of apprenticeships is the account of non-drinking alcoholics in Alcoholics Anonymous. As an apprenticeship, it seems less relevant to urban farming because the practice appears more therapeutic than product oriented. Yet, for a population of alcoholics seeking rehabilitation, a crucial element is learning not only how to speak in a meeting or call on mentors for help but also how to internalize a narrative that allows individuals to recast their stories in a hopeful and constructive way, conducive to staying sober (80–84). In a literate society, we are asked to "write our own stories," but more often than not that only means adopting and accommodating the narratives parents or neighbors, churches or educational institutions offer us.[4] In an urban area, difficult life choices involve conflicting stories that frame our actions. Many urban narratives normalize violence or hopelessness while others cast success as sparkling but distant, glorious but unattainable. Even as brilliant a series as *The Wire* can be terribly discouraging about the future in urban America, while the stirring story of some poor kid shooting hoops into the night who finally signs a big contract with the NBA can be inspiring but ultimately unrealistic for most urban youth. Spiritual storylines—the desperate addict who finds redemption at a mosque or church—can seem so removed from the temptations and threats of the street that young, unemployed, or disenfranchised people may feel that religious representatives are asking for a great commitment but offering little dependable help in exchange.

A farm in a city neighborhood can seem a shocking and surreal apparition, even while it appears handmade and actual. The visitor enters the front gate on a summer day and suddenly the sights and sounds and smells announce a new world built by collective labor and promising fruition and harvest. Children who come on a class trip or participate in a summer camp are usually assigned a task right away; they meet older children, young adults, and veteran growers working at all the jobs a season demands. A volunteer or new worker may end up doing something he or she initially thought distasteful, unfamiliar, or just plain impossible, whether it's spreading compost around tomato plants or picking Japanese beetles off cabbage leaves or fixing a hole in the shed roof on a hot day. The simple becomes daunting and then done. Nearly every farm experience involves a realistic struggle with danger: pests can ruin a crop, storms can damage a newly erected greenhouse, and local kids can vandalize property in the night. Gardens offer multiple lessons but seldom involve lectures or quizzes. The farm director may give instructions or draw up plans, but it's the doing that most defines a new narrative of labor and reward,

---

4. See Lauren Rosenberg's *The Desire for Literacy* (2015) for more on literacy's potential for "restorying" among disenfranchised people.

a timeline of actions and consequences, and ultimately the appreciation for the work of others and joy in cooperative effort.

The following sections describe two neighborhood-based farms in Philadelphia. Each is a "community of practice," within which people contribute their work at whatever level they can. Philadelphia Urban Creators' Life Do Grow Farm is a garden on two acres of abandoned land alongside a railroad line that runs through North Philadelphia. Most of its growers are local African American neighbors, with the help of some former and current Temple students as well as committed artists and activists. Growing Together is nearly three acres, also built beside a train track, in the South Philadelphia neighborhood of Point Breeze. Families from the Congo, Burma, and Bhutan grow crops there alongside longtime local residents and church parishioners. I chose these two farms simply because they represent diverse organizational approaches, missions, and demographics within the urban farm network of the city. As with the community arts organizations I discussed in the last chapter, it was difficult to choose a few to highlight among the many possible stories I could tell.

In each of the dozen or so farms I visited in 2016–2017, one or more leaders helped participants learn about farming as well as larger life lessons. Wherever I went, I met highly committed staff and volunteers who believed in what they were doing despite financial challenges, obstacles to good yields, fickle weather, and the inevitable trickiness of human interactions. Although I can't weed in my own home garden because of a bad back, I related to the farms most through my experience working on a Northern California vineyard and prune orchard when I was in my twenties (see *Writing Home* 2012, 102–12). I admire those who till and harvest, but I have particular respect for those who farm on formerly abandoned lots in underserved areas of the city. They give me hope for what can be done by ordinary people to enrich the lives of neighborhoods that governments tend to forget and the media portray as desolate. Urban farms are literacy projects in a profoundly democratic key. They remind me of Hal Adams's neighborhood writing groups and the epigraph to his journal: "every person is a philosopher." Unlike schools or adult basic education programs, urban farms embody literacy in and around productive activities without explicit instruction, standardized measurement, or specific job training requirements.

Philadelphia Urban Creators at Life Do Grow Farm

The Philadelphia Urban Creators staff members who run Life Do Grow Farm describes their history this way:

> The Urban Creators was founded in North Central Philadelphia 2010 by a diverse group of young people, unified by a vision to bridge the gap between isolated communities and transforming a 2-acre garbage dump into a farm. We spent our first year organizing door-to-door to gauge the interest and ideas shared by community members and stakeholders, and designing our theory of change. We spent our second year clearing away debris and planting the first seeds of our movement to remediate the polluted soils of injustice in North Philly. Our third year saw the transformation of this land into LIFE DO GROW; our urban farm, Community Resource and Innovation center, and our home. (Urban Creators 2014b)

Their account of the farm's origin touches on some distinctive qualities of the organization. In 2010 every member but one of the small group that founded the farm was younger than twenty-one. They were a mix of Temple undergraduates, neighborhood youth, and artist-activists looking to do something new and bold and collaborative in one of the poorest areas inside one of the most stressed sections of the city. Their impulse was toward community organizing first and farming second. In fact, the original group had little or no experience in agriculture—one codirector grew up in Manhattan, another other in Los Angeles, and the third in North Central Philly—but they had a passion for getting people together and "remediating the polluted soils of injustice." The land they adopted was indeed a two-acre relic of the industrial era that seemingly no one would build on, a triangular wasteland framed by a high wall that supported the elevated regional rail tracks on one side and on the other a narrow street running in front of dour concrete walls and corrugated metal sheets painted two shades of blue, then gray, and then blood red in successive properties. Even the Vision of Missions Tabernacle Church across the street seemed forbidding; everything said "Keep Out" on that unlovely block except the oddly luxuriant maple and honey locust trees shading parked cars.

But the rich and welcoming aspect of the block emerges as you come to know the people who constructed and sustain Life Do Grow Farm. The founding co-executive directors are Alex Epstein from New York, Jeaninne Kayembe from California, and Devon Bailey, who lives across the street from Life Do Grow. Their styles are quite different, but they share a devotion to effective organizing that will change lives. They all laugh easily and dream expansively. None have been afraid to work hard for the organization and the farm. Though at times they hanker for other climes and a more global reach, they have stayed true to their commitment to this patch of land and the people who live around it. Jeaninne is a spoken word performer, and black queer activist who can mesmerize an audience with her poetry. She came to Philadelphia as an artist and has gradually found new and innovative ways to use art in promoting social justice. She would agree that she's happier inspiring a crowd or talking with adjudicated youth than planting potatoes or making sure the greenhouse plastic sheeting is snug. Alex is a white Jewish activist who graduated from Temple with a degree of his own design, combining urban studies and geography, political science and sociology, social entrepreneurship and business. Before he started as a freshman, he had already cofounded a youth-led nonprofit (the NY2X Coalition), and organized several hundred young people in NYC to travel down to New Orleans after Hurricane Katrina and rebuild homes and support community organizing efforts in the Lower Ninth Ward. He wrote most of the original Urban Creators grants and guided the organization administratively as it navigated becoming a nonprofit, though he'd much rather have been knocking on doors to advocate for a local response to the big, bossy neighbor a few blocks away, the university.

A great many other people contribute to the character of Urban Creators, but I'll limit myself here to one other founding partner. He is Dev, a wise older African American man and self-proclaimed "mad scientist" of the group. Dev lives in the house across the street from the Life Do Grow Farm, his grandfather's house, a place his family has owned for several decades. As Alex often says when he introduces Dev, the young founding activists met Dev one night as they were moving some recycled building materials onto the lot to replace the ones that had been recently stolen from them. As Jeaninne and Alex were dropping off wooden pallets at 11:00 p.m. one February night, Dev came across the street to confront the two for illegally dumping in his neighborhood. They began a conversation, and it turned out it was Dev who had taken the previous batch of wood, thinking they were just foolish kids making a mess in the lot. He didn't see why the wood should go to waste, so he ended up using the pallets as firewood to heat his building across the street. It also turned out that Dev was a skilled carpenter who could build almost anything; soon he was helping them assemble their first garden beds, tool shed, greenhouses. Dev helped on their projects when he wasn't picking up jobs here and there.

At that time, everyone at Urban Creators was working on a fully volunteer basis. Once they received some money to run youth programs and raise organic crops for a vendor at the famous food market Reading Terminal downtown, they could pay Dev (along with Jeaninne, Alex, and a young farm manager) to join the team officially. Soon he was working regularly with them, not only building but mentoring the young people who attended the farm's after-school and summer programs. As the site and development director, Dev oversees projects, teaches skills and life lessons, and helps design other projects in the neighborhood that the Urban Creators pursue. The website in

2014 said he "channels the wisdom from experiencing troubled times and entanglement with the law to now be an example to the neighborhood youth" (Urban Creators 2014b). He knows the neighbors well and brings a sense of stability, dignity, and history to the organization.

Alex and Jeaninne put together an experienced board in preparation for their application for 501(c)(3) status. I served on the board of the organization from its beginning in 2014 until 2017, but I learned more than I contributed at meetings with my fellow board members: developers and city planners, agriculture consultants and activists. From the first meeting, we supported Urban Creators and were deeply impressed with the team's ideas and energy. At the same time, we were skeptical of the elaborate plans and dreams Alex and Jeaninne presented at the first few meetings. We warned them that they needed to establish a solid and thriving base in North Philadelphia before they thought about expanding to other sites in the city and other cities on the East Coast and beyond. We also urged them to hire a real farm director who had significant experience in raising crops under city conditions.

To their credit, Alex and Jeaninne listened to the board but didn't dim their enthusiasm for new projects. By the second summer of operation, they had secured a major award in collaboration with the city's Office of Public Safety on a Federal Justice Department grant to offer REGENERATION, a reentry program for adjudicated youth. Working with the Mural Arts Program (see previous chapter), they led a six-month workforce and leadership development program for fifteen formerly incarcerated young men who lived within the specific service sector of Police District 22, where the farm is located. The group tended crops, learned landscaping and carpentry skills with Dev, composed business plans and proposed social impact projects for the neighborhood, and painted a mural on those forbidding walls below the railroad tracks. The mayor came to the graduation ceremony at the end of the summer.

Within three years of gaining nonprofit status, Urban Creators listed on its website nineteen corporate and foundation funders, both national and local, in addition to twenty-two organizations with which it had partnered on one or more projects. The organization was able to bring in enough income to make a crucial hire: Kirtrina Baxter as the farm manager. Kirtrina had deep experience and training in urban agriculture as well as an MA in cultural studies, emphasizing social justice, African American traditions, and the politics of food. She had strong connections to other African American farmers in the region and had been deeply involved with the politically active group Soil Generation. This group calls itself "black-led, grassroots coalition of radical community gardeners and urban farmers" with a mission around food and environmental justice as well as community self-determination

(Soil Generation 2017). Her addition emphasized their commitment both to high-quality produce and active community engagement. Life Do Grow offers a regular farmer's market from April to November, distributing "squash, peppers, tomatoes, okra, figs, collard greens, kale, garlic, carrots, pumpkins, and all kinds of herbs" ("Farm" 2015) to neighbors and friends in addition to selling microgreens and other organic produce to vendors and restaurants. In July 2017 the farm celebrated its fourth annual Hoodstock, a daylong block party celebration of food, art, music, and "Radical Joy" that attracted hundreds of community members, artists, well-wishers, students, and local fans.

At the time I'm writing, Urban Creators seem to be successful in the crucial job of developing a new generation in the organization. Sonia Galiber, a recent Temple graduate of African American and Okinawan heritage, took over from Alex and Jeaninne many of the administrative and organizational duties as well as social media for Urban Creators. The organization also added an Americorps farm fellow named Stanley Morgan, a young Philadelphia native who brought tremendous excitement and commitment to the organization. The grant-funded position allowed him to become totally immersed in every aspect of the growing and building phases of the farm. In 2017 the farm added Keaira Jones and Nyseem Smith, two young people who had previously worked at Tree House Books (see chapter 5), to work on community connections and events with neighbors. Alex described this group of young people, along with the many local teens who have grown to be a part of the Urban Creator family over the past eight years, as the future leadership of Life Do Grow Farm.

Growing Together

Unlike Urban Creators, which was founded by young activists without institutional affiliations, Growing Together and its sister farm Growing Home were a result of two established and venerable organizations cooperating with neighborhood groups. In 2011 the Nationalities Services Center started a project it called the Refugee Urban Agriculture Initiative, hoping to use farming as a way to help its immigrant clients to integrate with their new communities. NSC provides language assistance, job training, and counseling for immigrants in Philadelphia. Communication is crucial to its operation. They offer translation services in more than 150 languages, interpreters for hospital visits and business meetings, and English classes for non-native speakers. Founded in 1921 as a part of a national organization for immigrant support, their original mission was to help immigrant women acquire English language proficiency and citizenship, but that initial emphasis has expanded to families and their needs, including food and housing in addition to employment

(Nationalities Services Center 2015). In short, literacy and language has always been at the heart of NSC's mission. They reasoned at the time of the Urban Agriculture Initiative launch that farming would help new arrivals to connect with their neighbors while also providing them a source of food and a way to acquire skills related to employment (Nationalities Services Center 2017).

NSC sought a partner that could provide agricultural expertise, and it found assistance from the Pennsylvania Horticultural Society, one of the largest nonprofits in the city devoted to the cultivation of plants and gardens. Established in 1827, PHS is the oldest of the city nonprofits I visited in my study. Its best-known project is the Philadelphia Flower Show, started in 1829 and today attracting more than 250,000 people each year to the largest and oldest gardening show in the United States. As celebrated as the Flower Show is, however, it is only one of many programs PHS pursues in the region. With more than one hundred employees, PHS has the resources and public presence to pursue an ambitious array of plans for "gardening, greening, and learning" (Pennsylvania Horticultural Society 2015). Its programming in 2017 included a regional partnership called Plant One Million, which commits to planting massive numbers of trees in the portions of Pennsylvania, New Jersey, and Delaware surrounding Philadelphia. Another ambitious project it continues to sponsor in 2019 is City Harvest ("City Harvest" 2015), a complex web of gardens and greenhouses throughout the city, including one greenhouse staffed by Philadelphia Prison System inmates who are trained by PHS professionals. Five PHS greenhouses supply seedlings to 140 gardens in the area and distribute the resulting produce to low-income families. In addition, PHS offers training courses for beginning and advanced gardeners to encourage vibrant horticulture practices that contribute to City Harvest ("Garden Tenders" 2017).

In the first growing season of 2015, Growing Together emerged through a cooperative effort of PHS farming staff Lisa Mosca and Adam Hill and NSC counseling staff, who recruited and trained gardeners to work on small plots within a 2.8-acre lot donated by the Church of the Redeemer in the Point Breeze section of South Philadelphia. It was a tremendous undertaking to clear the vacant and debris-strewn land, build raised beds, and pipe in water. More than two hundred volunteers worked that first year, and more than ninety-five thousand dollars went into waterlines, fresh soil, and compost, rehabilitating land that had once held factories along the train tracks. NSC initiated Entrepreneurial Gardens in 2016, offering plots and more training for gardeners who wanted to raise additional crops for sale.

Farmers in Growing Together are immigrants from the Congo, Burma, Nepal, and Bhutan, joined by Point Breeze residents as well as parishioners from Church of the Redeemer. In their sister farm, Growing Home, farmers work together in nationality groups on assigned plots of land. However, at Growing Together the organizers consciously mixed up nationalities in assigning plots. People from Africa and South Asia grow food alongside African American residents from the neighborhood. During a 2016 visit I made to the site, Adam told me that at first people were shy with strangers, but by the second year there was much more interaction and mutual support among participants. Sharing food as well as labor and advice helped cement relationships over the growing season.

In 2017 Lisa left PHS after twelve years, and Adam took on more City Harvest responsibilities in sites across town. PHS handed over more of the management of the farm to NSC Farm Manager Merthus Mbonigaba, a Congolese farmer and teacher who spoke better Portuguese and Swahili than English. Merthus understood the experience of the refugee farmers at Growing Together. His family had been forced to leave the Republic of Congo because of war and oppression, lived in a Namibian camp for seventeen years, and only arrived in the United States in 2015. As a way of bringing the familiar into their new home, Merthus introduced African eggplant and bitter melon to the farm (Jaramillo 2017). Adam still brought around a tractor now and then to cut grass along the sides of the property, and he supplied seedlings from City Harvest to the neighborhood gardeners, while Lisa often consulted with the Growing Together farmers, but as of 2017 Merthus handled most of the on-site problems and training.

Urban Farms as Literacy Sponsors

When I think about urban farms in Philadelphia, I am struck by the beauty of intentional efforts to raise healthful and affordable food in places many might regard as forbidding. At the same time, I also recognize the relatively un-self-conscious yet effective learning that farm participants experience while working together for a common purpose that seems to have nothing to do with literacy. Farms can help adjudicated youth reenter their old neighborhoods without falling back into self-destructive patterns. Gardens support immigrants new to American language and customs to feel a modicum of familiarity as they build their lives in adopted cities. A fenced-off half-block of land, where collards grow in rows and raised beds like rowboats carry string beans, cabbage, and okra, can also be a safe space, where one group of people reach a level of acceptance and communication with others who do not even share their language. Some farms are deeply tied to the neighbors and local institutions surrounding the tilled land while in others the farm founders only become intimate with locals through a long process of mutual education. Farmers may start off focused on crops, but in an urban setting kids and adults come by to ask questions, sample the produce, and tell the tenders how it was done in hometowns from Soviet Georgia to Georgia, USA. Farming in the city is always done within a fabric of relationships and social expectations that may have little to do with crop yield or soil management.

But what does urban farming have to do with literacy? When I started out to write this chapter, I felt certain the link existed, but I couldn't exactly explain to others what I felt to be true. Now I can identify two specific ways that literacy and farming go together. The first one involves the "habits of mind" that I referred to in the community arts chapter, both those tied to academic learning in "Framework for Success in Postsecondary Writing" and those more informal yet more capacious principles outlined by the Mural Arts Project. Farms nurture ways of thinking and acting that are quite congenial with literacy, even in fairly traditional definitions of that term. A farm manager can be a literacy sponsor for a new participant—emphasizing sequential operations, revision and editing, scientific knowledge, historical perspective— by teaching crop planning and management, the importance of weeding and pest control, all the while weaving in lessons about the physics of water flow, levers, or evaporation and inculcating a reverence for historical techniques or heirloom species. Farmers learn to interpret meteorological data, order seeds, and read manuals about planting times, soil pH, and crop nutrition. In this, urban farming follows a centuries-old function of agriculture: educating the young through apprenticeship in the lore and techniques developed over time by elders in a community of practice.

At the same time, farms—even more than art studios—thrust participants into a world not dominated by written or spoken language, forcing participants to reimagine the nature of literacy itself. The things we see and touch and taste aren't merely artifacts of written language, as modern city dwellers tend to assume. The physical world disrupts, sometimes rudely, our experience of language. Standing in a rainstorm, or watching a bee pollinate a cantaloupe flower, a person whose concept of eating is framed by refrigerators and fast food restaurants cannot hold on to the illusion that humans largely shape their own environment with products bought in a store. I don't mean this in a sentimental way, but I do recognize sentiment as a crucial element of language. We lose a sense of the traction and friction in language by learning words always in the context of other words, in school, in offices, even among friends sitting in a Starbucks. Direct interaction with natural environments refreshes language by bringing words in contact with palpable referents. *Harvest* isn't merely an evocative adjective used in October to sell pumpkin spice lattes; collecting corn, squash, beans as the weather turns cool not only demands hard labor but also reinforces a rich vocabulary of produce, ripeness, and eventual decay. And in African American communities, a highly skilled farmer such as Kirtrina Baxter serves a crucial purpose in reminding young and old North Philadelphia residents that people of African descent have a long, venerable, and deeply satisfying relationship to growing food and feeding their families from the land. A child cannot fully absorb this lesson in his own history simply by studying the biography of George Washington Carver in school once a year during Black History Month.

Both understandings of literacy—that agriculture teaches powerful habits of mind and that words have palpable referents in nature—are outgrowths of the open apprenticeships within these particular communities of practice, and both have similarities to the learning that takes place in community arts settings. Urban Creators has successfully built a community of practice that is both closely tied to the neighborhood it serves and capable of connecting individuals to artists, employers, and mentors from outside the neighborhood that they would not ordinarily meet in their day-to-day lives. If we think of literacy as the ability to access *conversations* bounded by certain norms, histories, and expectations facilitated by written symbols, then Life Do Grow shifts participants from one set of conversations to a different set, ones that hopefully lead to employment opportunities, insight on local social circumstances, and advocacy for the immediate community. The young men who joined REGENERATION came into the summer program immersed in the conversation of the street involving the drug trade, gangs, police, and government assistance as well as the specialized language of the juvenile justice system. REGENERATION plunged them into new conversations about agriculture and soil, murals depicting local events, and job possibilities in landscaping and other fields. They were *partial participants* in many activities because they were just learning how to paint, farm, compose poetry, and consider their lives in a wider domain, but they were *legitimate* because Life Do Grow gave them a respected social standing they had to earn every day. Some of the young men didn't complete the program for personal reasons or an inability to stay the course, but eleven of the original fifteen did stick with it. For the ones who lasted, the farm served not only as a mechanism through which organizations could cooperate for the sake of the group but also as a physical place to witness organic changes, a dramatic setting for new relationships, and a workshop for constructing one's identity anew. In this way, the young men served an apprenticeship similar to both a carpenter's training program and a nondrinking alcoholic's first months in AA: an extended opportunity to invent a new narrative for themselves among colleagues who cared about them and the practices they were learning.

Growing Together Farm represents another striking characteristic of urban farming in Philadelphia and beyond: networking and cooperation. This farm for immigrants and South Philly neighbors is a direct result of collaboration among organizations that are highly connected throughout the city. As I have mentioned, Pennsylvania Horticultural Society has a long history and a large presence in Philadelphia; Nationalities Services Center is not as commonly known but equally rooted in the city's history and positioned to work with a wide array of clients. The Baptist church that leased the land to Growing Together, the Church of the Redeemer, was founded in 1966 and, in addition to its worship services, supports a large Christian Education Center for youth and prospective pastors as well as a Community Development Corporation to encourage economic development and revitalize housing in the stressed Point Breeze neighborhood. These three institutions intersected in its diverse mission-driven commitments to make Growing Together a reality when no single entity could have created and sustained it alone.

Soon after I began exploring the farm culture in the city, I realized with pride and amazement that Philadelphia has a well-developed network of gardens and farms as well as food co-ops, distribution centers, and educational services associated with nutrition and organic food production. Just as farmwork requires constant cooperation among crews and volunteers to plow, seed, cultivate, and harvest food, single farms in a city are seldom isolated from other farms—the people who plant in vacant lots are almost always open for collaborations with others who grow seed stock, raise new crops, put on educational programs, and sell or distribute healthy food. Two examples must suffice. Adam Hill of PHS works with five seedling centers and dozens of gardens through his job at the City Harvest program. But in our conversations for this chapter, he mentioned many other groups in the city, such as Weavers Way Co-op (three food store locations and a productive farm of their own), Eastern Park Revitalization Alliance (an environmental and health organization supporting up to seven gardens and planting trees in the Strawberry Mansion area of North Philly), and The Farm at Bartram Gardens (extensive vegetable and fruit plantings in a forty-five-acre botanical garden, the oldest in North America, offering excellent educational programs for all ages). A second example is Kirtrina Baxter of Philadelphia Urban Creators. She actively connects the farm to predominantly African American farmers in the Soil Generators network. At the same time, she pursues other affiliations and informal activities that enrich her work at Life Do Grow, including her work as a community organizer for the Garden Justice League Initiative, assisting gardeners in town to gain access to arable land. Nearly every farm manager and director I met had multiple connections to other farmers, educational institutions, and food cooperatives. Many also had other vocations as artists, craftspeople, language teachers, and spiritual guides.

As I conclude this chapter, I'm sad I couldn't include accounts of the many other quality gardens and agricultural education projects in the city. The few examples I discussed will have to suffice, but much more can and should be said about the resources available in one of America's seemingly poorest cities. It's a striking paradox of American urban life that in exactly the places mainstream culture often sees deficit, poverty, and hopelessness, a watchful observer can also find fruitfulness, initiative, and a desire to rise. If you accept my argument that urban farms are literacy sponsors through their form of apprenticeship within a community of practice, then the urban farm system in Philadelphia is a superb example of the way sponsors can establish complex learning networks to expand and enhance their contributions to the region.

PART III

DAVID — **Learning Networks in Arkansas**

8 Health

My "homecoming" to Augusta, Arkansas, in 2007 was initiated by a concern for health—but in the years following, I developed a different perspective on health than I had expected.

I had lived in northwest Arkansas for only about a year when I happened to find myself in Augusta, and I should make clear from the outset three points about my rather unexpected presence there. First, before moving to Arkansas, I had lived in Chicago, the third-largest city in the United States, for twenty-one years, and I had become a bona-fide city dweller: I loved my life on the streets and in the neighborhoods. I loved the funky ethnic restaurants. I loved not having to drive. I loved the theaters, especially the storefront ones where I could see young actors and directors honing their craft for audiences of forty or fifty people sitting on folding chairs on makeshift risers. I loved the lovable-loser Cubs, the only team in town that played real baseball, abjuring the heinous designated hitter rule. When I left my job at DePaul University to take a position at the University of Arkansas, my new dean assured me that there were several direct flights daily between Fayetteville and Chicago and that lots of faculty members made that trek regularly. He never said so directly, but he hinted, "Why not think of Fayetteville simply as 'Chicago South?'" Or maybe that's just what I wanted to hear.

Second, Augusta sure as hell wasn't northwest Arkansas. Northwest Arkansas was in the midst of a boom. Stimulated by the growth of the University of Arkansas, Tyson Foods, J. B. Hunt Transportation, and Walmart's home office, the population was burgeoning. Good jobs were plentiful. Houses were mostly new and quite affordable. The schools were generally excellent. And northwest Arkansas had hills, trees, and four lovely seasons. Augusta, by contrast, struck me as troubled and perhaps even moving in the wrong direction. It was (and still is) a small town, about 2,400 people. Its houses ranged from middle-aged to old. Its one-street downtown clearly had once been a vibrant business district but now housed mostly vacant store fronts. Its high school seemed to have been frozen in time in the early 1960s, when it appeared to have been built. Two of the major employers in the town, both small factories, had shut down their operations. One had moved its production to Mexico. And it was flat—on the western slope of a geographic feature called the Arkansas Delta, where the Mississippi and its tributaries have leveled the land and deposited the rich alluvia that give rise to bumper crops of rice, cotton, soybeans, and milo. Northwest Arkansas is the Ozarks. The Arkansas Delta is the South. It's hard to envision the two regions' being in the same state.

Third, just being in Augusta in 2007 thrust me into the realm of what the poet John Keats called "negative capability," the state of holding two conflicting notions simultaneously. Or, to put it in more common terms, I experienced what that famous philosopher Yogi Berra called "déjà vu all over again," and it gave me the heebie-jeebies. Hailing from New Martinsville, West Virginia (population 5,000 or so), the seat of Wetzel County, where my branch of the Jolliffe family has lived since around 1830, I know all about small towns. On the one hand, everyone knows everyone else. People go to church together, shop at the same stores, go to the same athletic and cultural events (usually those connected with the town's high school), marry someone they met in school, settle down in a nice house, have two and a half children, work forty-five years at the same job, retire, die, get buried in the local cemetery. On the other hand . . . well, on the other hand one finds the same things as on the one hand. I loved growing up in my small hometown, but I learned quickly as an adult that I was not prone to romanticize small-town life. When I became a high school teacher in 1976 and took a job in Wheeling, West Virginia, then the "big city" (population around 50,000) in the Northern Panhandle, the principal of the high school I had attended in New Martinsville (Magnolia High, home of the Blue Eagles) asked me pointedly why I didn't "come back home" to teach. "Over my dead body . . . but more specifically, over yours," I wanted to respond.

So I was leery of Augusta. I could feel the tentacles of small-town life encircling me. It took just one afternoon for those tentacles to drop and their replacements, warm loving arms, begin to emerge. I had shown up in Augusta at the invitation of my new colleague Otto Loewer, the retired dean of the University of Arkansas engineering college, who had grown up in a little rice-farming village in the Arkansas Delta named Fair Oaks. Otto's brother was still running the family farm, and Otto had a warm place in his heart for his natal region. He had been one of the founders of a community organization called the Crossroads Coalition (so named for having its headquarters at the junction of Arkansas Route 1 and US Route 64 in Forrest City, Arkansas, literally the hub of commerce in the Delta), and one of the coalition's signature initiatives was health care. Someone in the health care community had told me that roughly three-quarters of a million dollars was ill-spent on health care in Arkansas because so many patients couldn't read well enough to follow directions on a prescription bottle or a care plan, so I decided to show up at the meeting in Augusta connected to the coalition's "pillar group" on health care.

The conclave was held at the American Legion Hut. "Hut" is the key term here—not the American Legion Hall or the American Legion Building but a long, dark, low-ceilinged log-and-cement structure that sits far down on the lovely but flood-prone banks of the White River. I don't recall what happened at that meeting—I probably talked a lot and popped off about my new job—but I remember vividly what transpired afterwards. A smallish man, probably a bit younger than me, approached me and asked politely, "Do you know something about education?" I allowed that I did—I'd been teaching for about thirty years by that time. And at that moment, a friendship, a partnership, a meeting of the minds was launched.

That inquisitor and soon-to-be partner was Dr. Steven Collier.

Steve Collier is a visionary, a dreamer, a doer. A native of Augusta—his father had been an automobile salesman and later a banker in the town—Steve graduated from Augusta High, went to Baylor where he earned a BA in history, then went to medical school at the University of Arkansas for Medical Sciences in Little Rock. A doc who still does daily rounds at Baptist Health Hospital in Searcy, twenty-five miles west of Augusta, Steve is also CEO of an organization called ARCare, which operates thirty clinics in small towns in eastern, central, and southern Arkansas. Before it expanded statewide, ARCare used to be called White River Rural Health Center, and I must admit that I like the old name better than the new. Otto Loewer always says that if you grow up in the Arkansas Delta, the banks of the White River are the closest thing you're ever going to find that resembles a beach.

When I met Steve on that day at the Legion Hut, he was trying to save his hometown. The aforementioned two small industries in Augusta had closed, leaving only the Bunge grain elevator, the Sloan toilet valve factory, and ARCare as major employers. The population was dropping, both in the town and in the schools, and the latter were having difficulties finding and retaining teachers. But two years earlier Steve had met a community organizer from Wynne, a somewhat larger town forty minutes east, named Bill Thomas. At that time, Marion, Arkansas—just slightly northwest of and across the Mississippi River from Memphis—was in the running to be the site of a new Toyota factory, and Bill had convinced Steve that if the new auto plant were to be built, the Delta economy would rumble to life and success would resonate in a hundred-mile radius around Marion. Augusta was inside that circle of potentiality, so Steve invited Bill to Augusta, and they walked through the derelict downtown, imagining possibilities. And Bill introduced Steve to Otto Loewer and the Crossroads Coalition.

Then in May 2007 the bubble of optimism popped. Toyota announced it was locating its new plant in Tupelo, Mississippi. The company cited "cleaner air quality" as the reason for choosing Tupelo over Marion, but insiders suspected that the decision had more to do with the potential workforces in the two locations than with environmental conditions. Could it really be possible that Mississippi was doing a better job of educating students (and adults) to participate in a high-tech workforce than Arkansas? What about all those jokes people had made for decades, when assessments suggested that Arkansas students were among the poorest performers in the country? If Arkansas wasn't in last place (in whatever metric was being applied), folks could always sigh, "Well, thank god for Mississippi!" Not anymore.

"That was a very dark day for us," Steve said in retrospect. However, he and others continued to have faith in the Crossroads Coalition, and for many would-be salvagers of the Arkansas Delta, Loewer was their lifeline. But unfortunately Loewer's resources were limited. When he retired from the deanship of the University of Arkansas College of Engineering, Loewer had been given some university funding to launch a center for economic development in the Delta, but those funds were drying up. I didn't realize it at the time, but I believe Loewer saw in me a new faculty member whose interest in the Delta had been kindled and who had a tidy endowment attached to his new job. Loewer was happy to introduce me to the good folks trying to save the Delta, and I was happy to meet them. "You were kind of a handoff," Steve admitted.

My next meeting with Steve came a month or so after the day at the Legion Hut, when he invited me back to Augusta for a meeting of a group called the Augusta Recovery Initiative, whose name suggests its mission. If any gathering around a conference table in a small-town medical clinic could be labeled momentous, this would have been it. Steve presided, but joining him at the table were, among others, ARCare's CFO, T. J. Whitehead, Steve's right-hand man; a youngish African American woman who worked as a nurse at the medical clinic but who also had been elected to the local school board; the minister of Augusta's most prominent African American church; a woman who had been writing the society column in the town's weekly newspaper for decades; a veteran math teacher from the high school; a US Navy veteran who had returned from service to take a data processing job with White River Rural Health; and a twentyish fellow, white, the local undertaker, who noted, "I've been burying way too many young people these days." The upshot of this meeting was this: the Augusta Recovery Initiative had been meeting for two years, trying to figure out ways to revive the town's economy, but the group had now decided that its major focus was not economic. They still wanted to attract new industries to occupy the sites vacated by the departed industries. But their new center of gravity was education. They determined that if they ever wanted to bring the town back, they needed to ensure that the schools were top notch, that if families moved to Augusta and enrolled their kids in the schools, they would get a quality education.

I was the newcomer to the group, and they asked me what I thought about this shift in direction. I allowed as how I was 100 percent in their corner, but I added a caveat: If we wanted to improve education, we couldn't limit ourselves to the schools. We had to expand our scope. We had to involve folks in the churches, the not-for-profit organizations, the businesses and industries, the library. I likened it to a corny movie from the 1970s, *Cold Turkey*, in which everyone in a small town promises to quit smoking. Everyone in Augusta, I proposed, needed to raise their hands and swear that he or she would work to improve reading and writing among citizens of all walks of life, understanding that improving literacy was key to improving the quality of life—personal, professional, economic, spiritual—in twenty-first-century America. And we had to emphasize literacy as *doing*: engaging people in networks where informed, thoughtful action motivated social change.

The Augusta Recovery Initiative folks apparently took my bait—at least Steve did. One of the first things he did after that meeting was to hire the miraculous Joy Lynn Bowen, a lifelong Augustan and a public school teacher who had retired early from the Augusta schools, as ARCare's education director and volunteer coordinator. Voila, I had a soulmate. In our nearly a decade of working together, Joy Lynn rarely said anything to me that didn't boil down to one of two questions, followed by a brief statement: "Is there a problem? How can we solve the problem? Let's get going." More on Joy Lynn anon.

I don't know any other directors of statewide health-care organizations, but I bet you that none of them adheres to a principle that I've seen manifest in Steve time and again: When he oversees the development and continuing operation of an ARCare clinic in a town, he believes that he (actually the corporation, but it starts with him) is responsible for improving not only the quality of health among the residents but also the overall health of the town. Steve deeply reveres his hometown and its region. He and his colleagues ask, "What does an ARCare community need to help its residents live more healthily in mind and body, more free from the stresses that everyday work and family life entail, and how can ARCare help?" Every ARCare location gets something "value added." McCrory, just eleven miles east of Augusta, needed a senior citizens' assisted living facility. ARCare built one. Cherry Valley, forty-two miles northeast, needed medical clinics right on the high school campus. ARCare built them. Brinkley, forty miles southeast, needed a diabetes education program. ARCare developed one.

In line with the Augusta Recovery Initiative's focus, the "value added" there was education. From the outset, Steve made it clear that our goal was never to "take over" the Augusta schools, but assuring the school leadership of that was never easy. Early in our work together, Steve and I scheduled a meeting with the superintendent of schools, a former football coach who was nearing retirement after decades of employment in the district, and I have rarely witnessed such wariness.[1] Here was the CEO of the largest employer in town and a university professor (from Chicago, no less!) wondering how we might "help" the schools. The meeting was tense, but the superintendent agreed to allow Augusta High School to participate in the Arkansas Delta Oral History Project, one of the first initiatives my office developed, in which students from small, rural high schools in the Delta would work in collaborative writing groups, each chaired by the University of Arkansas mentor, with each participant producing a substantial work—an essay, a short story, a play, a website—based on an oral history investigation proposed and carried out by each high school student. (See *The Arkansas Delta Oral History Project*.) This initiative gave us an in, something to *do* in the school other than simply

---

1. Have you noticed how many small school district superintendents and principals are former coaches?

talking to students and trying to help them see their way toward graduating and going on to postsecondary education—although Joy Lynn and I did lots of "simply talking."

With the superintendent's somewhat grudging blessing, the schools were now at least tentatively in play. We quickly launched a principal's book-of-the-month club in the elementary school, which involved supplying doctors' and dentists' offices with multiple copies of the book, all of which were immediately stolen, and to help students begin to think more realistically about going to college, we started sponsoring ACT tutoring sessions at the high school. The ACT tutoring seemed to take: in 2006, the year before we started offering the tutoring sessions, only 22 of the 48 graduating seniors from Augusta High School even took the exam and only 5 went to college; in 2009, 23 of the 29 graduating seniors were accepted to college, and collectively they earned $202,000 in scholarship support (Krupa 2009).

Steve then urged us to turn our attention to the larger community, and the idea of one-day education summits began to coalesce. We held three of them, each scheduled during the week before classes began in the fall. They were wonderful experiences, attended by folks from all walks of life in the town. A year before we started the education initiative, ARCare had purchased a structure that had been the stand-alone gymnasium for the former elementary school and had refurbished it as a community wellness center with a workout facility upstairs, a computer café in the back, and a full-size basketball court on the first floor. That court conveniently became a meeting space for the education summits, which involved a catered lunch, speeches, and group discussions.[2] The themes of the education summits, held for three consecutive years, were always the same: We must give our students more opportunities to learn—to read, write, talk, listen and think—than simply classroom instruction.[3] We must stress for everyone the importance of lifelong learning, in particular some kind of postsecondary education for high school graduates. We must impress on everyone that just because you're from a small town in rural Arkansas with a diminishing population and a troubled economy, that doesn't mean you can't or won't succeed in school and in your life beyond it.

With the one-day summits hitting the community at large with the educa-

---

2. I was on the dais at the first summit, along with Otto Loewer and a woman from Augusta who had received her PhD and gone on to teach entrepreneurship at a large university in Florida.

3. The summits maintained their vitality for all three years, but their attendance took a dip in years two and three when the superintendent would not allow teachers to miss one of the district's required in-service days prior to school's beginning in order to participate in the summit.

tion message, Steve called on the resources of ARCare to promote the message at an individual level. Five years before the community initiative got under way, Steve had established positions he called "ARCare Scholars in Residence," and he gave well-paying summer jobs in interesting corners of ARCare to promising students from Augusta. The first of these positions went to a fellow who, by the time I started my association with ARCare, had graduated from the state police academy and was a law enforcement officer in Augusta. When I began working in Augusta, one of the later scholars in residence had just completed her PhD in higher education at the University of Iowa—she boldly exclaimed that she wanted to return to Arkansas someday as the chancellor of the University of Arkansas at Pine Bluff, the state's only historically black public university. From my first day in Augusta, I was constantly assisted by a young fellow who was a high school junior then but with the scholar-in-residence support eventually was accepted into medical school at the University of Arkansas for Medical Sciences in Little Rock.

ARCare has added at least seven new clinics since I began working with folks in Augusta, and other regions are now showing interest in emulating the ARCare model of value-added health care. A group of counties in the far southwest corner of Kentucky, for example, has launched an organization called KentuckyCare to follow the ARCare path. So Steve is usually too busy to remain hands-on with the Augusta education initiative, leaving its day-to-day operation to Joy Lynn—and a bit to me, I'm happy to say. But Steve has continued to hold a brief for two aspects of the education initiative that he feels passionately committed to: getting students involved in the theater and sponsoring "challenge trips" so students can experience cultures beyond that of their hometowns and counties.

About the former: Having gone to Augusta High School during the day when it was standard practice for there to be a junior class play and a senior class play (as was the case at my alma mater, Magnolia High School, when I went there in the 1960s, by the way), Steve realizes how much students learn about language, reading, speaking, writing, confidence, community, and self-awareness by participating in a play, not only as an actor but even as a set builder, light runner, costume sewer, program hander-outer. Steve enthusiastically led ARCare's support of the White River Shakespeare Festival, an enterprise we ran in 2011, which involved students from Augusta High School and two neighboring ones meeting on five consecutive Saturdays to learn *The Tempest* by engaging in theater games about it, trying on its scenes, and writing creatively about it. When I brought a professional production of the play to Augusta, which was performed on a stage on the banks of the White River, just up the hill from the Legion Hut, the afternoon began with a performance of *The Tempest Tossed,* a thirty-minute curtain-raiser written and performed by the high school students themselves. Since that time, ARCare has consistently stepped forward to sponsor initiatives that get students into theater and theater into students. When the little professional company that I helped to found, the Classical Edge Theatre, wanted to bring its performances of "short Shakespeare" and its workshops on reading the Bard, understanding characters, and speaking a play's lines to a high school anyplace there is an ARCare clinic, the organization always found funds to make the touring gigs happen. When students from three Arkansas Delta towns asked me to help them get a drama program at their high schools—a task a bit beyond my capability—ARCare came forward to fund a week-long summer drama camp, held in Fayetteville and staffed by University of Arkansas theater faculty and graduate students, for high school sophomores, juniors, and seniors from small towns across the state.

About the latter: Like many people who went to high school in the seventies, Steve remembers the importance—and the fun—of senior trips. Even if these jaunts took the students to such nearby locations as Memphis or Little Rock, they frequently gave some students their first opportunity to venture outside the boundaries of their home counties to see what "city life" was all about: abundant shops that stayed open late, restaurants that offered ethnic menus, people from different ethnic and national cultures, transportation via buses and streetcars. The trips, moreover, were yet another bonding experience for the students—something other than classes and athletic teams that conduced identification with, and loyalty to, their peers, their school, their homes. So Steve has been an ardent supporter of the ARCare high school challenge trips. Each year between 2012 and 2018, students from selected ARCare community high schools have been invited to do the following: read a book (selected by me, I'm honored to say) and write a substantial essay about it; take the ACT at least twice and do better on it the second time; do a community service project; and make a brief presentation to the ARCare board. Students who complete these tasks successfully get an all-expenses-paid trip to some city for a long weekend of culture (there's always a play involved), sight-seeing, and—perhaps the most important element—a meeting with someone who lives in the visited location who has ties to Augusta and Arkansas: a university professor, a doctor, a government official. Joy Lynn and I led the first four of these trips, and we took groups to Stratford, Ontario, to see what I consider the best Shakespeare in North America, stopping at Niagara Falls on the way home; to Washington, DC, where we got to meet our US senator at the time, Mark Pryor, the most recent Democratic senator from the state; to Dallas, where we met the wonderful Greg Brownderville, a great poet, who's now on the creative writing faculty at Southern Methodist University and who's originally from rural Woodruff County, of which Augusta is the seat; and to Chicago, where we spent a great evening in the high-rise condo of a monumentally successful surgeon, an African American man who grew up in the Delta and now has a substantial practice, and influence, in the Windy City. When the Delta kids get back from these trips, they usually wonder aloud whether they'll ever be the same again. The answer: they won't be. Change is good.

Honest to god, Joy Lynn Bowen knows everyone in Augusta, Arkansas, and she probably knows their momma and daddy as well. Joy Lynn was two years behind Steve in Augusta grade school, and she recalls gleefully the day she came home in the autumn of her second-grade year and announced to her mother that she was going to marry Steve Collier. She didn't. Instead, she graduated from Augusta High School, started college at the University of Arkansas but transferred to Harding University, a Church of Christ institution in Searcy, married Bobby Bowen, another Augusta boy, had a lovely daughter Olivia, and began teaching in the Augusta schools. She was the gifted and talented coordinator for the schools, but that didn't put her in the rarefied air of working with only smart kids. Really, she connected with everybody. To everyone, she was "Miss Joy Lynn," and no student ever flinched when Joy Lynn would corner him or her and ask directly, "What are you going to do after you graduate? What's your dream? How are you going to make that happen?"

I honestly don't remember the first time I met Joy Lynn—it was probably at that first meeting of the Augusta Recovery Initiative that I attended—but I do remember one of the first tasks we undertook together. Given carte blanche to do pretty much whatever we thought was a good idea, Joy Lynn and I thought we needed to come up with a good name for our enterprise. Since we intended from the outset to try to support any effort to bring better critical reading and more effective writing to the forefront in the town, I suggested we call it the Augusta Community Literacy Advocacy Project. But then I realized that the last four words in this moniker could be abbreviated as CLAP, and Joy Lynn and I agreed that it probably wasn't wise to invite beneficiaries of our project to say, "I got the CLAP from the University of Arkansas." But we never got around to finding a better name. We were too busy.

Joy Lynn retired as ARCare's education director and volunteer coordinator in July of 2016—her second grandchild had been born earlier that year, her mother had died shortly thereafter, and the tug of family was understandably strong for her. So, as she departed, she and I sat down and simply tried to catalog all the projects we had undertaken in our years of working together. We started counting in 2007–2008 and got as far as 2014–2015, and we enumerated 221 separate "things" (projects, presentations, hostings, consultations, etc.) we had done together, ranging from putting "home literacy" tips in the envelope with all the citizens' December utility bills so that the family could doing something involving reading, writing, and conversing together (2007); sponsoring a music and literacy project for ninth graders (2008), giving them the chance to construct explanatory narratives connecting the selections in an "album" of their favorite songs; establishing the prototype of the Augusta Electronic Portfolio (2009), in which citizens were invited to create and share their positions on issues of the town's potential for growth; developing the Community Success Initiative (2010), in which students conducted research to create thumbnail sketches of people from Augusta who excelled in their chosen fields; hosting the White River Shakespeare Festival (2011) (more about that in the following essay); offering the region's first-ever after-school tutoring program at ARCare's new Center for Wellness and Education (2012); designing the pilot version of my office's new Students Involved in Sustaining Their Arkansas project, which supports high school students as they engage in a year-long process of developing plans to revitalize and sustain their hometown's quality of life (2013); making presentations about the CLA Project to the Crossroads Coalition and the local chamber of commerce (2014); and to supporting the campaign to expand the Woodruff County Library (2015).

Each of these 221 things evokes a story, the telling of which would occupy several volumes. But for the sake of economy and synecdoche, let me focus and expand on just five of them to provide a taste of how Joy Lynn worked to bring literacy as doing to the forefront of Augusta's consciousness.

The "come-to-Jesus" meeting with students in 2007. In the year before my work in Augusta got under way, a stark indicator of a lack of something—leadership, ambition, guidance, whatever—in the local schools emerged. In that year, as I mentioned earlier, forty-eight students had graduated from Augusta High School, but only twenty-two of them had even taken the ACT examination (the preferred examination for application to most of Arkansas's public colleges and universities), and only five of them had gone to college. It was also about this time that discourse began to circulate around the state about the troubling statistic mentioned in chapter 2: depending on when you looked at the data, Arkansas ranked either forty-ninth or fiftieth among the states in the percentage of adults who hold a college degree. Politicians, educators, policy wonks were justifiably concerned. As noted earlier, the worrisome reasoning went like this: if good jobs in the twenty-first century are going to require at least some college training—and perhaps at least a baccalaureate degree—and if Arkansas has a paucity of college graduates, then the state will have a very tough time attracting new businesses and industries that offer high-quality jobs.

Given both the local situation and the state discourse, Joy Lynn and I wondered what was going through the students' heads—why weren't they thinking about going to some kind of college? So with the help of the librarian at the high school, we held a closed-door meeting with about a dozen Augusta High School juniors and seniors: no parents, no teachers, no principals, no guidance counselors. Just Joy Lynn, me, and the students. And we asked them point-blank why they (or perhaps their classmates) weren't keen on going to college. Initially they were silent, but they soon began to open up. The first responses were the predictable ones: they thought that since they were from a small town and that kids from larger towns and cities were "smarter than they were," they wouldn't be able to cut the academic mustard in college. They were from a small town where everyone knows them, and when they went away to college they would just be a number, and if they got into any kind of trouble there wouldn't be anyone there to help them. But then the responses got a little more nuanced. Their parents regularly told them that they don't mind it if they went away to college, but they just don't want them to go very far. Their parents also regularly told them they didn't mind if they went away to college, but, according to the students, they parents would say—not directly, but in so many words—that they didn't want them to change very much, if at all.

Joy Lynn and I have reflected on that meeting countless times over the years. We realized at the time that the students' sentiments are not unique to Augusta—they express fears that many high school students confront before college. But in a small, rural town like Augusta, where relatively few adults have gone to college themselves, we realized that we would need to offer not only mentoring to the town's young people but also guidance and assurance to their parents and non-parental adults that going to college is not going to harm these students or change them to the point that they're alienated from their families. Joy Lynn and I determined that we needed to take every opportunity available to tell the Augustans the stories of folks from their own town, and other small towns in the state, who *have* succeeded in college and life beyond it. The Community Success Initiative (which we playfully labeled CSI) invited students to do small research projects on the achievements of Augusta natives and current residents. The ARCare challenge trips that started a few years later always featured contacts with successful Augustans.

The parents' home literacy workshop. Early in our collaboration, Joy Lynn and I did our best to get books into the hands and homes of young children in Augusta. ARCare funded the aforementioned principal's book-of-the-month project, and we promoted a competition in the elementary school called "the million-word challenge," which involved getting a huge total number of words read by the grade-school kids.[4] We realized early on, however, that getting books to the kids was only half of our responsibility. We thought it vital that we provide some guidance to parents about what to *do* with their kids and their books at home. In short, we wanted to conduce a *home* literacy environment that would be congruent with the school milieu.

So with the support of a modest grant from the Dollar General Foundation, we set up a ten-week family literacy program, intended for young parents and their children. We would help the parents understand not only how to read to their children but how to involve them in the world of the word through games, conversations, home projects. My sister Judy Fox, an expert teacher of early childhood literacy, came to Augusta to lead a workshop, kicking off the program. We provided each family with the three Bs, books, baskets, and bedside lamps—the first to read, the second to hold the books, the third to illuminate the whole process. In addition to teaching home literacy practices, our project would also teach the parents what we termed "marketable" computer skills for the adults—how to write on a word processor and how to understand and create a spreadsheet.

The project was well attended, but what surprised us was the clientele it drew. Our target audience was young parents with young children. Who showed up? To our delight, parents, grandparents, aunts and uncles, friends from down the street, friends from church. We quickly recognized a phenomenon that the literacy scholar Shirley Brice Heath has noted repeatedly, that childcare is often a communal activity—all sorts of folks look after kids. We even had adults come to the program who had no connection to young children at all—an elderly woman on the custodial staff at one of the ARCare buildings simply wanted to learn what we had on offer.

The spirit of this early family literacy program took roots more deeply in Augusta five years later, when ARCare, with substantial support from a federal grant, opened the twenty-thousand-square-foot Center for Education and Wellness, the first facility in the Arkansas Delta to offer before-school,

---

4. Joy Lynn and I were probably the only two people involved who remembered Abbie Hoffman's 1971 work, *Steal This Book*.

during-school, and after-school care and tutoring, provided by professionals well trained in the theory and teaching of literacy. And, of course, my sister Judy came back to Augusta to repeat her home literacy workshop for the clientele of the Education and Wellness Center.

College and Career Days. The first ARCare Wellness Center (the old elementary school gym that had been converted into a workout facility, computer café, and basketball court) came alive on these days. Tables surrounded the perimeter, and, of course, admissions representatives from many of the state's colleges and universities—two-year, four-year, public, and private—showed up at Joy Lynn's invitation. But so did other potential contacts for life after high school, military recruiters and potential employers. Among the latter: both local and state police departments; ARCare, the Bunge Grain Elevator, and the Sloan Valve Company, two other local employers in Augusta; the local utility companies; a handful of small businesses and contractors.

If the students thought coming to the College and Career Day would be just an opportunity to get out of school for a day and loaf around the facility, they had another think coming. Joy Lynn worked the crowd, finding someone who looked idle, probing the person about what his or her dreams, goals, aspirations were, then walking him or her over to a table and introducing the person to the presenter. She worked these events nonstop. Oh, and on the next day of school after the College and Career Day, the students were required in their English classes to write an essay about what they had learned and what their next steps in planning their future were.

High School Challenge Trips. About two decades ago, as I recall, a social scientific study addressed the following question: What subgroup in the general population would one expect to be the strongest source of *affirmation* for teenagers? Would it be their parents? Their peers? Their teachers? The answer: Non-parental adults—folks like scoutmasters, ministers, aunts and uncles, older folks who lived down the street. In short, adults who could treat the teenagers like the proto-adults they were becoming, listen to them, consider their emerging opinions seriously, interact with them honestly—and then send them back to their parents!

That's precisely what Joy Lynn did on the four ARCare challenge trips that we took students on—to Stratford, Ontario, followed by Niagara Falls; to Washington, DC; to Dallas; and to Chicago. Of course, Joy Lynn did lots of parental things: she purchased suitcases for many of the kids, especially those who had never been farther away from home than Little Rock or Memphis, both about an hour from Augusta. For the Canada trip, she made sure all the students had passports.[5] But mostly Joy Lynn used the trips to do her one-on-ones as the non-parental adult with the students.

There are scores of pithy quotations about how travel broadens the mind—my favorite is from Saint Augustine: "The world is a book, and those who do not travel read only one page"—and certainly all of them were borne out on our trips. On the Canadian trip, we not only saw some of the finest theater in North America, *Romeo and Juliet*, plus *The Who's Tommy* and *Fiddler on the Roof*, and got to witness the power of Niagara Falls from beside it and underneath it, but as we drove across rural Ontario in our van, we noticed how each farm had taken advantage of a government subsidy and installed gigantic solar panels to provide electricity, and we talked as a group about how governments can foster alternative energy policies. In Washington, DC, we witnessed firsthand how a US senator feels after spending all day on the Senate floor—young Mr. Pryor was polite and attentive when we finally got to meet him at nearly 6 p.m., but boy was he pooped—and we talked about the great demands that public service places on conscientious legislators. In Dallas we got one of the best questions ever from a student. We passed a store with the name Condoms to Go. One of the students, a bright young woman, looked at me and asked, "Dr. Jolliffe, aren't they *all* to go?" I had to think for a minute, but then I allowed that, yes, they are all to go. In Chicago we saw a stellar *Othello* at Chicago Shakespeare Theater, a production set in the present Middle East, and we talked about not only about the timelessness of Shakespeare's tragedies but also the interpersonal dramas that get played out in wartime. We ate deep-dish pizza and Greek food and talked about how ethnic cultures come to life in restaurants. We went everywhere on public transportation and talked about how life can—and often must—transpire without a car in big cities.

The notes Joy Lynn and I got at the end of each challenge trip were rewarding and heartwarming—and they came not only from the students but also from their parents. Especially for those who have had very little if any opportunity to learn to "read the world" via travel, its initial splash can be quite exhilarating.

The Lori Browning Story. Hailing from one myself, I've always known that small-town America is full of unrecognized talent, and Augusta was certainly

---

5. A side note: One of the kids who earned the right to travel to Stratford told Joy Lynn she was a bit afraid to go since Canada was a "foreign country." We assured the young woman that the Canadians spoke something like our own language and were generally friendly to Americans.

no exception. One of our finds in the town was Lori Browning, a junior at the high school when she came to our attention. Lori was the adopted daughter of the minister at Augusta's largest African American church and his wife, who was the secretary at the elementary school, and Lori had been noticed as a prodigiously talented writer from grade school on. She wrote stories. She wrote poems. She wrote plays. She was shy and thoroughly disliked public attention.

Joy Lynn gave me one of Lori's plays early on in my Augusta days, and I was absolutely blown away by it. Titled *The Devil's Oven*, it fleshed out vividly a story of questioning religious faith, dealing with domestic violence, and surviving drought in the cotton fields of the Delta. At that time, I was on the board of directors of TheatreSquared, a relatively new professional theatre company based in Fayetteville. One of T2's most innovative annual events was the Arkansas New Play Festival, at which six or seven new scripts would be workshopped and the T2 artistic staff would give studied consideration to the possibility of bringing one or more of the scripts under their wing for further development and perhaps eventually performance. A sidebar to the New Play Festival was a high school version of it. Young would-be playwrights from throughout the state were invited to submit their scripts for consideration, and if they were selected, T2 would link up the novice with talented young playwright named Clinnesha Dillon, who was on the University of Arkansas theater faculty at the time. After Clinnesha and the novice had worked up the play into a performable version, it would be read publicly by professional actors hired by T2.

Joy Lynn and I convinced Lori to submit her script for consideration, and, being on the board, I got an early notice, even before Lori did, that her script had been accepted. We needed to figure out some way to showcase Lori's achievement for the community, her reticence to have a public persona notwithstanding. Joy Lynn came up with a strategy. Lori *hated* high school athletic events, but she was a good soul and could occasionally be convinced to work at the concession stand at a game. Well, Augusta High School was playing a home basketball game, and Joy Lynn and Lori's parents subtly wheedled Lori into working the concession stand at the game. She was minding her business and doing so, and at halftime, Joy Lynn came and fetched her to center court, where she announced to the assembled crowd that Lori's play had been accepted in the young playwrights' competition at TheatreSquared and that it would be workshopped and performed in Fayetteville the following May. She presented Lori with a dozen red roses, and the crowd erupted in a long standing ovation.

When May rolled around and Lori's script was performed, about forty people made the four-hour drive from Augusta to Fayetteville to see the very compelling performance. As Joy Lynn, Steve, and others in Augusta pointed out, you may not be able to convince a thousand people to show up at an event just to honor someone for her achievement in the world of the word. But they will show up for a basketball game—and if you can throw a literacy celebration into the middle of it, well, why not? In a genuinely healthy community, people revel when they see the effects of literacy as action, literacy as doing, come to life.

Performance

They came from four small rural high schools in central Arkansas—Augusta, Bald Knob, McCrory, and Newport. They were an even dozen, three males and nine females. They were African American, Latinx, white. They drove through threatening flood waters—the White River was at a hundred-year high—on five Saturday mornings in 2011 to get to Augusta. They were Team Shakespeare. They came to write—and then perform.

They came from Springdale, Arkansas, mostly—a city of about seventy thousand whose Latinx population of about twenty-five thousand had grown by 18.5 percent between 2000 and 2010.[1] They were ten: four Latinos, three Latinas, two whites, and one African American—with the latter three included simply because they wanted to participate with their friends. Five of the Latinx folks were affiliated with a "club" they called Stitches. They told the story

---

1. All demographic data in this essay are gleaned from US Census Bureau data at www.factfinder.census.gov.

of their formation following a shooting at their high school that the media claimed was gang related. It wasn't. These young folks said they needed to stitch the community back together. They were the LatinX Theatre Project. Beginning in the winter of 2016, they came to write—and then perform.

They came from all over Arkansas, but most immediately they came from their cell block on Arkansas's death row in the Varner Supermax Prison in Gould, Arkansas. They were eleven: seven African American and four Caucasians. Ten were convicted murderers; one had been given a death sentence even though he simply participated in a robbery that "went bad" and ended in a murder committed by his accomplice. They ranged in age from their twenties through their sixties. The average number of years they had been on death row was twenty-one. They were the participants in the Prison Story Project's storytelling initiative. Beginning in the summer of 2016, they came to tell their stories and write—and eventually to witness their stories turn into a staged reading that has gained national attention.

I've always been a drama guy, but it wasn't until I began seriously to theorize literacy—to try to put together a definition of it and ponder how it works—that I started to understand how powerfully drama immerses one in the world of the word, even though I had been so immersed for most of my life. In the second grade, I was selected to be the narrator in the school's Christmas pageant, and I can still remember sitting at a reading desk on the auditorium stage, decked out in a white choir robe and red bow, bringing the house down by nearly falling asleep during the scenes when I wasn't reading the narration. When I was in junior high, I got my first legitimate break in the theater, playing one of the workhouse boys in *Oliver!* My buddy Steve Ratcliffe played a similar role, and he and I had one line to share—"we've brought the boy, ma'am"—which we were supposed to alternate delivering during the four performances of the play—but on opening night we couldn't remember whose turn it was to start, so I think we blurted out the line together. In high school, I was in every play I could get into, musical or not, and I think I decided to go to Bethany College in large measure because one of its theater professors (who became my lifelong friend and mentor) David Judy drove the ninety minutes from Bethany to my hometown, New Martinsville, to see me perform in the senior musical, *The King and I*.

After high school, I got deeply involved with an excellent community theater, the Towngate, in Wheeling, West Virginia, and had the opportunity to act in and direct both musicals and plays for that venue in the 1970s. I majored in English at Bethany but was in plays all four years, and as a senior I was asked to direct the musical, *Brigadoon*, which I happily undertook. As a high school teacher I taught English but directed a play every year, and when I finished my master's degree at West Virginia University, Bethany asked me to return for a one-year stint as instructor of English and theater, serving as acting department chair of the latter while David Judy was away on sabbatical. I directed four plays that year—I recall spending every evening in rehearsal. I applied to and was accepted into the graduate program in theater at Indiana University, where my scholarly hero, Oscar Brockett, taught at that time, but IU was unable to offer me an assistantship, so I opted to remain an English teacher, do graduate work in rhetoric and composition, and so on.

Though I took a break from acting and directing during my two decades in Chicago, I made it a point to see lots of performances in that great theater town, and when I moved to Arkansas in 2005, I rekindled my theater work, helping to launch (as a board member and later board president) TheatreSquared, Fayetteville's award-winning Actors' Equity regional theater; directing *The Tempest* for Trike Theatre in our collaborative project, the Team Shakespeare/White River Shakespeare Festival; cofounding and acting for the Classical Edge Theatre Company, which produces free outdoor Shakespeare and takes both performances and student workshops to schools throughout Arkansas; most recently playing a role in the Prison Story Project's staged reading of *On the Row*, a script developed in writing workshops with inmates housed on death row at the Varner Supermax Prison; and jumpstarting the LatinX Theatre Project in Springdale, which encourages folks in their late teens and early twenties to write and perform their own material.

As I hint in the vignettes that opened this essay, while I can see how a lifetime of working in the theater has shaped my perceptions of literacy, three projects in particular—Team Shakespeare, the LatinX Theatre Project, and the Prison Story Project's *On the Row* production—have equipped me with a bold claim about reading and writing dramatic texts. I maintain that doing so represents the quintessence of literacy experiences.

The art of reading and writing dramatic texts—texts in which characters flesh out a plot and grow and become some kind of entity (usually human) right in front of our eyes (whether those eyes are in our heads and minds as an audience member or as a closeted reader)—is radically different from writing or reading either fiction or nonfiction prose, whether the latter is thesis-driven argumentation or associative, discursive essaying. Dramatic texts—and note that I'm including most poems under this label along with plays, since poems are essentially monologues spoken by characters in a dramatic situation—call boldly for active, constructivist readings. One should always read a dramatic text like an actor; one should always teach a dramatic text like a director. One should constantly see the spectacle of the dramatic situation forming in one's mind. One should constantly ask, "How would you say that line? How would you behave as you say that line? How would others react as you say that line?"

When you're reading or writing fiction (particularly traditional or canonical fiction) and most nonfiction, you usually have the advantage of a narrator's voice or an arguer's voice that guides your construction of the text's reality. A narrator's voice generally fills you in on the details of context—time, place, prior circumstances—and often lets you know what the characters feel, think, and believe, either in the present circumstances or in past ones. The same holds true, of course, for associative, discursive essays, since for all intents the personal or expressive essay constructs basically the same kind of reality as a short story or novel does.

When you're reading nonfiction prose designed to demonstrate a proposition, explain a position, or argue a point, you experience, I maintain, even more contextualization than in fiction. In a demonstrative, explanatory, or argumentative text, the writer (and by extension the reader) has to create the context, introduce the issue, narrow its focus onto the point or proposition at hand, give some attention to what has been previously written about the issue, clarify why the present moment is timely and supportive of changed thinking and behavior, and then proceed not only to demonstrate and confirm the point via a visible, generally logical path but also to anticipate objections—roadblocks on the path to demonstration and confirmation—and downplay their significance and impact.

But when you're reading dramatic texts, especially those with little or no stage directions, all you have is the words on the page (or stage or screen) to create the context and to assist you as you make the point. And when you're writing dramatic texts, similarly, all you have is the words to invite your reader to create the context and make the point. In dramatic texts, just the words—not the narrator's or arguer's guidance—create the world. Words creating the world: the ultimate literacy experience.

"You can't teach these kids empathy." Or so said an English teacher in small, rural Arkansas town to one of the leaders of the joint Brown Chair–Trike Theatre Team Shakespeare project in the spring of 2011. Not solely to prove this teacher wrong, the Team Shakespeare project, which rolled out from February through May of that year in and around Augusta, Arkansas, *did* teach the high school student participants empathy—and a lot more too.

Team Shakespeare—what a crazy project, bringing together a motley crew of collaborators and a handful of quirky interests! First of all, it started, as have so many of the Brown Chair in English Literacy projects have, with the enthusiasm and support of Steve Collier (introduced in "Health"), CEO of ARCare, a statewide health-care organization based in Augusta and formerly known as White River Rural Health Center. As the previous essay notes, Steve is an ardent proponent of fostering community literacy as a means to improving the quality of life in small towns where ARCare operates clinics, and he thinks that having the opportunity for young people in those communities to perform in plays is an integral element in a community literacy initiative. What's more, he *loves* Shakespeare. So when I suggested to Steve that we could actually do Shakespeare in Augusta, where ARCare is headquartered, Steve was so taken with the idea he agreed to fund the initiative fully, with Trike Theatre, a very good young company based in Bentonville and led by my frequent collaborator Kassie Misiewicz, heading up the enterprise.[2]

Kassie's trust in me opened the door for my return to directing for the theater. Throughout the 1970s and into the 1980s, I had directed regularly for high-quality community and collegiate programs. I had directed everything from Shakespeare (*Romeo and Juliet*) to Chekhov (*The Cherry Orchard*) to Albee (*The Zoo Story*) to Lerner and Lowe (*Brigadoon*) to Neil Simon (*Come Blow Your Horn*). I had always been both fascinated and a bit terrified by Shakespeare's grandest romance, *The Tempest*, and even though I hadn't directed anything since 1993, when Kassie gave me the opportunity to direct that play with a fine cast of well-educated and experienced actors, I jumped at the chance. So Team Shakespeare was going to have a professional production of *The Tempest* that we could bring on tour to Augusta and also perform in Fayetteville.

But there was a quirk in the casting that led to a quirk in rehearsal. We were scheduled to do two performances of *The Tempest*, one in Augusta and one in Fayetteville. I was determined that the actors would be from both northwest Arkansas, where live theater thrives and a very good MFA program in theater at the University of Arkansas generates good actors, many of whom choose to remain in the region after they graduate, and from central Arkansas, where

---

2. Steve and my other Augusta collaborator, Joy Lynn Bowen, whom readers also got to know in "Health," dug up the archives of an Augusta Shakespeare Club that had thrived in the early twentieth century, and when Joy Lynn found old photographs of this club's members, she and Steve were able to point out several folks who still had relatives living in Augusta.

Augusta is located and where live theater is quite rare. Fortunately, the cast of *The Tempest* divides rather neatly into three chunks: the "island" folks (Prospero, Ariel, Caliban, Miranda, and the presumed-drowned Ferdinand), the "comic shipwrecked" folks (Stephano and Trinculo), and the "bad guy" shipwrecked folks (Antonio, Alonso, Sebastian—although there's one "good guy" in their midst, Gonzalo). I was able to cast the first two chunks with experienced actors from northwest Arkansas and the third chunk with actors who either worked for ARCare or were connected with the small but good theater program at Arkansas State University's branch campus in Beebe, about thirty miles southwest of Augusta. So, having divided the script into French scenes, I was able to rehearse with the first two chunks of cast members regularly in Fayetteville, drive to Beebe for a handful of long weekends to rehearse the third chunk, then bring everyone together just before the initial performance to merge all the scenes.[3] Whew!

Once the plan for the play was in place, all sorts of affirmative mojo began to develop around the incipient production. First of all, an old Augusta family, the Gregorys, had a son-in-law, Peter Smith, who happens to be a reader in Renaissance literature at the University of Nottingham in Trent and a Shakespeare scholar with an international reputation. His in-laws and ARCare friends convinced him to come to Arkansas and launch a statewide lecture tour—in schools, libraries, and club meetings—about how important it is for "common folks" to experience live Shakespeare. Second, I had an acquaintance on the music faculty at the University of Arkansas at Little Rock, Bob Boury, the son of a prominent family in Wheeling, West Virginia, where I had lived and worked from 1974 through 1980. I had tracked him down at the university a couple of years earlier and had learned that he had composed a series of lovely art songs, based on *The Tempest*, for contralto and tenor. I began to see the outlines of a festival emerging: Peter Smith would give lectures. Bob Boury would provide a lovely concert or two. We would do a professional production of *The Tempest*.

All we needed was an educational component. We knew we wanted to involve high school students in the enterprise, and we aimed to craft something of an experiment: a boot camp introduction to the arts of theater, to the world of Shakespeare in general, and to *The Tempest* in particular. To help us with this initiative, Kassie and I recruited a husband-and-wife team whose edgy artistic work we were coming to know and love. Erika Wilhite had done an MFA

---

3. A French scene is a scene in which the beginning and end are marked by a change in the presence of characters onstage, rather than by the lights going up or down or the set being changed.

in acting at the University of Central Florida, and her husband, Rodney Wilhite, had been accepted as a poet in the MFA program in creative writing at the University of Arkansas. With this team in place, we traveled around to the high schools in and near Augusta to see if we could find students who would be willing to devote several Saturdays to what we believed was an incredibly cool arts project. If they could get themselves to Augusta early on Saturday mornings for five weeks, we would engage them in studying *The Tempest* in depth; engaging in theater games, improvisation, and scene study to understand it; and writing creatively about the themes and issues raised in the play.

And recruit we did. We got a dozen kids from four high schools: Augusta, Bald Knob (fifteen miles to the east), McCrory (twelve miles to the west), and Newport (thirty miles to the north). They were clearly eager to do something like this, because, oh, the challenges they faced driving into Augusta during that spring. From the middle of April to the middle of May, two major storm systems had dumped torrents of rain in the delta of the Mississippi River, both on the Mississippi side and the Arkansas side. That and a substantial runoff from the winter's substantial snow had caused record-breaking flooding not only on the Mississippi but also on its tributaries, including the White River, on which Augusta sits. The kids from Bald Knob, McCrory, and Newport had to navigate roads covered with backwater, bridges perilously close to being flooded out, and continuing storms raining so hard their windshield wipers couldn't keep up. The congruence of dealing with storms and floods and working on *The Tempest* was uncanny.

But the dozen kids showed up each time and happily threw themselves into what Kassie and Erika, in a retrospective interview, labeled "a full immersive experience in the play—really immersive for all the folks involved: the actors, the teaching artists, the producer." (That last would be yours truly, by the way.) Each of the five Saturdays offered some mixture of the same elements, all designed to help the young participants develop a critical reading of the play and learn to write effectively themselves. We did table work with the play itself—getting the words into the mouths of the young actors and ideas into their minds, teaching them to work from the original text to contemporary paraphrase and back to the original text; scene work, figuring out who the characters are and what they had done and been *before the scene begins* and what each character hoped to accomplish in the scene; tableaux, the creation of "frozen pictures" at the beginning, middle, and end of scenes, allowing the actors to transition their thinking from words on the page to active bodies on the stage; creative writing, allowing the youngsters to write imaginatively, in poetry or prose, about the themes, issues, and quandaries they were constructing as they worked through the scenes; and improvisation and theater games, activities designed to help them build their characters and their relationships to other characters as they came to understand the play.

The youngsters richly rewarded the effort that Kassie, Erika, and Rodney put into experience. "The kids were very green, very eager," Erika noted. "The first time they encountered a metaphor—Prospero's staff as an emblem for his magic and his authority, for example—they were gleefully surprised. The world of the theater was so new to them." Indeed, the whole idea that a person could spend his or her life working in the arts was completely novel to them. Erika related a story about one of the young women asking her, "what do you actually *do*?" Explaining that she was a theater artist by profession, Erika noticed that the young woman was carrying her band instrument, a saxophone, and mentioned she could be on her way to becoming an artist herself, awakening her to the prospect that art could potentially sit at the center of her life as well. The young girl simply smiled in silence.

Looking back on the experience, both Kassie and Erika were able to give voice to the ways such an immersive theater experience both builds empathy and leads to the richest of literacy experiences. Kassie, who runs a successful theater program for preschool and elementary students in Bentonville, noted that in the nineteenth and early twentieth centuries, families would often read plays aloud together for bonding and entertainment. "And even today," she added, "when we read stories aloud to young children, we emphasize the characters' voices—we make them come alive." She proceeded: "Similarly, when we work with scripts in the theater, it's all about inferencing. We have to develop the empathy among characters. We have to make creative choices about characters and their motivations and objectives, and we do that through the empathy that comes from being those characters in imaginary circumstances. In novels and stories, someone is either doing that for you or helping you to do it." Erika added a point about the power of drama in literacy education. "If you release students from a steady diet of writing formal expository prose and give them the license to write real-person dramatic dialogues," she said, "then you can get to your literacy goals a lot more successfully, particularly with the kids who are not already good readers and writers." In a jumble of quotations, one thought tumbling into another, Kassie and Erika (I can't recall exactly which one said what) concluded: "The way your heart and mind can really grow is through theater. To be alive and to be challenged with conflicts. To really look at humanity. This is what drama does. This is what you have to do with acting."

To cap off the five-week experience, the Team Shakespeare participants eventually wrote a twenty-minute curtain-raiser they called *The Tempest Tossed*. They performed it right before the start of our full production of *The Tempest*, and they built it out of this situation—which was not completely fictional: Their classmates at Augusta, Bald Knob, McCrory, and Newport high schools repeatedly asked them, "What the heck have you been doing for the past five Saturday mornings?" So their play told the story of the play, with each of the five major characters—Prospero, Ariel, Caliban, Ferdinand, and Miranda—offering his or her or its perspective on the convoluted plot. But *The Tempest Tossed* also told the stories of their perilous journeys to Augusta, through springtime 2011 tempests, showing how their travels and travails helped them come to a deep understanding, not only of how a Shakespeare play works but also of how they bonded by reading, writing, and performing drama together and how the immersive experience made them new kinds of readers and writers, different literate beings than they had ever been before.

Oh, brave new world that has such creatures in it.

They called themselves "Stitches," and their name holds an unusual backstory. In 2014 there was a shooting outside Springdale High School. The local media went into shrieking mode: "It's gang warfare," the media cried. "No, it's not," these young people said. "It's a shooting." They coalesced, a dozen or so of them, into an informal club, with the remarkable Samuel Rivera Lopez as their unofficial convener. They said their mission was to stitch the community together.

In December 2016 a core group of Stitches sat with me around a table at my favorite taqueria in Springdale, El Cunado, trying to get a bead on this gray-haired, gray-bearded professor whom Sam Lopez had said they needed to meet. They were all, quite simply, beautiful—even their names: Oscar Bravo, Audrey Romero, Martin Garay, Ever Geronimo Villalobos, Joaquin Vela, Sativa Vela, and, of course, Samuel Rivera Lopez. In English I ordered the enchiladas verdes. They ordered in Spanish, the others covering for the one who claimed she didn't speak Spanish. We ate. And to get the conversation moving, I asked them where they were from. From most of them, I got what I expected. Sam had been born in Mexico and had moved to Austin, Texas, when he was seven and then to Springdale as a teenager. Martin had been born in El Salvador and Audrey in Mexico, and each had moved to Los Angeles before coming to Springdale in their teen years. And so it went, around the table, until we got to Sativa. "I'm seventh-generation American," she said. "I'm from Ohio." And she was the one who said she couldn't speak Spanish.

That quirk, that complication in my questioning, led to the theme of the first devised theater production of the LatinX Theatre Project.[4] The play was called *Follow Me@Tio Sam*, and it grew out of the question that I posed to the Stitches members around the table at Taqueria El Cunado: "Where are you from?" The initial material for the play was written by five members of the Stitches group between the first of February and the middle of March 13, 2017, and these five and an additional five actors continued to build the script, workshop style, in rehearsals from March 14 through April 17. The play opened on April 18 at Northwest Arkansas Community College and was performed four times between then and May 3 to large, enthusiastic audiences in three venues. At one of the talk-backs, a middle-aged Latina stood up and announced, "I've been living in northwest Arkansas for twenty-two years, and this is the first performance of anything where I feel at home." A board member of the Arts Center of the Ozarks, one of the collaborating organizations sponsoring the project, claimed that *Follow Me@Tio Sam* was the most important artistic work ever performed at that venue.

Here's how it all came about. In 2015 a venerable institution in Springdale, Arkansas, the Arts Center of the Ozarks, was struggling to stay open after fifty years of sponsoring community theater, a community chorus, and art classes. There was some thought that perhaps the ACO was no longer offering the kind of programming that appealed to Springdale, a city with a strong working-class ethos. Springdale is home to Tyson Foods and to George's Inc., a large chicken processing company. Factory jobs at those two companies, along with the burgeoning construction, home-building, health-care, and service industries in the region have helped to make Springdale the home not only to a growing Latinx population but also to the largest Marshallese population outside the Marshall Islands themselves. If the ACO couldn't make itself more amenable to diversity, the thinking went, it wouldn't survive.

So the ACO took two bold steps to reorganize. First, it replaced its thirty-five-member board of directors with a twelve-member one, making sure to include representatives of the "new" Springdale on it. Second, they got a legend in the northwest Arkansas arts scene, Jenni Taylor Swain, to come out of retirement and serve as the center's interim executive director. Jenni had previously been the vice president for programming at the Walton Arts Center

---

4. Devised theater is a creative process in which an ensemble develops a play script or musical score by means of collective writing and workshopping. Using devised theater techniques, the LatinX Theatre Project has developed and performed four more plays since its inception, and the project is ongoing.

in Fayetteville, which had opened in the 1980s with the support of the City of Fayetteville, the University of Arkansas, and, of course, the Walton Family Foundation. In her new role, Jenni quickly went about trying to schedule programming that would speak more directly to the "new" Springdale.

Because my literacy outreach work had taken me so regularly into the Springdale schools, I had come to know (and admire greatly) Marsha Jones, the associate superintendent who not only helped to run the schools but also sat on the ACO board of directors. Marsha knew my penchant for arts-oriented literacy projects, so she brokered an introduction between Jenni and me and urged us to get together and start brainstorming.

I met Jenni for coffee and related to her my many experiences of moving through the hallways of Springdale High School, noting the large Latinx population, and wondering what might be happening in the schools that would allow those youngsters to experience, affirm, and validate their culture through the arts. When both of us sensed that the answer to that question was probably "not much," I decided to take action.

First, I immediately got in touch with my former colleague Henry Godinez, who had taught in the Theatre School at DePaul when I was there and had since moved to a position at Northwestern University. Henry is the founder and former artistic director of the Chicago Latino Theatre Festival. I asked Henry whom he knew who had good experience in community arts, community organizing, and Latino theater. He told me that I absolutely must meet Laura Crotte, a Latina from Veracruz who had lived in Chicago for nineteen years and excelled in all of those areas. Fortunately, I had a trip to Chicago planned already, so I got in touch with Laura and scheduled a breakfast meeting near her home in Logan Square, one of the hippest, most vibrant Latinx neighborhoods in the city. I must ask the reader a rhetorical question: have you ever had an initial meeting with someone at which one lightbulb after another not only comes on but pops on brightly and even sizzles? That's what happened in my meeting with Laura. In her I found an experienced, Actors' Equity performer who had done community organizing, parent education, social-justice-oriented theater, devised theater.[5] Our talk over chilaquiles was boom, boom, zip, zip, idea, idea. Before breakfast ended, I had arranged for her to come to northwest Arkansas just to talk to folks and see what we might do.

Laura visited us for three days in early December 2016, and we met with actors, artists, directors, designers, not-for-profit folks, superintendents, principals, teachers, and most vitally with Sam Lopez and Sativa Vela from Stitches.

---

5. Actor's Equity is the union of professional actors.

By the time I put Laura back on the plane to Chicago, the idea for the LatinX Theatre Project was launched.

For starters, we found young people—in their last few years in high school and their first two years in college—who would write. The Stitches group was an obvious choice for this "center-of-gravity" group. I met and brought on board a bright young Latino poet, Vicente Yepez, who was in his second year of the four-year Master of Fine Arts in Creative Writing program at the University of Arkansas. Vicente agreed to meet with five members of Stitches—Sam, Sativa, Ever, Martin, and Audrey—for four hours on Saturday morning and four hours on Sunday afternoon every weekend from the first of February through the middle of March. Vicente followed a procedure that I understand is standard practice in the university's long-standing Writers in the Schools program, one that we also have used in the Prison Stories Project, described later in this essay. Vicente would read a poem aloud to them—some of his own and some by other poets—that dealt, perhaps even tangentially, with the "where am I from" theme. Next, he would have one of the Stitches writers read the poem back to the group. Then he would give them a prompt to write in response to—a prompt that grew out of one of the themes and motifs in the original work. This remarkably generative procedure would go on for several hours, and Vicente would conclude by giving the writers a prompt they would compose in response to before the next weekend's meeting.

After five weekends of these intensive writing sessions, all the writers' material went to Ashley Edwards, director of theater at Northwest Arkansas Community College and an outstanding playwright in her own right. She agreed to shape the material into an actual play. Meanwhile, Michael Landman, head of the directing program in the University of Arkansas Master of Fine Arts in Theatre, saw an opportunity: he and his wife, Janie, had repeatedly shown their social justice bona fides in the community, and now they were learning Spanish in anticipation of possibly spending *lots* of time outside of Donald Trump's America. He agreed to direct the play.

So, after about five weekends of writing group activity, two weeks of playwright activity, and quick auditions to fill out the cast beyond the original five Stitches writers, a play emerged called *Follow Me@Tio Sam*, every word of which had been composed by the writers working with Vicente. Michael started rehearsals on March 29, 2017, with a cast that had almost no experience on the stage. On April 18 we opened. From the outset, I had anticipated that the performers would do a staged reading, with script in hand, as we do in the Prison Stories Project plays, sketched out below. But no! Ashley and Michael insisted the actors get off book, find their characters, and perform an actual play. And they did!

Follow Me@Tio Sam begins with the entire ensemble, lined up across the front of the stage, speaking directly to the audience and forecasting the "where am I from" motif that would continue throughout the play.[6]

AUDREY
> I am manifested as the word of revolution.

NOAH
> I am where anyone else is from. Where they tell you you're from.

DAMIAN
> I heard the roads in America were paved with gold. I didn't know I would have to be paving those roads.

EVER
> Just another dream of the America they see.

MARTIN
> From the dreams of the Aztecs to the dreams of the past tense.

SATIVA
> Your American dream is my American struggle.

EMILY
> Listen to the voices of the unheard.

DANIEL
> In the land of milk and honey, we're the ones who die for a slice of the American pie.

COCO
> Brown birds like us, where do we nest?

SAVANNAH
> This will never end for them. We see controlled immigration, they see families being torn apart.

SAM
> In the land of liberty, why do we live in fear of reality?

The play unfolds as the story of a young would-be politician named Damian who is originally from El Paso but who has moved to Springdale, Arkansas, and is now running for elected office. He has learned about the reputation of one Sam Valdez, a twenty-year-old artist, from local lore. Two years earlier, while still a high school student, Sam had given a reportedly fiery, pro-immigrants-rights speech as part of the high school's spring talent show. Damian shows up in Sam's garage, trying to meet him, because he had seen a version of Sam's speech on YouTube and wants to connect with a young Latinx

---

6. In the following excerpt, the speakers are identified by the first name of the actor playing the role.

population who would be willing to speak out publicly in support of his candidacy. Sam, working on one of his beautiful, large-scale murals at the time, initially wants nothing to do with Damian and politely tries to dismiss him. But, as Sam notes, "I've got people showing up," and over the next few minutes, the Stitches folks and several others begin to filter into the garage, just to hang out and be together.

The other characters, particularly the six additional Latinx folks, but the others as well—two white women and an African American man—are predictably suspicious of the suited-and-tied Damian. When Martin, one of the Latinos, asks Damian, "you're not from immigration are you?" and Damian pauses for a moment before answering, everyone jumps. But Damian wins their trust and gets them to settle in and answer his questions: Where are you from? What's it like to live in Springdale? Why did you come here? Why do you stay here? But the play isn't dominated by didactic expositions. Instead, it's rich with the stories the Stitches writers told in their writing group and that they and the other members of the cast added as the script grew in the workshop-oriented rehearsal process. There's the story of the high school teacher who decides to sponsor a discussion of race in her class and not only won't allow the students to express their ideas but even gives a little speech of her own about why there needs to be a "white history month." There's the story of the Sunday school mother who "jokingly" boards the children on the bus with the announcement, "Okay, beaners in the back, crackers in the front." There's the story of the assistant principal who butchers the kids' last names when trying to pronounce them and asks, "can you say that in English, please?" There's the story of the mother and father whose marriage dissolves when the father leaves the United States to return to his homeland, opining to his son that "I'm a better man in Mexico." The stories are acted out with glee, verve, sadness—genuine pathos. And *Follow Me@Tio Sam* ends on a resoundingly positive note: The entire cast—Latino, Latina, Black, and White—agree to appear en masse at Damian's political rally and support him.

The final scene, in fact, is a vision of Damian's political rally:

DAMIAN
   Now, may I introduce, Sam's Garage.

DAMIAN steps aside.

The Ensemble sings as a chorus:
   The salvation I see can be found within me. Judgment has clouded the air that I breathe. Despite, I'll do my time and take all my chances. Because life

is good no matter the circumstances. Because there is nobody that can take this dream from me.

Each character freestyles a rap, embodying his or her "Where am I from" motif.

The play ends with a reprise of the chorus.

I think it was clear to all involved that *Follow Me@Tio Sam* exemplified the dynamic I'm trying to unpack in this essay: the acts of writing and performing drama giving voice to young writers who had not been given that opportunity before, allowing them to create and understand their identities and their worlds in newly vital ways. Here's a perspective from one of the Stitches writers, Sativa Vela, who acted a substantial role in the play:

> Since I was young, anytime someone asked where I was from or whether or not I spoke Spanish, I was told by my peers, "so you're not Mexican, because you're never been there" or "you don't speak Spanish, so you can't be Latina"; therefore, I never thought of myself as Latina. I've always identified as American because of the Latinos around me, and the lifestyle established by my mother, made me feel so distant from my culture. I don't have any family because they all live out of state, so the only brown people I am close to, other than my immediate family, are friends I have met at school. Even then, I felt like an outsider. I thought that if I established myself with a label like "Mexican" or "Latina," it wasn't fitting. At the start of this project, I was very hesitant, but I love theater. I thought this may be a big opportunity for my friends, and maybe I could help, but this isn't my fight. After having the actual opportunity to sit with them and hear their stories, and realizing I can relate, it gave me a feeling that I could contribute. It made me feel closer to parts of my culture that were already established, and parts I was too scared to embrace. This opportunity made me feel closer to my Latin roots. I know that I am American, and I, like most of my family, have grown around American culture, but that does not change the color of my skin. I have come to realize that this project is bigger than me. It is about MY people. It is about the people who have been suppressed for too long. This is more than just a play. It's a statement. It's a movement. We are not just speaking for ourselves, but for every person born subjected by their skin color.

There you have it: literacy as conversation as identity formation as cultural bonding.

Ashleigh Burns, the LatinX Theatre Company's set designer, added a brief coda about *Follow Me@Tio Sam*: "The end product was so powerful, each and every artist shared so much with our audiences, not afraid to be vulnerable at times. The talents of this group are mind-blowing, and the hard work showed. I am unbelievably proud to have been a part of such a unique work, and so honored to work with this amazing group of people." Me too, Ashleigh.

It's a four-hour drive from Fayetteville to Gould, Arkansas, site of the Varner Supermax Prison, home to the twenty-nine men currently resident on Arkansas's death row. Kathy McGregor, the founder and project director of the Prison Story Project; Matt Henricksen, the project's creative writing director; and I made that trip one Saturday a month from May through October of 2016. We would drive to Gould in Kathy's Impreza, get ourselves checked in through security, work for two hours with the writing group composed of the nine death row inmates who had volunteered to meet with us in person and been cleared for the project, then drive the four hours home, decompressing and ruminating on the astounding scene we had just been part of.[7] In a nutshell: the Prison Story Project that eventually produced *On the Row*, a staged reading of the inmates' work, represents the most vital and important artistic endeavor I've ever participated in. It portrays more vividly than any project I can envision the ultimate power of literacy to empower, to evoke agency, to give a voice to an otherwise voiceless population.

The Prison Story Project emerged from the myriad experiences Kathy brought to the initiative. A professional storyteller, a former union organizer, a hospice nurse, and a songwriter, she moved to Fayetteville early in 2012 to be near her daughter and family, especially her grandchild. Later that year, she began conversations with Reverend Suzanne Stoner, associate rector at Saint Paul's Episcopal Church, about ways to interact with women incarcerated at the Northwest Arkansas Community Correction Center, where women could be imprisoned for up to two years, usually for felonies that involved some combination of prostitution, trafficking, and substance abuse. Saint Paul's had established an outreach to the correction center, taking communion to the inmates on Sunday nights and offering confirmation and baptism to anyone interested.

---

7. Two additional inmates agreed to write for the project but did not want to meet with us and the group in person.

Looking for a way to tap into her many talents, Kathy conjured up an idea that she thought, wisely so, would enrich the lives of the imprisoned women and the folks from the outside who might work with them. Kathy gathered a group of folks who would volunteer to meet with interested prisoners in a circle to listen to and tell each other their stories. The group met twice a week for two hours over a four-month period. And thus the Prison Story Project was born.

The University of Arkansas is the home of a renowned Master of Fine Arts in Creative Writing program, and Fayetteville has lots of really good writers around town, so the Prison Story Project team wasn't hard to assemble. The incomparable Katie Nichol, the initial creative writing director, established the Prison Story Project method that has been used since the first iteration. Accompanied by other volunteers, Katie would bring rich, evocative poems to the circle, and she or another volunteer would read the poem aloud. Then one of the inmates would read the poem aloud. Then the leader would give the participants a prompt that grew out of the themes, issues, or motifs in the poem. Then the women would write and share their work with other members of the group and with Katie and her fellow volunteers. Kathy, Katie, and the volunteers made it clear from the outset that the Prison Story Project was not an opportunity for the prisoners to write about how thoroughly it sucks being in jail or how they weren't guilty. The Prison Story Project represented an opportunity for the inmates to write about themselves: where they came from, how they had lived, whom they love or had loved, what went wrong for them, and how they envisioned their lives after they were released. And write they did, in reckless abundance.

Eventually all of the writing done by the women in the writing groups went to a local actor and playwright, Janelle (Jonny) Schremmer, who assembled it into a script, with every word taken from the women's writing. The staged reading was called *Stories from the Inside Out*. Then, directed by Jonny, local actors, most of them professionals, having graduated from the University of Arkansas Master of Fine Arts in Acting Program, performed the staged reading twice, once inside the jail for an internal audience—not only the inmates who had participated in the writing group but also the entire jail population—and once for an external audience—the general public. The performance was held in the parish hall at Saint Paul's Church, which seats about 250. The performance was jammed.

The Prison Story Project continued its work, which is ongoing to this day, with two iterations a year at the women's correction center, but the project took a bold step in 2014. Getting to know the women housed at the Community Correction Center, Kathy and her team discovered that many of the inmates had husbands, boyfriends, fathers, uncles, and friends who were incarcerated at the Randall L. Williams Correctional Facility, in Pine Bluff, Arkansas, about three and a half hours southeast of Fayetteville. Kathy got permission to run a two-day intensive project at Randall Williams, which produced a stunning script that was performed not only for the inmates housed at Randall Williams but also for the women at the Northwest Arkansas Community Corrections Center. I saw the latter, and I can swear it was one of the most moving pieces of theater I've ever seen, as the incarcerated women listened to professional actors read the stories—of confession, contrition, apology, and love—written by their loved ones.

But it was actually the former, the internal performance at Randall Williams, that radically changed the course of the Prison Story Project. In the audience was the warden of the Varner Supermax, home of Arkansas's death row. Kathy had been trying to get an in at Varner, so she had invited the warden to attend. He came to two performances at Randall Williams, and after he saw the second one, Kathy asked him about the possibility of a project on death row. Kathy wrote a proposal, which went back and forth for a couple of months. Eventually, the proposal was approved, and thus the seed was planted for the project, the first one in which I was an active participant, that generated *On the Row*, the hour-long script written by eleven men condemned to death by the state of Arkansas. Kathy wrote to all thirty-four men held on death row at the time, asking if they wanted to be part of the project. Eleven said yes. Beginning in May 2016, the Prison Story Project would be on death row.

The warden made it relatively simple for us to get through security on our monthly visits. We couldn't bring in anything that might be passed to the inmates: no wallets, loose money, watches, phones, computers. To get in we took off our shoes and belts and walked through a metal detector. Then we were patted down. Then we had to exhibit the bottoms of our feet. Then we had to stand with our hands above our heads and do a 360-degree turn in an x-ray machine. Then we had to sign in. Then we had to pass through four electric gates, all controlled by guards in a watch tower. Then we had to walk about one hundred yards along an electrified fence topped by razor wire. Then we had to rap on the metal door of the visitation section and wait for a guard to let us in. Then we had to wait for the nine prisoners who worked with us in person to be brought in. Simple as that.

The visitation area for death row at Varner has been constructed in a big rectangular room about 50 feet by 150 feet. Its main feature is the visitation cells: eight adjoining cells on each side of a hallway, around eight feet wide and forty feet long. The sixteen cells front onto one side of this hallway; on the back side of each cell is a plexiglass window with vents. If a prisoner goes a year without any disciplinary actions, he is permitted to interact with visitors through the cell bars—the visitors can sit in the interior hallway and make physical contact with the prisoner—touching, shaking hands, but no hugging or more intense displays of affections. If the prisoner has not earned—or has lost through unacceptable behavior—his right to "contact" visits, he must interact with visitors through the plexiglass window. We were fortunate to be permitted to lead the writing group from the center hallway, so we could hand the prisoners copies of poems we were working with and legal pads and pens, which we brought with us but which we had to get back from the prisoners at the end of each session.

Because Arkansas law forbids any death row prisoner from ever being in the same room with another human being (except in court, of course), each of our nine participants was placed in one of the visitation cells, and it took more than a half an hour to get the men in place for the workshop session. Each of the nine had to be led individually from the cell block to the visitation area. Each prisoner was chained and shackled at the neck, at the waist (with hands behind their back), and at the ankles. Each prisoner was held by two armed security guards, one on each side. After each prisoner was placed into his visitation cell, the guards would reach through and remove the shackles and chains. At the end of our workshop, the process would reverse. The guards would come to get each prisoner, shackle him at the neck, waist, and ankles, and lead him back to the death row cell block.

Kathy, Matt, and I were in the middle hallway during both of these routines. That's when we had some of our best one-on-one conversations with the prisoners.

I'm not allowed to use the prisoners' real names, so I'll give them pseudonyms, but let me describe the nine of them who actually met with us, using the notes I took at the first session.

Sam, one of the two white men, was already in one of the visitation cells when Kathy, Matt, and I arrived. I'd say he was in his late sixties, and he sat in a wheelchair. He was dressed in an Orthodox Jew's yarmulke and prayer shawl. (We would later discover through his writing and *inaction*—we met on Saturdays—that he was indeed an Orthodox Jew, having converted while in prison. His devotion to his faith prohibited his working on Saturday, so Kathy would take notes for him, and we'd leave the prompts for him to write in response to once the Sabbath ended—which he did, brilliantly.) Sam wore very large, old-fashioned hearing aids and told us regularly that he had trouble hearing what was going on during the writing group sessions.

Kramer was the other white guy. I'd say he was in his early fifties. He struck me initially—and continued to do so over the months—as one of the kindest, sweetest people one could ever hope to meet. He repeatedly told us how much he enjoyed our sessions, and he never stopped smiling. Through his smiles he effusively apologized for not being a good writer—in his estimation. He loved to draw pictures and write poems resembling greeting-card verse. His interactions with the other participants were minimal, to say the least.

Then there were the African Americans. Korey was one of the two youngish ones. (I later discovered that he was not yet forty but had been on death row for twenty-one years.) Korey was very up, very focused, very much a player. Somehow, even while incarcerated, he had managed to start his own 501(c)(3) not-for-profit organization, designed to raise public awareness about the death penalty. Korey's ultimate goal was, and is, to get a new trial, get out of prison, and build an international museum about the death penalty. From his cell, he had orchestrated exhibitions of art works that had been displayed throughout the United States and Europe.

Korinthian was as low key as Korey was keyed up. Korinthian revealed quickly his primary identity. A former gang member—he had been taken in by the Black Gangster Disciples at the age of nine—he had experienced a true religious conversion in 2005 and had become an ordained minister in a fundamentalist church based in Canada. On the first day, Korinthian shared with us the book he had written and self-published about his life in the gangs, his conversion, and his dedication to keeping young people away from drugs and out of gangs. He not only was working on a second edition of his book but also was developing board games that young kids could play to learn about the perils of bullying, drugs, and gangs.

Demetrius was clearly the youngest one of the nine—I'd say he was in his mid-twenties, and I later discovered that he had only been on death row for two years. For some reason, it took the guards an inordinate amount of time to figure out which cell to put him in. Demetrius, I quickly discerned, was renowned as the best rapper on the row. Once he was in place, the discourse among the seven African American prisoners code-switched from "white" English, with which they were speaking to Kathy, Matt, and me, to African American vernacular English.

Arthur was the oldest—I imagine well into his sixties. He moved slowly. He talked slowly. He wrote little. He struck me as about as dangerous as the Sunday school superintendent in the little Methodist church I attended as a kid.

Ron, in his fifties, was very big and quite vocal. Though it diminished over the span of our working sessions, Ron carried a medium- to large-sized chip on his shoulder. From the outset of the project, he wondered what was in it for us—were we simply just a bunch of do-gooders?—and what was in it for him. He was constantly hungry and asked us repeatedly if we could get him a pen pal or send him some money so he could get food from the price-gouging commissary.[8]

Derrick, a relative youngster (I'd say around forty), resided intellectually on another planet. By all appearances he was always thoroughly medicated. When he came into focus and concentrated on the reading and writing at hand, he would utter, and write, long, magnificent pieces, breaking into both Hebrew and Arabic at times and populated by archaic monsters and filled with the most arcane theology one could ever imagine.

And then there was Andre. Six foot seven, close to four hundred pounds. At our first session, Andre sat like a caged bear in the back of his cell. He never made eye contact with us. He never commented on the poems being read or on his fellow participants' writing. He would hunch over the metal desk in the cell and write and then turn and hand me or Matt or Kathy what he had written. Then he would go back and face into his corner.

At the beginning of our second meeting, something miraculous happened. Andre turned around. He interacted with us and the rest of the group. He commented on the poems. He listened to his fellows' work and commented wisely on it. He shared his work willingly. And he wrote copiously, from then until the end of the project. And, my god, what he wrote. In my forty-two years as a teacher, I have never encountered a writer who has a more perceptive eye, and better-tuned ear, a stronger voice than Andre's.

I came to love these men. I have had no greater privilege in my life than working with them as writers and as human beings. I know of no greater irony than the state of Arkansas's intention eventually to kill them.

Early in *On the Row*, one of the actors reads the following letter, which Andre had written in response to our initial inquiry to the thirty-four men who in early 2016 resided on death row:

---

8. We discovered as the project progressed that the inmates were fed breakfast at 4:00 in the morning, lunch at 10:00 in the morning, and dinner at 2:00 in the afternoon. After that, there was nothing else to eat unless one had purchased snacks from the commissary to keep in his cell.

Dear Ms. McGregor,

    I've received your information but I'm not sure as to how my life story could help you or anyone. My so-called dad beat me, broke my bones and kept me chained to an old truck I used to sleep under. My mom was a whore who allowed him to abuse me rather than her. There was no child protective services. At ten years old, I was sold for $600 and a case of Kentucky Bourbon. My life had been nothing until I escaped at age 16 and took to the streets. I wish you the best with your project. There are some true characters here on the row. But I don't see how my life story could help anyone.

    Sincerely . . .

To the contrary, *On the Row* demonstrated powerfully how the life stories of Andre and the other writers could mean something to pretty much anyone who encountered them.

The premiere performance day for *On the Row*—October 8, 2016—was an ecstatic experience. After our final Saturday writing session on September 3, 2016, everything that the eleven inmates had written over the previous five months had gone to Troy Schremmer, the project's theater director and an outstanding actor in his own right. Somehow, between September 3 and October 8, Troy assembled the script.

Having served as a writing assistant for the once-a-month Saturday sessions at Varner from May through September, I was honored to be given a role to play in the staged reading. The Prison Story Project had hired six of us actors to perform, and there were eleven voices represented, so each of us had a character or two whose texts mostly went to us, but we also had the opportunity to read portions of other prisoners' works besides those of our primary character. My primary was Sam, the Vietnam veteran and Orthodox Jew.

The nine inmates who had agreed actually to meet with us were led into their individual cells and unshackled, and with the exception of Sam they quickly moved to and leaned on the cell bars to get as close to the performance as possible. We performed in the same hallway where we had led the Saturday sessions, so the experience was a bit like performing in a subway car. Kathy had hired an old musician friend from Memphis to come and provide instrumental musical bridges between the scenes, and she made sure we actors were positioned as close as possible to our primary characters. We launched into the performance. The inmates hung on every word. As the sixty-five-minute performance concluded, many of them tried not to let any of the others see they were crying.

By some miracle, Kathy had persuaded the warden to let us bring snacks and drinks. As we distributed the goodies—soft drinks, chocolate milk, donuts, sausage rolls—the inmates shouted kudos to each other and lavished praise on the performance. At the end of the hallway, Kathy turned to Matt and joyfully uttered the sentence that has become part of the Prison Story Project lore: "Can you believe that here, on the darkest corner of America, in the midst of a culture of death, we're having a party?"

Sam, of course, could not join in the party, but Kathy had made a point to bring him a special snack: bagels and cream cheese and lox. She handed it to him through the bars. He held the goodies in his lap for a moment, then wheeled his chair to the back of the cell where there was a small metal table. He placed the bread, cheese, and fish on the table and said a blessing. He turned his wheelchair back toward Kathy. Tears were streaming from his eyes.

We started doing public performances of *On the Row*—to large, enthusiastic audiences—soon after its "world premiere" in Varner on October 8. We did two performances on the campus of the University of Arkansas, where coincidentally the "common reading" book that fall was Bryan Stevenson's *Just Mercy*, a riveting account of the efforts of the author's Equal Justice Institute to defend prisoners on death rows. We performed to packed houses at Saint Paul's Episcopal Church in Fayetteville and at the 21C Hotel in Bentonville.

But shortly after the turn of the year, an announcement from Arkansas politics threatened to change the fortunes of the Prison Story Project and *On the Row*. On February 27, 2017, the governor of Arkansas, Asa Hutchinson, announced that the state, which had not executed anyone for a dozen years, intended to execute eight men over eleven days—two executions a day on successive Tuesdays and Thursdays—in April. Of the eight inmates scheduled to die by lethal injection, four of them were among our eleven writers.

In the wake of the political and social turmoil stirred up by this announcement, the Prison Story Project learned that the Arkansas Department of Corrections, officials of which had seen a videotape of a performance, intended to rescind its tacit permission for us to do public performances of *On the Row*. We checked with our American Civil Liberties Union lawyer to see if the Arkansas DOC could stop us. The lawyer replied: "Maybe." We decided to proceed with public performances, a decision that has rendered us personae non gratae in Arkansas's prisons.

Throughout the spring of 2017, the Prison Story Project was at the forefront of efforts to stop the scheduled executions and abolish the death penalty in Arkansas. And beginning on April 17, we held vigils at Saint Paul's to pray for the men about to be executed. When the final execution took place on April 27, two of our project participants had received stays of execution, but two were executed—one on April 20 and one on April 27. Excerpts from the final statements of both of these men—eloquent, thoughtful, contrite—have been included in performances of *On the Row* since then.

Somewhat to our surprise, *On the Row* has developed legs. Shortly after the October 8, 2016, premiere, I began to write about the project and the experience on social media. My friend Veronica House, who teaches at the University of Colorado in Boulder and who helped to found the Conference on Community Writing, was in the midst of planning the biennial conference, scheduled for October of 2017. She asked if I could bring the production of *On the Row* to Boulder and perform it for the conference. I allowed as how it would be prohibitively expensive to transport all six actors and our musician to Colorado, but I came up with an alternate plan. I would fly to Denver in August and audition local actors in Denver and Boulder to read the roles. Since the production is a script-in-hand staged reading, if the actors had the script for six weeks or so ahead of the performance, we could gather at the University of Colorado the day before the performance and put the production together. The plan worked. I found outstanding actors in Denver and Boulder (and one from Fort Collins), and our musician, Rich Moore, lives in Denver, so we rehearsed, running the show twice, on October 18 and performed it to a huge crowd—around four hundred people attending the conference—the next afternoon. The performance soared.

In the audience that day were community literacy specialists and scholars from colleges and universities around the United States, and soon requests from other institutions began to emerge. Following the same local-talent plan we had used in Colorado, in 2018 we mounted productions at the University of North Carolina at Asheville, at Notre Dame University, at Wheeling Jesuit University, and at my alma mater, tiny Bethany College in West Virginia. Folks all over the country were experiencing the powerful words of these eleven inmates.

In late 2018 and in 2019, two organizations, the Mid-America Arts Alliance and the Whiting Foundation, provided the Prison Story Project with generous funding to support tours of *On the Row*. We took a forty-five-minute version of the play to high schools in Fayetteville, Little Rock, and Pine Bluff, Arkansas, and we performed the same version at the Harrisburg Juvenile Detention Center near Jonesboro. We offered the full production at Arkansas State University and a large Episcopal church in Memphis. In the summer of 2019, we took the full production to Episcopal churches in Kansas City, Wichita, Tulsa, and Dallas. Another tour to juvenile justice centers in Arkansas awaits, even as I write this. High school students have been rapt by the production and pepper us with questions afterward about working with and getting to know the death row inmates. Audiences at the churches have stayed for our post-show talk-backs, contributing to rich, often impassioned, discussions about the death penalty.

The words of eleven inmates have created a world that, I would hazard, few of our audience members ever thought they would inhabit. Literacy is action. Literacy is doing.

I can't do justice to the death row inmates' power and eloquence by talking *about* it, so let me share a bit of the method we used to elicit the writing that eventually made its way into the script of On the Row.

Exhibit A: Here is the assignment, created by Matt Henricksen, that we left with the prisoners so they could write during the month between two of our visits:

> In this packet I've included a 3-page poem by Nazim Hikmet, who spent 35 years in prison for his political beliefs. The poem is called "Things I Didn't Know I Loved" and is basically a long list of basic aspects of the physical world and his praise for them. He doesn't mention loving any general ideas, such as freedom, family, and romance, perhaps because he already knew he loved those things. One technique that often leads to good writing is to focus on very simple things or small details rather than starting with a big idea or emotion. Notice how Hikmet says "I didn't know I loved the sky" and then goes on to describe its sights and sounds. He praises each thing he didn't know he loved by describing it in extensive detail.
>
> *NOTE: the poem incorporates places and other references specific to Hikmet's travels in Russia. Do not worry about those words: they are names of places he visited and names of people he knew or knew of. He could as easily be saying "Memphis" and "Elvis."*
>
> THE PROMPTS
>
> For your writing assignment, begin each line with "I didn't know I loved" and then name a physical object, natural or man-made. Try not to talk about people, ideas, or emotions—focus on physical things we might all overlook. For example, "I didn't know I loved my car" or "I didn't know I loved the

rain." Then describe the sights, sounds, tastes, smells, and/or touch in a way that shows your love for them. Take "love" however you like: the word has a lot of different meanings and degrees of intensity.

For a second assignment, read the poem "Inventory" by Günter Eich. Look around you at your possessions. Focus, at least at first, on the physical objects. You can simply list your possesions, but you are also welcome to say anything about them that you wish. You might also choose to expand from physical possessions to mental, emotional, and/or spiritual possessions. However, please begin with physical objects.

[You are welcome to complete both prompts or just one of them. Also, don't forget you can mail us your homework assignment—describe the best day of your life to someone who hates you, and try to convince them you deserved to have a good day.]

Yours,
Matt (and Katie!)

Here is a seventy-word sample of Hikmet's poem, just to provide a sense of what the inmates were using to jumpstart their own writing. (See Academy of American Poets 1962.)

> it's 1962 March 28th
> I'm sitting by the window on the Prague-Berlin train
> night is falling
> I never knew I liked
> night descending like a tired bird on a smoky wet plain
> I don't like
> comparing nightfall to a tired bird
>
> I didn't know I loved the earth
> can someone who hasn't worked the earth love it
> I've never worked the earth
> it must be my only Platonic love

What follows is the portion of *On the Row* that grew out of their work on the first prompt.[9]

"I didn't know"

---

9. Once again, the names of the speakers are those of the actors reading the roles, not the inmates who wrote them. Because six actors performed *On the Row* and eleven inmates wrote the material, there was not a perfect correspondence between actors and writers.

DAVID
> "What do you miss most about being free?"
> A prisoner on Arkansas' Death Row was asked,

BRANDON
> "I miss being trusted,"

DAVID
> He responded without hesitation.

BRANDON
> Everyday
> Death row prisoners,
> From the time they open their eyes,
> Until they close them at night,
> We're constantly reminded:

TROY
> You're not to be trusted.

EMMANUEL
> Distrust dines inside the cell
> with death row prisoners
> For breakfast, lunch and dinner.

AUSTIN
> Distrust showers with us,

TROY
> Goes to the bathroom with us,

BRANDON
> Is present with us
> when we bow our knees to pray to God.

EMMANUEL
> It tucks itself in
> under the sheets at night with us,

KERRY
> A constant companion.

BRANDON
> I never realized how much of a blessing
> Trust is.
> Until I came to know just how much of a curse
> Distrust is.

KERRY
> I didn't know
> I loved an unlocked door
> And an unlocked window so much,

Until I was no longer able to freely exit a room
Or let up a window.
That fresh air rushing in on you
And the outside elements,
As it skates across your skin,
Leaving chill bumps in its wake.

DAVID
I didn't know
I loved nature
With all of its different colors
And sceneries,
Like a long walk through a wooded forest trail!

BRANDON
I didn't know I loved having those blisters,
Cuts, and scrapes on my hands
From a hard day's work on the construction site.
Those cuts and scrapes
Are worn as a badge of honor,
The evidence of a working man.

AUSTIN
I didn't know
I loved being able to reach down
Into my blue jeans pocket
And fiddle with the coins there.
I would grab a handful,
Run them in between my five fingers,
Being soothed by the sound
Of the change
As each piece brushed against the other.
That sound has always been comforting,
A language in itself:
I'm not broke!

TROY
I didn't know I loved a steak dinner;
To savor the smell
As it lay in the flames of the grill
And to enjoy the savory taste on my tongue
As my teeth devour it in a wolf fashion!

EMMANUEL
I didn't know

> I loved having pockets on the sides of my pants.
> Without them there's the feeling of nakedness.
> No pockets,
> No keys,
> No money to fill the pockets.
> Who knew a person could actually feel less
> Valuable without the companion of pockets?
>
> TROY
> I didn't know I love a good ink pen;
> I could have wrote a lot better with a good one.
>
> KERRY
> I didn't know
> I loved the smell of fresh morning air.
>
> BRANDON
> I didn't know
> I loved the smell of mowed grass
> and lawn mower smoke.
>
> DAVID
> I didn't know
> I loved the feel of grass on my bare feet
> as I walked across it.
>
> EMMANUEL
> I didn't know
> I loved the feel of sand between my toes
> as I walked outside in the dirt.
>
> KERRY
> I didn't know
> I'd love again the sound of the arrow
> slicing through the air
> as these memories
> pull the drawstrings of my heart.

Here is a thirty-three-word segment of the poem (Eich 2007) the second prompt asked the inmates to respond to:

Inventory
   by Günter Eich

This is my cap,
this is my overcoat,
here is my shave kit

in its linen pouch.

Some field rations:
my dish, my tumbler,
here in the tin-plate
I've scratched my name.

And here is the portion of *On the Row* that was crafted from the inmates' responses to the poem:

Inventory

BRANDON
    These are my shoes.
    Here are my socks,
    These are my T-shirts.
    These are the clothes
    That I personally have bought
    And refer to as possessions.
EMMANUEL
    Here is my toothbrush and toothpaste,
    These are my razors,
    These are my pants and shirts,
    Blankets and sheets—These are all issued.
    I only use them for a while.
AUSTIN
    Here is my radio, I love every station!
TROY
    These are my color pencils
    That I draw pictures and make cards with
    If only to provide a smile
    To someone else for a few minutes.
Pause.
AUSTIN
    Compared to the vast amount of things
    I want to possess
    I sense nothing but sorrow
    Loss, regret, and shame
    For having achieved,
    And then failing so terribly.
DAVID

This is my Yarmulke
This is my Siddur (prayer book)
This is my Tallit (undershorts with fringes)
Here is my Tanach (Bible, Prophets and Writings)
These clothes aren't mine
They belong to the State.
The pen with which I write,
And this paper I bought,
They are my greatest gifts.
With them I speak
To the world and my loved ones.
This is my cage:
A steel door painted gray,
Walls painted off white,
Metal sink and toilet.
This is my heart:
It aches sometimes.
These are my pills
Which stop the ache,
Which will one day
Kill me.
These are my tears:
They don't wash away
Pain, loneliness, or anger.
They serve no purpose,
They just are.
These are my hands:
They don't work so well anymore.
Once they were strong,
Once they caressed my wife,
My children, my grandchildren,
—Perhaps one day
My great-grandchildren, I have
But have not seen
These are my legs:
They don't work so well anymore.
They carried me through childhood,
Through jungles and deserts,

They lept from airplanes,
And stood by graves, cribs
Beds, and Time.
This is my life:
It held more joy than sorrow
Lots of memories, although
Some are lost.
There is more of it
Behind me than in front;
But it was full.

On the Row concludes with a very unconventional epilogue. The script ends with a powerful section labeled "I Am Done," and as each actor finishes, he walks to the edge of the stage and drops his script into a large garbage can before exiting the auditorium.

Then the following happens:

The ACTORS return to the stage and bow to the audience. TROY introduces each ACTOR and the MUSCIAN. He explains that after the "inside performance" for the writers on Death Row, they wrote to Kathy. The ACTORS go back to the trash can, take out their scripts and read the following:

EPILOGUE

AUSTIN

Dear Kathy:
As I send this to u, I want u to know that after sleeping and clearing my mind, I'm still trying to wrap my head around what I witnessed yesterday, (Saturday). The presentation that you presented to us from our writings was some strong and deep shit on many levels . . . and much of what was actually written by us was just sharing things on the surface.

DAVID

Dear Ms. McGregor,
Greetings and Blessings:
I am writing to thank you and the other project members for the presentation at Varner last Saturday.
The lox and cream cheese and the bagels were a

delightful surprise. It had been eleven years since I last tasted lox and bagels. I choked back tears as I said the blessings over bread and fish. Thank you to all for reminding me what it feels like to be human.

TROY

Dear Kathy,

WOW! What a wonderful program y'all prepared. We all were left with a great feeling of how our writings all came together and performed! Thank you so much!

Love you, take care!

P.S.

We are the broken ones
That with your help were patched up
To shine like new.

BRANDON

When they first reached out to me through the mail asking me whether or not I wanted to be a part of the project I wasn't sure what to make of it. [But] from the first class to our final class I enjoyed the journey of writing and being creative. I appreciated seeing new faces of the people coming in to the prison to help me find my voice, sharpen it, and even adjust it.

I got the chance to interact with fellow prisoners that I'd been around for over 15 years on a level we had never ventured onto before. We got the chance to see each other in a different light. Through one another's writings, we could see the real person, the true human being. When previously had you asked me about this or that person, I would have told you he was pure monster. But now not anymore. Through our individual and collective writings the potential was visible. It felt so wonderful doing something worthy, something bigger than any one of us; to be doing something different other than the status quo.

Had our efforts and time not produced anything

more out of coming together writing and reading aloud our writings, most of us, if not all would have been content with what we had received thus far.

[But] from the beginning of the project we were told that upon completion of the writing stage of the program there would be professional actors who would come in and act out our character / writings. I thought I was prepared for the live performance. I had no clue what I was in for. The performance blew me away! I tell you the truth, hearing someone else read aloud my writings and perform it was an outer body experience for me. My thoughts were, "Wow! Did I write that piece? Was that really me?" The performance was surreal! It was touching, deep, eye-opening, liberating! I found myself crying on the inside, careful not to show it on the outside. I wasn't alone here!

I also felt myself feeling sorry for the guys who missed out. During the performance, I remember not wanting it to come to an end. You see, something special was taking place. Dreams were being realized once again; hope was in the eyes of condemned men. We were being shown our humanity; our worth. That we have something to offer, too. We too matter, no matter what horrible things we did (or didn't do) in the past to land us on death row.

I call the day of the performance on October 8, 2016 my greatest day on the row, [a day] that I got to share with friends.

Thank you and God bless prison story project.

Conclusion

Constructing Hope through Conversation

> Through words and other actions,
> we build ourselves in a world that is building us.
>
> —Ira Shor, 1999

Until this chapter, we've largely stayed away from making direct comparisons between urban and rural literacy environments. Not that we haven't thought about similarities and differences over the years—in fact we jokingly called this book *The City Mouse and the Country Mouse* in the early stages—but we've felt that putting too much emphasis on differences would distract us from the real lessons we were both learning in parallel from projects and people we knew. At many times, our work with nonprofits, schools, foundations, government agencies, and various communities seemed so much alike that we hardly bothered to talk about differences. We still see overwhelming similarities within and among the projects we write about, and we often find that the assumption of difference between urban and rural locations short-changes both of them at once. Urban and rural populations have each suffered because of caricatures and stereotypes over the years; shallow generalizations isolate and stigmatize rather than humanize the very real inhabitants in city and countryside alike. In the end, communities discriminated against historically often come to resemble one another. They share both common problems and also common on-the-ground solutions.

Of course we know similarities and differences matter, and comparisons deserve attention now that we've had time to share with readers some stories from our two regions. We also know that Philadelphia can't stand for all urban centers any more than the Arkansas Delta can stand for every rural area. Our approach in this chapter is to return to the strategy of LEARN as a way of comparing our two literacy environments, considering resources and needs in Philadelphia and Arkansas in a way that we hope frames them both as rich places to live and hopeful places to work. Too often in the past, the portraits of city and country settings project communities in such crisis that readers wonder why people don't simply flee from those local predicaments. On the contrary, we see people who love their neighborhoods and prefer to work toward better conditions right where they live.

LEARN across Communities

Perhaps the most obvious difference between our two home regions is population. According the US Census estimate in 2017, Philadelphia is the sixth-largest US city with 1,580,863 people, within a larger metropolitan area of more than 6 million people and a state ranked fifth in population. Philadelphia has experienced seven straight years of population growth, although the city is decidedly smaller than in the 1950 US Census total of 2,071,605. The World Population Review lists Philadelphia's population density within the city-county limits as 11,782 people per square mile. By contrast, US Census 2017 estimate for the population of the entire state of Arkansas as 3,013,825, ranked thirty-third in the nation but growing at a current annual rate of 0.53 percent. World Population Review estimates Arkansas's overall population density at fifty-six people per square mile, but this includes the two relatively densely populated areas around Little Rock and Fayetteville. Thus, by population statistics the two regions seem radically different indeed.

	Philadelphia	Arkansas	Bentonville	Woodruff County
Total Population 2017 Estimate	1,580,863	3,013,825	49,298	6,571
White (non-Latinx)	34.6%	72.5%	73%	69.9%
Black	43.9%	15.7%	2.6%	26.3%
Latinx	14.8%	7.6%	9.4%	1.7%
Asian	7.7%	1.6%	10.6%	.3%
Native American	0.8%	1.0%	1.1%	0.5%

The two areas where David has been most active in Arkansas are the northwestern counties near Fayetteville, the home of the University of Arkansas, and the eastern counties near the Mississippi River, known collectively as the Delta. Table 1 shows a demographic comparison between Philadelphia and areas in Arkansas. The town of Bentonville, just north of Fayetteville, is one center of the LatinX Theatre Project he discusses in chapter 9. The rural county of Woodruff is where David did extensive work, described in chapter 8, with the White River Rural Health Center in the little town of Augusta. For our purposes here, we will make only a few observations about these comparative demographics because we don't want to belabor the point that Philadelphia is larger and more dense, or that Augusta has to fight hard just to retain its single high school. We are much more interested in pointing out current or potential learning networks within and among the seemingly disparate locations we've written about.

Another difference that leaps out between Philadelphia and the two locations in Arkansas is demographic diversity. In Philly, the white population is a smaller portion of the whole in comparison to the two-thirds of the population identified as people of color while in all of Arkansas the nonwhite population is only about 25 percent. This translates into a different power dynamic among the social groups within our two areas. A larger portion of the city government in Philadelphia is controlled by black and Latinx politicians and policy makers than has been the case in most of Arkansas, though the history of Little Rock is more complicated in that regard than in more rural areas. The Latinx population in Philadelphia is also a significant enough cultural component of the city that the Puerto Rican, Mexican, Dominican, and South American people cannot be dismissed as marginal. The culture of any northeastern American city does not seem as predominantly Caucasian as most of Arkansas feels, which is not to say that the art museums, universities and colleges, and Western classical music establishments do not project a decided Eurocentric dominance in Philadelphia, as in Boston or New York. At the same time, corporate and private wealth in both our areas is still largely concentrated in Euro-American hands, and the people who are least well served by public services and affordable housing remain the nonwhite population in both Philadelphia and Arkansas.

An outcome of the disparity between city and country populations is that there are simply more resources concentrated in a Northeastern city like Philadelphia. When we first started working on this book, David invited Eli and his wife, Wendy, to Arkansas for a conference on the arts and literacy held in Fayetteville. In preparation for the conference, he invited every community arts partner he worked with in the area for a meeting with the two northerners. We met in the back room of a local Mexican restaurant, and we had a fine lunchtime conversation among fifteen or so people. Afterward, we speculated about how big a room we'd have to rent to bring everybody in community arts together in Philadelphia. We guessed we could not have gotten away with fewer than 80 to 100 invitees if we didn't want to insult a great many organizations, and we might have had to make room for more than 150 if any group wanted to send more than two representatives.

David could concentrate on partnership building and still leave room for fostering new groups that were struggling to emerge. In Philly Eli learns about new projects in unexpected parts of the city regularly. Too often, the Philadelphia arts community also hears about the demise of long-standing organizations that have run out of funding, split into factions, or failed because of strategic mistakes. David has seen organizations grow and thrive or falter and close; however, the scale is more manageable even though the impact from the success or failure of any one organization might be greater in a small town or a rural area. Both Philadelphia and Arkansas are environments where dynamic cultural changes occur, but the sheer bulk of the city brings the mixed blessing of multiplicity within the feast or famine of foundation and donor funding that all nonprofits experience.

One more difference we can mention here is land use and economic growth. Neither of us is a financial analyst or economist, nor is tax law uppermost in our minds when we think about our shared work. And yet the tax base for urban and rural regions represents both similarities and differences in the resources and needs of these civic constituencies.[1] In Philadelphia, as in many other cities, gentrification has been shaping the growth of neighborhoods since at least the early 2000 (Young), fueled by tax abatements to encourage real estate development put in place in the 1990s (Blumgart). In truth, the change of a block or neighborhood from low value to high value is "a natural phenomena that has been with us since Benjamin Franklin," as Temple professor emerita Carolyn Adams has pointed out (Young). Philadelphia had been losing population until urban neighborhoods started becoming attractive to young, white, and wealthy residents, and the city depends on these new residents for revenues and renewed national reputation. Yet, at the same time as all the new apartment buildings, rehabbed row homes, and hip coffee shops bring life to areas where there had been vacant lots and boarded-up corner stores, the changes have also brought rent and tax increases for longtime residents and pressure on people of modest means to sell out and move away from their old neighborhoods. The new Philadelphians aren't as concerned about

---

1. Here, as in many other places, we are following Deb Brandt's (2001) recognition that economics and literacy are deeply entwined. As noted earlier in the book, we believe the future of writing studies must include much more extensive interdisciplinary training in order to contextualize understandings of composition, literacy, and rhetoric.

public schools as they are about restaurants, entertainment, and shopping, so the city emerging in the early twenty-first century looks sharper and taller, more appealing for those with money in their pockets, but it's not necessarily a better place to raise kids on a worker's budget.

Recent development has been fueled in part by tax abatements and special deals for builders. Wealthier residents pay more city wage taxes but the city loses income on incentives. At the same time, the city has rewritten the tax valuation system to catch up with the skyrocketing new prices. For example, a house in the traditionally African American neighborhood of Point Breeze was valued at $27,000 for tax purposes in 2012 and reassessed at $420,000 only two years later (Young). The city council has passed some legislation to ameliorate these massive reassessments for long time homeowners, but the overall consequence is that whole areas of the city have become whiter and wealthier, while people of color have had to move further away from Center City or outside the city limits altogether. One might think that people moving to the suburbs could find better schools and services there, but people in search of lower rents are not moving to suburban school districts with the capacity to fund schools amply. One can envision a time when schools in the city improve significantly, when day services for the elderly are more prevalent and better funded, where rec centers provide fascinating workshops for families to learn art techniques and multicultural perspectives, but these facilities might no longer serve communities that include children and adults from working-class and minority families. Literacy educational needs for children and adults might therefore become better met in gentrified sections but neglected in other neighborhoods of the metropolitan area.

It would be optimistic to label economic growth in rural Arkansas "sluggish." In contrast to the few urban areas in the state, rural Arkansas continues to struggle in terms of population, economic indicators, socioeconomic stress, and education. Data provided by the University of Arkansas Agricultural Extension Service in its 2017 "Rural Profile of Arkansas" substantiate that claim. While the state's population grew 2.1 percent between 2010 and 2015, almost all of the growth was in urban areas. Delta counties lost 4.1 percent of their population during that period. At the center of the Delta, down the Mississippi southwest of Memphis, Phillips County alone lost 11 percent of its population and Monroe County 9.2 percent. Outmigration from the Delta counties resulted in population losses ranging from 2,000 to 6,000 people annually between 2000 and 2015. The remaining population in the Delta counties is older (median age 42) than in the urban counties (about 38). There are more "dependent" people—aged younger than 17 and older than 65, and therefore not fully in the labor force—in the Delta counties than in the urban regions.

Between 2010 and 2015, the Delta lost about 1,000 jobs in finance, about 300 in financial services, nearly 2,000 in government, and about 200 in farm and forestry.

These losses in population and jobs have been accompanied by socioeconomic stress, health-care issues, and declines in educational enrollment and attainment. There are pockets of extreme poverty in rural Arkansas: In nineteen counties, 25 percent or more of the population live under the federal poverty level. In the Delta counties, 36 percent of all children live in poverty. The infant mortality and overall obesity rates are high: fourth in the nation in the former and sixth in the latter. In rural Arkansas, there are just about 69 primary care physicians per 100,000 people, in contrast to 166 in urban areas. Between the 2007–2008 and 2016–2017 academic years, rural Arkansas experienced a 7 percent decrease in public school enrollment, as compared to a 9 percent growth in the entire state. Public school enrollment in the Delta counties declined 15 percent during that period ("Rural Profile of Arkansas" 2017).

While the economic pictures in our two areas seem markedly distinct, we recognize a common challenge. Growth experienced by urban centers does not "lift all ships" or trickle down to people who have been traditionally underserved by poorly funded schools and neglected health and human services. Among the most pressing literacy needs in both our areas is the need for self-advocacy: people need to be able to tell their stories, articulate shared hopes for their communities, demand a place at the political conference table. They need to feel that they can engage in the conversation about what America— rural and urban—needs to be, and they need educators in colleges and universities to see their young people as worthy prospective undergraduates and graduate students, professionals and leaders in the future.

For this reason, one literacy characteristic more similar than different in our two areas is access to higher education and advanced training. The college data website CollegeSimply lists ninety-five colleges within fifty miles of Philadelphia, including two- and four-year schools; historically black colleges and universities; technical, proprietary, and vocational colleges; and research universities. A search in the same website lists forty-eight entries in the state of Arkansas, including a comparable variety of institutions serving a range of students after high school. For both locations the challenge is the same. Students from wealthier families and more enriched K-12 schools will regard college as their natural next step after high school, while students with modest means may look at college as distant, forbidding, and unaffordable. Though specific solutions to the problem of access may be different in the two locations, the central issues remain the same. Students everywhere need adequate academic preparation, familiarity and comfort with postsecondary schools, a strong sense that their potential will be recognized in college, and financial support to make higher education possible.

A profound lack of college guidance counseling is one of the more glaring results of the lean financial years for the Philadelphia School District. In December 2013, Kevin McCorry reported for the local public broadcasting station WHYY that in 2012 "the district employed 384 full-time counselors for 141,143 students—an overall ratio of one counselor for every 367 students," but after the funding crisis and layoffs in the summer of 2013, "the district employs 218 full-time counselors for 131,463 students—an overall ratio of one counselor for every 603 students." Many of these counselors work in elementary schools or focus on a long list of traumas and discipline-related issues among students, which leaves even fewer to help with college guidance. The ratio has come back to something under 380–1 across high schools (College Transition), but students certainly have few people to help with the shift to college. Edison High School, with 1,057 students in 2018–2019—31 percent English language learners—has 168 seniors. Edison employs an overall counseling staff of three, for a ratio of 352–1 in the school as a whole, but the number focused on college guidance, in a neighborhood where trauma from violence and poverty is common, cannot be gleaned from the public record. The most storied magnet school in the district, Central High School, in 2018 had 2,397 students in grades 9–12, including 548 seniors. The counselor team includes five people for the whole school, two designated as college advisors, for an overall ratio of 479–1 student to counselor and a college guidance ratio of 274–1. By contrast, Harriton High School, in a wealthy suburban school district outside of the city, reported an enrollment of 1,206 in 2018–2019, with a graduating class of 282. Harriton has six counselors, three of whom assuming primary responsibility for college access guidance, for an overall ratio of 201–1 high school students to counselors and 94–1 seniors to college counselors.

The availability of college counseling in Arkansas high schools also varies dramatically from site to site. Consider two schools in the Delta: Brinkley High School in Monroe County has one counselor to serve the 247 students in grades K-12; Helena Central High School in Phillips County has two general counselors and two college counselors to serve 641 students in grades 7–12. By contrast, in Northwest Arkansas both Fayetteville High School (1,911 students in grades 9–12) and Bentonville High School (1,910 students in grades 9–12) have eight guidance counselors.

College is nearby for Philadelphia students, but for all the visibility of Temple, Penn, Drexel, Villanova, Saint Joseph, and La Salle on TV basketball games, school district students who are not part of special programs or helped by church organizations can still only see life beyond high school as a distant dream. Many students leave school before finishing high school at all (witness Edison High School's 2018–2019 entering ninth-grade class of 383 and graduating class of 168), and those who do attain a diploma need much to go right before they can even enter college, let alone persevere to a degree. Admirable programs such as Philadelphia Futures (see chapter 5) exist to help individuals, and every college in the area has some sort of support for city students who find their way to matriculate, but the Philadelphia School District child from a low-income home must be remarkably self-motivated, persistent, intelligent and lucky to become a college graduate. Often district students start at Philadelphia Community College and transfer to a local school, usually Temple, but the way is hardly easy or smooth. Indeed, the way is often unpaved, dimly lit, and lonely. Temple, which offered a number of more or less successful programs to support Philadelphia students in college during the seventies and eighties, when the university needed more enrollment, closed its last official program for at risk students, the Russell Conwell Center with its Summer Bridge, in 2015.[2]

Given the proximity of colleges and universities in Arkansas, there is no logical reason why any citizen should feel a psychic distance from higher education. In a state of just over 3 million people, with the aforementioned forty-eight colleges and universities, counting two-year public and online private schools, there are few corners of the state where one can't drive to a postsecondary institution in less than an hour. These facts notwithstanding, the discourse about educational attainment, particularly about college and university enrollment and graduation rates, often embodies a sense of emergency, if not outright panic. Nationally, almost 70 percent of high school students enroll in some form of postsecondary education after graduation. In 2017, the last year for which relevant data were available, only 48.2 percent of Arkansas high school graduates entered college. Nationally, about 34 percent of adults twenty-five or older hold a bachelor's degree. In Arkansas that number is 21 percent—ranking it forty-eighth in the country, ahead of just Mississippi and West Virginia in that category. The reasoning that underlies the sense of urgency about these statistics is clear: if good jobs in the future are going to require a college education, so the thinking goes, then Arkansas is going to have

---

2. This chapter is not the place to discuss such a complex problem as transfer and transition from high school to college. Others have written extensively on the issue, and much work still needs to be done. Eli has written about this topic in *Because We Live Here*. David and his colleagues have written about the high-school-to-college transition in *The Arkansas Delta Oral History Project*. Rachel Edwards has published a useful annotated bibliography on high school to college transitions in CompPile.

a difficult time encouraging businesses and industries to locate here, given the relatively anemic level of educational attainment in the state.

The state holds an unusual relationship to the educational stature of its flagship university, the University of Arkansas at Fayetteville, where the Brown Chair in English Literacy, occupied by David from 2005 through 2018, is housed. The university is located in the far northwest corner of the state, over five hours by automobile from the farther corners of the Arkansas Delta. In fall 2018 a mere 1,026 students who listed home addresses in the fifteen counties of the Delta were enrolled there, in contrast with 3,741 students from Washington County and 3,063 from Benton County, the two northwestern-most counties in the state, and 1,098 from Pulaski County, where Little Rock sits in the middle of the state. The campus has historically had a difficult time attracting minority students. In fall 2018, for example, only 4 percent of the undergraduate population was African American and 9 percent was Hispanic. According to 2018 population estimates, the overall population in the state is 79 percent white, 16 percent African American, and 8 percent Latinx.

While the legions of Razorback athletics fans cover the state (even though there are Division I programs at four other universities in Arkansas), apparently not everyone considers the University of Arkansas at Fayetteville their intellectual home base. The university does not sponsor an extensive program of academic outreach programs to the seventy-two counties in the state, so when the Brown Chair in English Literacy would appear in the rural corners of the state—in regions east of Little Rock and into the Delta—we could often be met with befuddled responses. Folks in those parts of the state had literally never encountered such programming from the state's flagship university.

Despite the differences, literacy challenges in both Philadelphia and Arkansas involve underserved communities for whom large economic factors don't work in their favor. Our goal for LEARN at this point is to identify issues that future community literacy researchers and educators should explore for a more detailed picture of the literacy environment in any given region. We offer one last example that, in our estimation, suggests the rich possibilities of extending literacy work into action within a given region based on the perceived needs of the participants.

SISTA

One group of literacy educators, the Walton College of Business Communication Center at the University of Arkansas, has already risen to this challenge. A project called SISTA—Students Involved in Sustaining Their Arkansas— was launched by the Brown Chair in 2015 as an outgrowth of the Arkansas Delta Oral History Project, which had been ultimately phased out in 2013. The

Arkansas Delta project had run for seven years, and more than three hundred students from predominantly rural high schools had created original work, under the mentorship of University of Arkansas undergraduate students, by following the Arkansas Delta Oral History Project process: identify some topic or issue from local history or lore, do some background research on the topic, plan and conduct an interview with someone who had an informed perspective on the topic, transcribe the interview, and then write about the topic in whatever genre seemed most appropriate to report on the investigation—an academic paper, a piece of short fiction, an individual poem or series of poems, a pamphlet or brochure, a website, and so on. As the book published by Syracuse University Press, *The Arkansas Delta Oral History Project* (Jolliffe et al. 2016) demonstrates, the initiative produced a rich vein of student work, all of which contributed to the efforts to vivify the history and culture of the Delta and stem the forces of depopulation and stagnation.

A salient problem with the Arkansas Delta Oral History Project was the tendency for some of the student work to slip into excessive nostalgia. Especially when they interviewed older people who had lived in the region their whole lives, the students' projects often reflected a "those-were-the-good-old-days" perspective. But, unfortunately, the good old days in many corners of the Delta were not, in a word, "good." The past times were frequently dominated by racism, class divisions, and other socioeconomic inequities. David and his colleagues at the University of Arkansas looked for way to re-tool the project to avoid this disproportionate backward gaze.

SISTA seemed to solve the problem.[3] In SISTA high school students, again with the mentorship of a University of Arkansas student, would propose projects that they believed would revitalize or sustain some aspect of life in their hometown or home region. With the mentor's support for a full academic year, the students, whom we named SISTA fellows, would do background research on their topic and then conduct one or more oral history interviews with people who knew something about the topic. Equipped with these two bodies of material, the students would then write a grant proposal, recommending a specific course of action to be taken in relation to the topic that would improve life in the town or region. As the students were working on their documents—an academic paper about the background research and interviews and the grant proposal—we hosted them in Fayetteville for a weekend to give them the opportunity to provide interim reports on their projects and to take advantage

---

3. The project was originally named SISA, for Students Involved in Sustaining Arkansas, but David's friend and frequent collaborator Kassie Misiewicz, whom we meet in "Performance," took one look at the acronym and opined, "Brother, you need a T in there someplace." Thus SISA became SISTA.

of a writing workshop, focusing on the grant proposal, offered by the Walton College of Business Communication Center.

During the three years SISTA operated—one year as a small pilot program and two with a dozen students working either individually or in teams—the fellows generated an array of fascinating and ambitious proposals: a healthy-cooking clinic, a music school where volunteer teachers could offer lessons, a green-grocer farmers' market, a county tourism authority, a plan to improve the irrigation of rice crops, a public art trail, a repurposed air force base converted into a Cold War museum, a paddleboat facility for tourists. It was a joy to see their ideas made concrete in grant proposals.

As their SISTA year ended and the students finished their documents, the office of the Brown Chair got busy trying to find funding to implement the projects. We succeeded in doing so with only one of the proposals—the one to establish a county tourism authority in northeast Arkansas—before David's retirement date arrived. But SISTA has now been taken over by the Walton College of Business Communication Center, and students from throughout the state continue to develop projects that combine the backward gaze of oral history and the forward prospect of specific actions to improve the state.

When we look at what's possible for education, the arts, business development, health, and many other civic needs, we recognize that local, state, and federal governments must fund most of the essential services necessary for the overall well-being of a region. Government responsibility remains imperative even with the conservative tide against higher taxes that support public works and social welfare; in the United States, government is still in charge of schools and roads, parks and recreation, immigration rules and public health. Yet the corporate and nonprofit sectors can play an important part in networks of literacy sponsorship. Philanthropic groups are, perhaps, the most available funding partners for literacy educators and activists who would like to construct networks that foster literacy as conversation rather than literacy as a measurable and quantifiable skill. For this reason, we devote the next section of this chapter to the issue of funding networks of literacy sponsorship, after which we will offer first-person accounts of our endeavors to find financial support for our literacy outreach work.

Networks and Money

Both of us have been able to do what we've done over the years in part because we've been fortunate to tap into funding for projects and partnerships. The money hasn't made things happen; our great fortune has been the allies and friends from various walks of life who over the years helped construct hope for communities through their ideas and hard work. But there's no doubt that timely grants and dependable support have helped bring ideas to fruition and paid people to pursue the good work they envisioned. Each of us has had our own history with grant writing and cultivating donors, so we decided to speak in our own voices for a part of this concluding section. Before we each tell our stories, however, we want to outline four principles that we share in our approach to seeking money for literacy projects.[4]

- Always work with partners from the community you wish to serve, and see local institution building as a central part of the work.
- Develop an idea you would pursue whether you receive the grant or not.
- Recognize that prospective donors can be partners too.
- Balance short-term gains with long-term goals (tactics versus strategy).

Perhaps these are more or less self-explanatory, but we will briefly comment on each below. In certain ways, each is a face of an overall approach that values reciprocity, democratic engagement, and praxis—that is, theory and practice in constant dialectic relationship with one another.

Partnership and Institution Building

One of the big issues in developing a network of literacy sponsors is that institutions sponsoring literacy are not equal in status, power, or visibility. If an idea for a teen health magazine or a play to be performed in a senior center comes primarily from a university teacher or a recreation center director, then the resulting event may not reflect the concerns of the community, develop leadership skills among youth or elders, or change the way legislators see a neighborhood. The event becomes a device for announcing the skills and commitments of the director and writer but not the actors, and the school or center becomes stronger while the neighborhood itself remains relatively mute. Our goal is to create mechanisms for people to join public conversations, but this means that the home institutions people hold dear—whether that is caregivers for young children in Augusta or the Stitches group in Springdale or the mentors at Tree House Books—also gain recognition and respect along with the ostensible sponsors of a given event.

---

4. Eli has written about principles for community literacy taken from Saul Alinsky's approach to community organizing. These principles for grant writing are somewhat more specifically focused on funders, but Alinsky—with his roots in David's longtime domicile, Chicago—is still an influential thinker for us both.

Productive Ideas Don't Depend upon Funding

Anyone who writes grants knows about the trap of "chasing the money." To some extent, every grant has to fit an audience, and one can't ask for money to teach argumentation through sports if the foundation proscribes any support for sports in its charter. On the other hand, a group that devises a project that strains its mission to seek money from a foundation's new fund will find itself either to have wasted good grant-writing time on a foolish venture or, perhaps worse, suddenly receive funds to do a project they aren't really prepared or enthusiastic to make a reality. Both of us have started projects we believed in before we knew we had full funding because we felt certain the project just had to exist. At other times, we've done projects that didn't turn out as we'd hoped because, in the end, the money was there more than the spirit was. For example, years ago Eli was working with Steve Parks on a publishing venture called New City Community Press. One of the books New City published had considerable backing from a local funder and became a beautiful book that was actually better produced than others in that same series of publications. However, the book didn't sell well and, to some extent, generated bad blood in exactly the area of the city it highlighted. Many in the community perceived the book as representing more elites than average people (see Parks *The Republic of Letters* for a fuller account of New City Press).

Donors Are Partners Too

Projects arise usually because of an urgent need within a community or region. Usually the idea of seeking a grant comes after the initial ideas have been formed. Too often inexperienced grant seekers view funders as the sugar daddy source for money to solve local problems the funders themselves probably don't understand or recognize. This is a fatal misreading of the situation. Yes, we've certainly met our share of clueless do-gooders or people who donate out of an abstract noblesse oblige impulse that has more to do with ego than commitment. However, we have more often worked with foundation program officers and family donors who both know a great deal about the issues they are funding and also care passionately about the outcome of their gifts. All of the Brown Chair projects supported by ARCare and the Arkansas Community Health Foundation, for example, emerged from these two entities' clear desire to improve the general quality of life in ARCare communities. Moreover, foundations and donors often know a great many other people and organizations interested in the same issues. The right funder can be an excellent partner in developing a literacy network.

Funders have a legitimate desire to know what the project is designed to do as well as what will signal that the project is working. One of the challenges and gifts of writing grants is that the process forces the organization or coalition of organizations involved in the grant to understand and articulate what it is they really want to accomplish at a moment of their existence. By requiring the writers to be detailed rather than vague, specific about local objectives rather than eloquent about global goals, and hard-nosed about what will signify success rather than overly ambitious about changing the grand scheme, a grant can improve an organization even if the money doesn't come through. A philanthropic organization that does not fund a project in the initial round may become a strong ally as the funders get to know the nonprofit's record and the nonprofit refines its means and methods.

Balancing Tactics and Strategy

The field of community literacy has had a long-running debate over the relative merits of tactics, often associated with Paula Mathieu's important book *Tactics of Hope*, and strategies, represented by the foundational work of Linda Flower in such books as *Community Literacy and the Rhetoric of Public Engagement*. We don't want to enter the controversy here except to say that both our distinguished colleagues are correct. Projects should be designed so that people see beneficial consequences right away, but significant structural change shouldn't be sacrificed for immediate results. Short-term tactics to make something happen, particularly in communities with urgent needs like the homeless population Mathieu writes about, allow for direct action and hands-on collaboration with the people most affected. Strategic thinking, following a longer-term perspective and involving slower-moving but powerful institutional partners such as universities and city government, can improve the literacy climate for a great many people together over time. We don't see these two orientations as mutually exclusive, nor do we agree with those (not Mathieu or Flower) who tend to see tactics as more aligned with a leftist position and strategies as more conservative. To us, the work must go on at multiple levels, in multiple time frames, in order to foster the greatest number of approaches to pressing problems that are too complicated to have unitary or static solutions.

Longevity need not be the most desirable outcome, but adaptability and flexibility are almost always necessary to address knotty local problems. We have both watched projects that succeeded brilliantly for a few years because of a good idea and some very energetic activists and then ceased, not sadly but appropriately. We have also witnessed admirable nonprofits grow and change according to productive strategies that continue to unfold and alter with the times. Conversely, we've seen small nonprofits close before they could reach their full potential and others grow into agencies with so much power or stability that they resist any community input not blessed by the agency itself. Sometimes survival becomes the goal to the exclusion of a nonprofit's original mission, and that drive to survive can be annoying, disturbing, or downright destructive. We can't help but observe that universities—education nonprofits that swell into vast corporate entities—can sometimes prioritize survival over mission to such an extent that "education" becomes a catchword with little significance to the overall operation.

Financing Community Literacy Projects: A Personal Excursus by David Jolliffe

I may not be the best person to ask about how to secure financial support for community literacy projects. In the last two institutions where I have worked, I have been fortunate to have guaranteed sources of funding for projects I have developed.

During my thirteen-year tenure as the Brown Chair in English Literacy, I benefited from the support of two prominent foundations, the Brown Foundation of Houston, Texas (after which the endowed chair is named) and the Walton Family Foundation. The former emerged from Brown and Root, one of the most successful—and politically connected—construction companies in the United States, while the latter manifests the philanthropy of the huge Walton fortune amassed by the retail success of Walmart. The Brown Foundation contributed one-half of the initial endowment of the chair, while the other half was provided as part of a $300 million gift—the Walton Family Gift—to the University of Arkansas's capital campaign in the early 2000s. The Walton Family Gift was used, among other purposes, to support portions of chair endowments across the universities' colleges. In addition to part of the endowment of the chair, I also received support for one of my school-based projects—Razorback Writers, an after-school initiative in middle schools in Springdale and Rogers, Arkansas—and one of my "performance" projects, the LatinX Theatre Project, from the Walton Family Foundation. Acknowledging that some readers might have political or ethical issues with the sources of funds that gave rise to these foundations, I can attest that the support I received from them was completely hands-off—I was never either encouraged or discouraged to shape the outreach activities of the Brown Chair in any particular direction.

The endowment funded, at least in part, the Arkansas Delta Oral History Project and its successor, SISTA; the Razorback Writers After-School Program and its successor, the Arkansas Studio Project; the LatinX Theatre Project;

the Prison Story Project; and the Hawkmoth project, which involved students from small rural high schools creating a literary magazine.

I have also been supported by two relatively modest additional grants: one from the Women's Giving Circle at the University of Arkansas, which financed the purchase of several personal computers for the Woodruff County Literacy Council, and one from the Dollar General Literacy Foundation, which allowed the Woodruff County Literacy Council to partner with the Brown Chair in a series of family literacy workshops for families and caregivers of preschool and elementary school children.

At DePaul University, where I taught from 1994 through 2005, I was the beneficiary of support from the Steans Center for Community-Based Service Learning, enabling me to lead projects that offered writing tutorial services, provided by trained DePaul undergraduates, to students at two large inner-city high schools in Chicago and that provided conversational partners to Latino and Latina families in learning circles at a community settlement house in the southwest corner of the city. In short, I have been a very lucky man!

In contrast to "sexier" corners of education—for example science, technology, engineering, and mathematics (STEM)—there are not abundant funding programs for literacy projects. The aforementioned Dollar General Literacy Foundation and the Wish You Well Foundation both offer grants, usually ranging from the low four figures to about $15,000, to support family and community literacy. But my experience applying for grants suggests that funders perceive literacy in the strongly autonomous sense, as basic decoding of print materials and the simplest encoding of "functional" documents. Support for applied, engaged literacy-as-conversation projects such as the ones detailed in this book generally falls outside the purview of literacy project funders.

So how does one go about finding funding for projects that, say, help people learn to read critically and write effectively while engaged in urban farming or community arts or regional sustainability initiatives? There are two possible answers to this question: First, look for partnerships with entities—foundations, corporations, school systems—that are consciously dedicated simply to improving quality of life, be it health, education, job creation and placement, educational achievement, housing, and so on. A state, region, or municipality might have a community development council or a public education foundation. Find out what these entities do and then latch on. As I explain in chapter 8, I was fortunate early in my time in Arkansas to connect with White River Rural Health Center (later ARCare), which to this day announces its mission as focusing on the overall health of the communities it serves with clinics, not simply on the physical health of its citizens. ARCare went so far as to form the Arkansas Family Health Foundation to support improved quality-of-life initiatives in towns with clinics, and a great deal of my work as the Brown Chair intersected with these generously funded projects. Second—and this might sound a bit deceptive, but so be it—unless you're proposing to do something that looks like traditional, autonomous literacy work, don't refer to your initiative as a "literacy" project. Tell folks that you're providing books and reading lamps to families with young children, or that you're helping young people create grant proposals for projects that will revitalize and sustain their communities, or that you're working with prisoners to help them prepare for citizenship after incarceration by engaging them in a storytelling project. In short, emphasize what your project will *do* for community development.

New City Writing and What That History Might Mean: A Personal Excursus by Eli Goldblatt

Most of my experience with fundraising and grant writing comes from projects involving New City Writing, the community engagement arm of the writing program based in the Temple English Department. Founded in the spring semester of 1997, soon after I was hired at Temple to be the university writing director, New City Writing emerged from a federal Fund for the Improvement of Postsecondary Education grant in the College of Arts and Sciences to explore ways faculty could be rewarded for service to the community surrounding the university. At the time, Geography and Urban Studies Professor Carolyn Adams was dean of the college (later to become the College of Liberal Arts), and she strongly supported the mission to develop literacy partnerships with organizations in North Philadelphia and other nearby urban neighborhoods. Steve Parks and I wrote the initial charter for what was then called the Institute for the Study of Literature, Literacy, and Culture, a long title meant to position the institute among the disciplines of English, philosophy, and anthropology. Parks was the first director, and he soon began referring to the institute by our "street name," New City Writing. When Parks took a position at Syracuse University in 2004, I assumed the directorship.

Soon after Dean Adams established our institute, we realized we needed money to pursue more ambitious projects. Both Parks and I have recounted the story of our connection with the John S. and James L. Knight Foundation elsewhere (Goldblatt 2007, Parks and Goldblatt 2000, Parks 2010) but the short version is that through my alma mater Cornell University, which had received Knight money for its writing program, I reached out to a sympathetic program officer at the foundation named Rick Love. He took an interest in the approach we had developed to connect internal innovations in a university writing program with the construction of external initiatives, an undertaking we called Literacy in Action. With the help of nearly $1 million from Knight over the course of five years and three grants, we established a modest but dependable endowment to fund projects inside and outside the university. Temple's College of Liberal Arts, then led by interim dean Morris Vogel, contributed to the endowment fund. In addition to various events and programs to encourage writing in the disciplines within academic departments, we started our external efforts by sponsoring a graduate student from African American Studies, Suzanne Henderson, to facilitate a writing group for early teen girls in Norris Homes, a housing development then bordering Temple to the south. Under the name New City Community Press ("New City Community Press" n.d.), we produced books written by and for communities of Mexican farm workers (*Espejos y Ventanas/Mirrors and Windows* 2004), the Chinese community in Philadelphia (*Chinatown Live(s)* 2004), people with disabilities (*No Restraints* 2002), and a racially integrated working-class South Philadelphia neighborhood (*The Forgotten Bottom Remembered* 2003). We also briefly published a magazine called *Open City* that collected writing by people throughout the city. In this way, writing instruction within the university became stronger while community writing projects grew in North Philadelphia and beyond.

Along the way, I learned about the large and small foundations that nonprofits in Philadelphia typically approach for funding. I worked with grassroots organizations in African American and Latinx North Philadelphia, especially Tree House Books (chapter 5) and Open Borders Project (Goldblatt 2007, Goldblatt 2008), to attract money for operating budgets and special initiatives. Serving on boards for these and other organizations, I've come to see how important relationship building is to fundraising. I'm not much of one for cocktail parties, finding them less useful than meetings over coffee and lunch, but I developed connections and sometimes friendships with program officers and foundation directors who consider grants, citizens who serve on foundation boards, or consultants who advise nonprofits on board matters. Philadelphia, for all its size and complexity, functions as a small town once you've started learning the philanthropy networks. Hearing the criteria for grant deliberations has been enlightening for me, not only as a grant writer but also as a scholar interested in how networks of nonprofits fit together, grow, and sometimes become undone. In recent years, I've also started placing graduate and undergraduate students as interns in nonprofit administrative offices, and that has helped me understand the granting process and the people who work in fundraising even more.

Individual donors have also been a significant part of New City funding. In 1996 I had my first meeting with an interested alumnus who wanted to give money to Temple. He provided a small gift to the First-Year Writing Program because he was so grateful for the lessons he learned in a basic writing course many years before. I didn't know what I was doing at the initial conversation over coffee, but as I listened to him I recognized that here was a man, for all his wealth, determined to reach out to young people who might be as lost as he once had been. Working with the development office of the university, however, was often frustrating because its priorities left little room for writing or community literacy, and university priorities dictated what a professor could ask outside sources to fund. Then in 2005 an enlightened College of Liberal Arts development director connected me with a couple in Chicago named Sue and Bob Wieseneck. They had been giving money for scholarships to the college for some years, but no one had ever asked them before what they most wanted to fund. The college flew me out to meet them, and they responded to an idea I had to start a summer program for high school students called the Temple Writing Academy. The Wiesenecks went on to fund the academy for four years, starting in 2006, until I could no longer run the program when I took over First-Year Writing, but at that point they were excited enough about literacy in North Philly to become mainstay donors of Tree House Books. For twelve years the Wiesenecks have been supporting New City Writing projects, and in that time I have come to know them as friends and nearly as family. This is certainly an instance where conversation led to powerful actions.

I would mention only one other funded adventure that I think particularly pertinent to a book on learning networks. Starting around 2010, a national project called Instructional Rounds (see City et al. 2009 for a more in-depth description) was administered in Philadelphia by a well-established educational nonprofit named the Philadelphia Education Fund and originally funded by CITI Foundation's Post-secondary Success Project. From 2011 to 2015, Temple's First-Year Writing Program participated in this collaboration, which encouraged discussion and understanding across educational levels by bringing high school and community college English faculty to observe first-year writing and other early college humanities classes at Temple and then sent Temple faculty to observe in two city high schools. A few other colleges in the areas teamed with additional high schools, and the whole group met to discuss the results of all these visits and consultations. Instructional Rounds was a well-conceived large-scale effort that took different forms in four or five other sites around the United States. I found it a highly effective way to teach teachers and administrators across levels, to foster a much-needed conversation about how students move from school to college and what educational institutions could do to help with fraught transitions. The considerable funding for stipends and conference time mattered, but what made Instructional Rounds work best was the way the conceptual approach portrayed every member of the literacy network as a valuable and worthy contributor.

This brief history doesn't cover all New City Writing projects or other nonprofit work I found myself drawn to over the years, but I hope it conveys my core understanding that the allies and lessons I encountered on any one project became invaluable for my later work. For example, during my time in the early 2000s as board chair at Open Borders in Latino North Philadelphia, I met Helen Cunningham, then the executive director of a small but influential foundation named for Samuel Fels (based on the fortune generated from his family business selling Naptha, a household laundry detergent popular in the late nineteenth to early twentieth century). Helen became not only a friendly advisor to me for Open Borders and later Tree House Books but a wise guide who helped me understand philanthropy outside of academic circles, the virtue of a sustainable business plan for a nonprofit, and the necessity of seeing funders as partners and not merely money dispensers. Fels Foundation didn't always give my partner organizations money, but even when they turned us down, I learned a great deal about addressing urban needs with integrity and meaningful community participation.

Together Again: A Coda

Mark Twain once said that the only person permitted to refer to himself as *we* is the King of England or someone with a tapeworm. Well, neither Eli nor David has royal blood, and as far as we know, we are free of parasites. In any case, we return now as "we" and offer this coda, circling back to the theme of hope that explicitly launched this chapter and that we have tried to inscribe implicitly throughout the book.

As we complete *Literacy as Conversation*, both of us have recently retired. But this book is not an exercise in nostalgia. We have filled it, of course, with stories in reckless abundance—tales of what we have learned by working with projects in our home bases of Philly and rural Arkansas, accompanied by ruminations on what we have learned in the process. Neither of us sees himself as having a legacy that someone needs to continue. We do hope, though, that our readers—in academia, in foundations, in think-tanks, in government, in not-for-profit organizations—will resonate with our experiences. Community initiatives can invite people from all walks of life into conversations framed by and enriched through writing. Those conversations draw out unfolding meanings from webs of relationships. In short, they vivify lives with genuine literacies.

Bibliography

Academy of American Poets. 1962. "Things I Didn't Know I Loved, by Nazim Hikmet—Poem." Translated by Randy Blasing and Mutlu Konuk. Academy of American Poets. https://poets.org.
"A City Transformed: The Racial and Ethnic Changes in Philadelphia over the Last 20 Years." 2011. Philadelphia: Pew Charitable Trust Philadelphia Research Initiative.
Adams, Hal. 1995. "A Grassroots Think Tank: Linking Writing and Community Building." *Democracy & Education: The Magazine for Classroom Teachers*, 1995.
Adams, Hal, and Janise Hurtig. 2002. "Creative Acts, Creative Insights: Adult Writing Workshops in Two Chicago Neighborhoods." In *Community Partnerships (Case Studies in TESOL Practice Series)*, edited by Elsa Auerbach, 147–58. Alexandra, VA: Teachers of English to Speakers of Other Languages.
"A Day in My Life." 2018. *Live Connections*. https://www.liveconnections.org/programs/education/news/49-news/blog/education/440-adayinmylife.html.
Adler-Kassner, Linda, and Elizabeth Wardle. 2015. *Naming What We Know: Threshold Concepts of Writing Studies*. Logan: Utah State University Press.
"American Fact Finder." n.d. US Census Bureau. https://factfinder.census.gov.
Arkansas Literacy Council. 2017. "How Many Adults Can't Read?" https://www.arkansasliteracy.org.
Asian Arts Initiative. 2014. "Pearl Street Project." http://asianartsinitiative.org.
Asian Arts Initiative. 2018. "Home." http://asianartsinitiative.org.
Ayers, William, Caroline Heller, and Janise Hurtig, eds. 2016. *Every Person Is a Philosopher*. New York: Peter Lang.
Baker, Sheridan. 1962. *The Practical Stylist*. New York: Thomas Crowell.
Bakhtin, M. M. 2017. *The Dialogic Imagination: Four Essays*. Austin: University of Texas Press.

Bakhtin, M. M., Caryl Emerson, Michael Holquist, and Vern W. McGee. 2010. *Speech Genres and Other Late Essays*. Austin: University of Texas Press.

Barga, Michael. 2013. "The Long Depression (1873–1876)." Social Welfare History Project. http://socialwelfarelibrary.vcu.edu/eras/civil-war-reconstruction/the-long-depression/2013.

Bazerman, Charles, and David R Russell. 2003. *Writing Selves, Writing Societies: Research from Activity Perspectives*. Fort Collins, CO: Wac Clearinghouse.

"Best States Rankings." 2019. *US News and World Report*. usnews.com.

Blackmer, Lane. 2013. "Weavers Way and W. B. Saul Team Up to Bring Composting to NW Philly." WHYY, May 13, 2013. http://www.whyy.org.

Brandt, Deborah. 2001. *Literacy in American Lives*. Cambridge: Cambridge University Press.

Brandt, Deborah. 2014. "Literacy Is a Resource." YouTube. January 17, 2014. https://www.youtube.com/watch?v=yWUb3BaqABY.

Britton, James. 1994. "Shaping at the Point of Utterance." In *Landmark Essays on Rhetorical Invention in Writing*, edited by Richard E. Young and Yameng Liu. Davis, CA: Hermagoras Press.

Bruffee, Kenneth. 1984. "Collaborative Learning and the 'Conversation of Mankind.'" *College English* 46 (7): 635–52.

Burgee, Daryl Kwasi, Stanley Crawford, Kofi Asante, Tommy Smart, Nana K. A. Boafa, and El Sawyer. 2008. "Renaissance on Sacred Ground." Vimeo. Scribe Video Production.

Caldarelli, Guido. 2007. *Scale-Free Networks: Complex Webs in Nature and Technology*. Oxford, UK: Oxford University Press.

Cavazos, Alyssa. 2016. "Translingual Oral and Written Practices: Rhetorical Resources in Multilingual Writers' Discourses." *International Journal of Bilingualism*. doi:10.1177/1367006916629225.

Chappell, Ian. 2018. "India Could Beat This English Side in England." ESPNcricinfo, June 10, 2018. http://www.stats.espncricinfo.com.

City, Elizabeth A., Richard F. Elmore, Sarah E. Fiarman, Lee Teitel, and Andrew Lachman. 2009. *Instructional Rounds in Education: A Network Approach to Improving Teaching and Learning*. Cambridge, MA: Harvard Education Press.

"City Harvest." 2015. Pennsylvania Horticultural Society. https://phsonline.org.

Clark, Andy. 2008. *Supersizing the Mind: Embodiment, Action, and Cognitive Extension*. Oxford: Oxford University Press.

"College Search in Arkansas." n.d. Accessed December 2, 2018. https://collegesimply.com.

"Colleges near Philadelphia." n.d. Accessed December 2, 2018. https://colleges simply.com.

"Company Overview." n.d. Spiral Q. http://www.spiralq.org.

Contassot-Vivier, Sylvain, Jean-François Couchot, and Pierre-Cyrille Héam. 2018. "Gray Codes Generation Algorithm and Theoretical Evaluation of Random Walks in N-Cubes." *Mathematics* 6, no. 6: 98. https://doi.org/10.3390/math6060098.

"Crime in Philadelphia: West Mt. Airy." 2018. *Philadelphia Inquirer*. http://data.philly.com.

DeMillo, Andrew. 2007. "Arkansas Town Fails to Win Toyota Plant." *Tulsa World*, January 10, 2007. tulsaworld.com.

Doe, Sue, Natalie Barnes, David Bowen, David Gilkey, Ginger Guardiola Smoak, Sarah Ryan, Kirk Sarrell, Laura H. Thomas, Lucy J. Troup, and Mike Palmquist. 2011. "Discourse of the Firetenders: Considering Contingent Faculty through the Lens of Activity Theory." *College English* 73 (4): 428–49.

Dorogovtsev, S. N., and J. F. F. Mendes. 2003. *Evolution of Networks: From Biological Nets to the Internet and WWW*. Oxford: Oxford University Press.

Duffy, John, Julie Nelson Christoff, Eli Goldblatt, Nelson Graff, Rebecca Nowacek, and Bryan Trabold. 2014. *Literacy, Economy, and Power: Writing and Research after Literacy in American Lives*. Carbondale: Southern Illinois University Press.

Edwards, Rachel. 2012. "Alignments and Alliances: Smoothing Students' Transitions from High School English to First-Year College." WPA-CompPile Research Bibliographies 20. Council of Writing Program Administrators. http://comppile.org.

Eich, Gunter. 2007. "Inventory." Translated by Joshua Mehigan. Poetry Foundation. https://poetryfoundation.org.

Estrada, Ernesto. 2011. *The Structure of Complex Networks: Theory and Applications*. Oxford, UK: Oxford University Press.

Ewell, Maryo Gard. 2011. "Community Arts: A Little Historical Context." Grantmakers in the Arts. https://www.giarts.org.

Fallon, Roberta. 2016. "Olanrewaju (Lanré) Tejuoso Talks of His Sculptural Community Project." Artblog, December 7, 2016. https://www.theartblog.org.

Fallon, Roberta. 2017. "Grimaldi Baez Is Teacher, Community Art Practitioner, Printmaker, Drawing Machine Maker, Driven by Commitment to Social Justice and Hatred of Poverty." Artblog, April 14, 2017. https://www.theartblog.org.

"FAQ." n.d. Philadelphia Office of Adult Education. http://philaliteracy.org/.

"Farm." 2015. Philadelphia Urban Creators. http://phillyurbancreators.org.
"Final Report 2017." 2017. Philadelphia Futures. https://www.philadelphiafutures.org.
Fleisher Art Memorial. 2015a. "History." https://fleisher.org.
Fleisher Art Memorial. 2015b. "Make a Gift." https://fleisher.org.
Foucault, Michel. 1972. *The Archaeology of Knowledge*. Translated by A. M. Sheridan Smith. New York: Pantheon Books.
"Framework for Success in Postsecondary Writing." 2009. Council of Writing Program Administrators. http://www.wpacouncil.org.
Friends Council on Education. 2019. "Home." http://friendscouncil.org.
FullMedia. 2019. "How Do You Measure Readability?" fullmedia.com.
"Functional Literacy." 2019. UNESCO. http://uis.unesco.org.
"Garden Tenders." 2017. Pennsylvania Horticultural Society. https://phsonline.org.
Gee, James. 1989. "Literacy, Discourse, and Linguistics: Introduction." *Journal of Education* 171, no. 1: 5–25.
Goldbard, Arlene. 2010. *New Creative Community: The Art of Cultural Development*. Oakland, CA: New Village Press.
Goldblatt, Eli. 1995. *'Round My Way: Authority and Double-Consciousness in Three Urban High School Writers*. Pittsburgh: University of Pittsburgh Press.
Goldblatt, Eli. 2007. *Because We Live Here: Sponsoring Literacy beyond the College Curriculum*. Cresskill, NJ: Hampton Press.
Goldblatt, Eli. 2008. "Story to Action: A Conversation about Literacy and Organizing." *Community Literacy* 2 (2): 45–56.
Goldblatt, Eli. 2012. *Writing Home: A Literacy Autobiography*. Carbondale: Southern Illinois University Press.
Goldblatt, Eli. 2020. "Imagine a Schoolyard: Mobilizing Urban Literacy Networks." In *Mobility Studies in Composition*, edited by Bruce Horner and Anis Bawarshi. Logan: Utah State University Press.
"Go See the Village of Arts and Humanities' First SPACES Exhibition before It Closes Next Week." 2017. Streets Department. February 2, 2017. https://streetsdept.com.
GREENandSAVE Staff. 2017. "Greens Grow: Indoor Farming Plus Made in USA LED Grow Lights: Profile 1.4." IGrow. https://www.igrow.news.
Greensgrow. 2013. "About Us." https://www.greensgrow.org.
"Growing Together Garden Clean-Up." 2017. Nationalities Service Center. https://nscphila.org.
Heath, Shirley Brice, and Brian V. Street. 2008. *On Ethnography: Approaches to Language and Literacy*. New York: Teachers College Press.

Helguera, Pablo. 2011. *Education for Socially Engaged Art: Materials and Techniques Handbook*. New York: Jorge Pinto Books.
Holley, Marc J. 2013. "School Consolidation." *CALS: The Encyclopedia of Arkansas*. Accessed October 21, 2018. https://encyclopediaofarkansas.net/.
Horner, Bruce, and Anis Bawarshi, eds. 2020. *Mobility Studies in Composition*. Logan: Utah State University Press.
Hurtig, Janise, and Hal Adams. 2010. "Democracy Is in the Details: Small Writing Groups Prefiguring a New Society." *New Directions in Adult and Continuing Education* 128: 15–25.
Jaramillo, Catalina. 2017. "Seeds from Home Help Refugees Grow Roots in South Philly." WHYY. https://whyy.org.
Jewish Farm School. 2014. "Mission." https://www.jewishfarmschool.org.
Jolliffe, David A., Christian Z. Goering, Krista Jones Oldham, and James A. Anderson Jr. 2016. *The Arkansas Delta Oral History Project: Culture, Place, and Authenticity*. Syracuse, NY: Syracuse University Press.
Keats, John, and Hyder Edward Rollins. 2012. *The Letters of John Keats. Volume 1*. Cambridge: Cambridge University Press.
Kelly, Ursula. 2009. "Learning to Lose: Rurality, Transience, and Belonging: A Companion to Michael Corbett." *Journal of Research in Rural Education* 24 (11): 1–14.
Kirsch, Irwin S., Ann Jungeblut, Lynn Jenkins, and Andrew Kolstad. 2002. "Adult Literacy in America." National Center for Education Statistics. https://nces.ed.gov.
Klein, Betsy, and Maeghan Vazquez. 2018. "Trump Falsely Claims Nearly 3,000 Americans in Puerto Rico 'Did Not Die.'" CNN. September 14, 2018. https://cnnphilippines.com.
Koch, Kenneth. 1970. *Wishes, Lies, and Dreams: Teaching Children to Write Poetry*. New York: HarperCollins.
Krupa, John. 2009. "Augusta Seeing Literacy Project Pay Off." *Arkansas Democrat-Gazette*. arkansasonline.com.
Lave, Jean, and Etienne Wenger. 1997. *Situated Learning: Legitimate Peripheral Participation*. Cambridge, UK: Cambridge University Press.
Learning for Life. 2018a. "Our Impact." Center for Literacy. https://centerforliteracy.org.
Learning for Life. 2018b. "Poverty and Literacy." Center for Literacy. https://centerforliteracy.org.
Lee, Trymaine. 2013. "Who Is Going to Help Me? In Philly Schools, Life without Counselors." MSNBC. September 25, 2013. msnbc.com.
Lipke, Andrew, Ezechial Thomas, and David Bradley, producers. 2016. *A Day*

in My Life. CD. Philadelphia: Live Connections/The Philadelphia Cultural Fund.

Liptak, Adam. 2018. "Supreme Court Delivers a Sharp Blow to Labor Unions." *New York Times*, June 27, 2018.

Luetzow, Darcy, ed. 2009. *The Ave* 2 (1). Tree House Books.

Luetzow, Darcy, Lauren Macaluso, and Eli Goldblatt. 2014. "Garden in a Vacant Lot: Growing Thinkers at Tree House Books." In *Service-Learning in Literacy Education: Possibilities for Teaching and Learning*, edited by Valerie Kinloch and Peter Smagorinksy, 27–44. Charlotte, NC: Information Age Publishing.

Mahiri, Jabari. 1998. *Shooting for Excellence: African American and Youth Culture in New Century Schools*. Urbana, IL: National Council of Teachers of English.

Mahiri, Jabari, ed. 2004. *What They Don't Learn in School*. New York: Peter Lang.

Mancinelli, Danielle, ed. 2009. *The Ave*. 2.2. Tree House Books.

McCorry, Kevin. 2013. "Philly School Counselors Struggle to Help Seniors with College Plans." WHYY. December 21, 2013. https://whyy.org.

McCorry, Kevin. 2014. "Despite Budget Cuts, Students Reap Essential Lessons at Philly's Saul Farm School [Photos]." WHYY. December 4, 2014. https://whyy.org.

Melamed, Samantha. 2017. "North Philly's Makeshift Memorials Inspired a Nigerian Artist's Monumental New Work." *Philadelphia Inquirer*. January 5, 2017. inquirer.com.

Mezzacappa, Dale. 2015. "How Much Does Pennsylvania Spend on Public Schools, and How Are Costs Shared?" WHYY. https://whyy.org.

Mural Arts Philadelphia. 2015a. "About." https://www.muralarts.org.

Mural Arts Philadelphia. 2015b. "Our Process." https://muralarts.org.

Nasr, Joe. 2009. "Jac Smit (1929–2009): Father of Urban Agriculture." City Farmer News http://cityfarmer.info.

"National Assessment of Adult Literacy." n.d. National Center for Education Statistics. Accessed July 16, 2018. https://nces.ed.gov.

Nationalities Service Center. 2015. "Our History." https://nscphila.org.

Nationalities Service Center. 2017. "Refugee Urban Agriculture Initiative." May 16, 2017. https://nscphila.org.

"New City Community Press." n.d. http://newcitycommunitypress.com.

Ng, Meei Ling. 2015. "Meei Ling Ng's Grow Food Where You Live Develops New Urban Farm at a Chinatown North Homeless Shelter." Asian Arts Initiative. http://asianartsinitiative.org.

Ng, Meei Ling. 2017. "Grow Food Where You Live." Video. Asian Arts Initiative. http://asianartsinitiative.org.
"North Central Neighborhood in Philadelphia, PA." n.d. City-Data. city-data.com.
The Official Jane Schaffer Writing Program. n.d. Accessed December 12, 2018. http://janeschaffer.com.
"Olanrewaju Tejuoso." 2018. I-Open. http://www.i-open.org.
"Olanrewaju Tejuoso Begins Work with Discarded Materials." 2016. Village of Arts and Humanities. http://villagearts.org.
"19133 Zip Code (Philadelphia, Pennsylvania) Profile." 2016. City-Data. city-data.com.
Ong, Walter. 2001. "Writing Is a Technology That Restructures Thought." In *Literacy: A Critical Sourcebook*, edited by Ellen Cushman, Eugene Kintgen, Barry Kroll, and Mike Rose, 19–31. Boston: Bedford St. Martin's.
Parks, Steve. 2009. *The Republic of Letters*. Syracuse, NY: New City Community Press/Syracuse University Press.
Parks, Steve. 2010. *Gravyland: Writing beyond the Curriculum in the City of Brotherly Love*. Syracuse, NY: Syracuse University Press.
Parks, Stephen, and Eli Goldblatt. 2000. "Writing beyond the Curriculum: Fostering New Collaborations in Literacy." *College English* 62, no. 5: 584–606.
Pennsylvania Horticultural Society. 2015. "History." https://phsonline.org.
"Philadelphia College Admissions Consulting." n.d. College Transitions. Accessed November 2, 2018. collegetransitions.com.
Philadelphia Futures. 2018a. "About Us." https://www.philadelphiafutures.org.
Philadelphia Futures. 2018b. "History." https://www.philadelphiafutures.org.
Philadelphia Youth Network. 2017. "Blueprint for Success." January 11, 2017. https://issuu.com/pyninc/docs/pyn_annualreport2017-web.
Rediker, Marcus. 2017. "The 'Quaker Comet' Was the Greatest Abolitionist You've Never Heard Of." Smithsonian. August 15. smithsonianmag.com.
Reid, Michael, ed. 2009. *The Ave* 4 (1). Tree House Books.
"Results of 2019 ACT Aspire Exams Released." 2019. *Arkansas Democrat-Gazette*. July 2, 2019. arkansasonline.com.
Rosenberg, Lauren. 2015. *The Desire for Literacy: Writing in the Lives of Adult Learners*. Urbana, IL: National Council of Teachers of English.
"Rural Profile of Arkansas." 2017. University of Arkansas Division of Agriculture: Research and Extension. https://www.uaex.edu.
School District of Philadelphia. 2012. "District Scorecard: District Performance Office." https://www.philasd.org.

School District of Philadelphia. 2017. "District Graduation Rates Increase Again." https://www.philasd.org.

School District of Philadelphia. 2018a. "About Us." http://www.philasd.org.

School District of Philadelphia. 2018b. "General Information." https://dashboards.philasd.org.

School District of Philadelphia. n.d. "Charter Schools." Accessed 2015. https://www.philasd.org/.

School District of Philadelphia. n.d. "Charter Schools Office." Accessed 2015. https://www.philasd.org.

School District of Philadelphia. n.d. "District Schools." Accessed 2015. https://www.philasd.org.

"School Spending." 2013. OpenPAGov. http://openpagov.org.

Settlement Music School. 2010. "History." https://settlementmusic.org.

Shepelavy, Roxanne Patel. 2015. "Charter Schools Are Better Than District Schools. Unless They Aren't." *Philadelphia Citizen*. May 6, 2015. http://thephiladelphiacitizen.org.

Shirley Brice Heath, Brian V. Street, and In Language. 2008. *On Ethnography: Approaches to Language and Literacy Research*. New York: Teachers College Press.

Shor, Ira. 1999. "What Is Critical Literacy?" *Journal of Pedagogy, Pluralism, and Practice* 1, no.4.

Smallwood, Scott, and Alex Richards. 2011. "How Educated Are State Legislators?" *Chronicle of Higher Education*. June 11, 2011. chronicle.com.

Smit, Jac, Joe Nasr, and Annu Ratta. 2001. "Trends in Urban Agriculture." In *Urban Agriculture: Food, Jobs, and Sustainable Cities*. Philadelphia: Urban Agriculture Network.

Soil Generation. 2017. "Soil Generation." https://soilgeneration.org.

"Statistics." 2014. Archdiocese of Philadelphia. http://archphila.org/statistics.php.

Strauss, Valerie. 2016. "Hiding in Plain Sight: The Adult Literacy Crisis." *Washington Post*, November 1, 2016. washingtonpost.com.

Sullivan, Mecca Jamillah. 2006. "Tree House Books Young Writers Program 2005–2006: Report." New City Writing Files.

"The Condition of Education." 2018. National Center for Education Statistics. https://nces.ed.gov.

"The Problem." n.d. Center for Literacy. https://centerforliteracy.org.

"The Village of Arts and Humanities: A Multifaceted Arts Organization Dedicated to Community Revitalization through the Arts." 2018. Village of Arts and Humanities. http://villagearts.org.

"2019 Report." 2019. Arkansas County Health and Roadmaps Project. https://www.countyhealthrankings.org.

Urban Creators. 2014a. "Home." http://www.phillyurbancreators.org.

Urban Creators. 2014b. "Story of Us." http://www.phillyurbancreators.org.

Waldheim, Charles. 2010. "Notes toward a History of Agrarian Urbanism." *Places Journal*. November 4, 2010. https://placesjournal.org.

Wan, Amy J. 2014. *Producing Good Citizens: Literacy Training in Anxious Times*. Pittsburgh: University of Pittsburgh Press.

Webster, Daniel. 1968. "The Afro-American Dance Ensemble Ile-Ife. 1968. http://ileife.org.

"Welcome to AOPS Catholic Schools." 2019. Archdiocese of Catholic Public Schools. http://www.aopcatholicschools.org.

Welk, Michelle. 2010. "Timeline: A Brief History of Charters." *The Notebook*. June 10. https://thenotebook.org/articles/2010/06/10/timeline-a-brief-history-of-charters/.

Wenger-Trayner, Beverly, and Etienne Wenger-Trayner. 2015. "Introduction to Communities of Practice." https://wenger-trayner.com.

"What Is PIAAC?" 2018. National Center for Education Statistics. https://nces.ed.gov.

Whittaker, Richard. 2014. "A Conversation with Lily Yeh: Art for Social Transformation." http://www.dailygood.org.

Windle, Greg. 2016. "2 Philly Charters Cited for Disproportionately Suspending Students with Disabilities." *The Notebook*. March 29, 2016. https://thenotebook.org.

Windle, Greg. 2017. "In Philadelphia, School Police Outnumber Counselors." *The Notebook*. March 16, 2017. https://thenotebook.org.

826 Valencia Workshop Teachers. 2005. *Don't Forget to Write: 54 Enthralling and Effective Writing Lessons for Students 6–18*. San Francisco: 826 Valencia.

Young, Earni. 2014. "Changing Philadelphia." *Philadelphia Inquirer*. October 23, 2014. inquirer.com.

"Zeroing In on Place and Race—Measure of America: A Program of the Social Science Research Council." 2018. Measure of America. https://measureofamerica.org.

Index

ACT test. *See under* standardized testing
Adams, Hal, 83–85, 86, 89, 96, 97, 102
African American, 58, 64, 72, 118, 125, 138, 188; Black Gangster Disciples, 164; Black Humanitarian Center, 89–90; Black Lives Matter, 22; Black Panthers, 61; churches, 41, 133; communities, 28, 51, 65, 66, 83, 93, 116, 124; dancers, 89, 90; mayor, 48; in Philadelphia, 42, 103, 184, 197; politicians, 182; vernacular English, 164; writers, 42, 60
Alcoholics Anonymous (AA), 115, 124
American Legion Hut, Augusta, 131, 133
apprenticeships, 113, 115, 123, 124, 126
ARCare, 40, 50, 131–36, 150, 151; Center for Wellness and Education, 139, 142; high school challenge trips, 137, 141, 142–43
architects, 79, 110
Arkansas: County Health Ranking and Roadmaps project, 37; Department of Corrections, 168; Department of Education, 38; KKK in, 42; legislature, 39; Literacy Councils, 33; New Play Festival, 144; Reading Initiative for Student Excellence program, 38; Studio Project, 194–95
Arkansas Delta, 37, 51, 130, 131, 184, 185
Arkansas Delta Oral History Project, 16, 40–41, 49, 96n1, 134, 187n2, 188–90; funding for, 194–95. *See also* SISTA
Arkansas State University, 151, 169
art exhibits, 92, 164
arts, 78, 93, 104, 105, 126; and literacy, 182; and process, 90–91. *See also* community arts

Arts Center of the Ozarks (ACO), 154, 156
arts organizations, 103, 107
Arts Plus Literacy workshop, 103, 105
Asian Arts Initiative (AAI), 79, 82, 103, 104, 107
Augusta, 49, 131; Community Literacy Advocacy Project, 138; education initiative, 136; Electronic Portfolio, 139; high schools in 130, 133, 135, 146, 152, 182; Recovery Initiative, 133, 134; schools, 134, 138; Shakespeare Club, 150n2
AYP (Adequate Yearly Progress), 38, 39

Baez, Grimaldi, 52–53, 89–90, 92, 95, 98–99, 105, 106; a Puerto Rican artist, 93–94; and "sewing circle," 97, 101
Bakhtin, Mikhail, 14, 18
Baxter, Kirtrina, 119, 124, 125
Bond, Ira, 103, 104
Bowen, Joy Lynn, 46, 50, 51, 133–41, 144–45, 150n2; and ARCare challenge trips, 137, 141, 142–43
Brandt, Deborah, 7, 21, 24, 36, 183n1
Bretz, June, 66, 67
Brix, Michael, 66, 67
Brown Chair in English Literacy, 10, 35, 36, 40, 188, 190, 194, 196; projects, 40, 41, 150, 192; Trike Theatre Team Shakespeare project, 148, 149, 150
Browning, Lori, 143–44

charter schools, 30, 31–32
churches. *See under* religious institutions
Clark, Andy, 19–20

211

Classical Edge Theatre Company, 137, 148. *See also* theater
clubs: agricultural buying, 114; Augusta Shakespeare Club, 150n2; book-of-the-month, 135; comedy, 22; Graphic Sketch Club, 78; informal 154; meetings, 151; social, 113; Stitches, 146–47
cognitive research, 19, 20
college: admissions, 38, 72, 142; Arkansas Baptist, 35–36; Bethany 148, 169; community, 94; Haverford, 72; historically black, 185; in Philadelphia, 63, 68, 186, 187, 196; of Agriculture, Arkansas, 49; of Art, Massachusetts 94; Pierce, 65; students, 58, 63, 64, 65, 68, 70, 198
Collier, Dr. Steven, 131–35, 137, 138, 145, 150
community arts, 82, 91–92, 94, 110, 156, 182, 183; organizations, 23, 24, 80, 83, 86, 90, 103; projects, 84, 89
Community Correction Center, 162–63
community development, 91, 195
community literacy, 33–34, 46, 83, 150, 169, 188, 194
"community of practice," 112–16, 124
community organizing, 96n1, 117–18, 125, 131, 132, 135, 137, 156, 191n4, 199; in Chicago, 84, 195
Community Success Initiative (CSI), 139, 140–41
community theater, 147, 154, 156
corporations, 62, 125, 190, 195
Crossroads Coalition, 131, 132, 139
Crotte, Laura, 156, 157

death row inmates, 147, 170. See also *On the Row*
detention centers, 23, 169
Dewey, John, 11, 102
dialogue, 102, 106
Du Bois, W. E. B., 27, 42
DuBois, Vashti, 64, 67

826 Valencia (children's literacy program), 61, 73, 74

elementary school, 12, 31, 80, 81, 82, 84, 135, 141, 186; Duckrey, 61, 65, 68; students at, 62, 63, 70, 153, 195
English departments, 5, 21
Epstein, Alex, 117, 118, 119

faculty, 17, 18n2, 20, 83; DePaul University, 34, 129, 195; Northwestern University, 156; Syracuse University, 196; Temple, 196, 198; University of Arkansas, 36, 151, 137, 144; University of Colorado, 169; University of Pennsylvania, 74
Feldman Brandt, Beth, 80, 103, 105
festivals, 67, 144, 151, 156. See also White River Shakespeare Festival
Fleisher, Samuel, 78; Fleisher Art Memorial and Settlement Music, 79, 80
Follow Me@Tio Sam. See under LatinX Theatre Project
foundations, 75, 180, 183; Arkansas Family Health Foundation, 192, 196; Stockton Rush Bartol Foundation, 80, 103, 105; Brown Foundation of Houston, Texas, 35, 194; CITI Foundation, 198; Dollar General Literacy Foundation, 141, 195; Samuel Fels Foundation, 199; Ford Foundation, 91; John S. and James L. Knight Foundation, 196–97; Walton Family Foundation, 156, 194; Whiting Foundation, 169; Wish You Well Foundation, 195
Fox, Judy, 36, 141
"Framework for Success in Postsecondary Writing," 84–87, 88, 104, 123
Freire, Paulo, 11, 102
funding, 75, 190, 192–93, 197–99; for Hawkmoth project, 194–95; White Williams Scholarship Fund, 71–72

galleries: Alley Gallery, 79; art, 89, 90, 92, 95, 96, 97, 99, 101
Garay, Martin, 154, 157, 158
gardens, 11, 18, 89, 107–8, 110, 115, 125
graduate students, 5, 17, 35, 59, 187, 197; Indiana University, 148; in Rome, 94; Temple University, 60, 61, 94, 119

Gramsci, Antonio, 83, 85
grants: Federal Justice Department, 119; Fund for the Improvement of Postsecondary Education in the College of Arts and Sciences, 196; Pew Arts, 91; Taller Puertorriqueño, 103; to support family and community literacy, 195. *See also* funding; grant writing
grant writing, 63, 93, 105, 189, 191–93, 196, 197
Growing Together. *See under* urban agriculture

Hall, Arthur L., 89, 90
health care, 18, 24, 33, 40, 52, 76, 131, 134, 136, 185
Helguera, Pablo, 96–97, 100, 102, 104
Henricksen, Matt, 161, 164, 166, 168, 170–71
Henry H. Houston School (K-8 school), 81, 82
high schools: in Arkansas, 134, 146, 147, 152, 169, 186; in Augusta, 130, 133, 135, 146, 152, 182; Augusta High School, 131, 134, 136, 138, 139, 140, 144; Challenge Trips, 137, 141, 142–43; Edison High School, 186, 187; faculty of, 140, 148, 198; inner-city in Chicago, 195; Lane Technical High School, 34; Magnolia High School, 136; in New Martinsville, 130; in Philadelphia, 31, 186, 198; W. B. Saul High School, 114; Springdale High School, 154, 156
high school students, 72, 134, 137, 139, 144, 187, 194–95; to involve, 150, 151; summer program for, 198
higher education, 5, 20, 43, 88, 136; access to, 21, 185, 186; in Arkansas., 187–88; *Chronicle of Higher Education*, 37; Philadelphia Higher Education Network for Neighborhood Development, 29
Hill, Adam, 121, 122, 125
Hispanic populations, 28, 30, 32, 43, 51, 72, 90, 188
homeless populations, 7, 79, 83, 84, 104, 106, 107, 193
hospitals, 24, 27, 113, 120, 131

Hunt, J. B., Intermodal Transportation, 37, 130
Hurricanes: Katrina, 118; Maria, 42–43, 53
Hurtig, Janise, 84, 85

immigrants, 14, 23, 27, 78–80, 112, 116, 158; gardens of, 11, 122; Growing Together Gardens, 120, 121, 125; language support for, 23, 119; Refugee Urban Agriculture Initiative, 119
Instructional Rounds, 198–99
interstate highway commerce, 37–38, 39

Jackson, Joanne, 59–60, 62, 66
Journal of Ordinary Thought, 83, 84
Judy, David, 147, 148
juvenile justice system, 124, 170

Kayembe, Jeaninne, 117, 118, 119, 120
laptop computers, 13, 19
Latinx, 45, 83, 197; population, 23, 48, 74, 146–47, 154, 155–59, 181, 182, 188; youth, 23, 30, 40
LatinX Theatre Company, 160–61
LatinX Theatre Project, 52, 147, 148, 182; *Follow Me@Tio Sam*, 152–53, 154, 155, 157–61; funding for, 194–95
Latinx Youth Theatre Project, 40–41
Lave, Jean, 113, 115
LEARN, 10–12, 27, 181–88
learning networks, 5, 8, 12, 21–25, 33, 182, 198; in community arts, 103–6; of literacy sponsorship, 12, 21, 75–77, 86, 105. *See also* networking
Leonard, Natacha, 60, 62
libraries, 23, 27, 28, 47, 51, 75, 133; Library Free of Philadelphia, 68; Library of Congress, 22; Tree House, 58, 64; Woodruff County Library, 139
Life Do Grow Farm, 117, 118–19, 124, 125. *See also* urban agriculture
literacy, 24, 38, 71–75, 76, 86, 100, 196; in action, 139, 197; among disenfranchised people, 115n4; challenges, 188; community, 191n4; environments, 180–81; experiences, 68, 153; family, 141, 195;

literacy (*cont.*): home workshop, 50, 141, 142; learning, 8, 12, 88–89, 97, 101–2; meanings of the term, 5, 7, 12–15, 82–83, 85, 104; needs, 27–32, 33–41, 184, 185; projects, 10, 194–96; scholars, 7, 12, 141; sponsors, 21–23, 75, 88, 96, 190; US Department of Education and the National Institute of Literacy, 35; Woodruff County Literacy Council, 195. *See also* 826 Valencia

Little Rock, Arkansas, 47, 137, 142, 169, 182, 188; black college in, 35–36; population of, 17, 181, 182; University of Arkansas in, 131, 136, 151

Loewer, Otto, 36, 131, 135n2

Lopez, Samuel Rivera, 154, 156, 157, 158

Macaluso, Lauren, 63, 65, 66, 67

magazines, 22, 191, 195; *The Ave.*, 63; *Journal of Ordinary Thought*, 84; *Open City*, 197; *Popular Mechanics*, 111

magnet schools, 31, 186

MAP. *See* Mural Arts program (MAP)

Maxton, James (Big Man), 89, 91

McGregor, Kathy, 161, 162, 163, 164, 166, 168

Mighty Writers, 73, 74, 76

Misiewicz, Kassie, 150, 151, 152, 153, 189n3

Mosca, Lisa, 121, 122

Mural Arts program (MAP), 87–88, 104, 105, 119, 123

museums, 23, 49, 97, 164, 182, 190; Philadelphia Museum of Art, 79

music schools, 78, 79, 81, 151; Settlement Music School, Philadelphia, 78, 103

musicians, 78, 104, 167, 169; Andrew Lipke, 81; Rich Moore, 169

National Adult Literacy Survey, 12, 13

National Assessment of Adult Literacy, 12–13, 33

National Center for Education Statistics (NCES), 12–13, 32

Nationalities Services Center (NSC), 119, 121, 125

Native Americans, 101, 181

networking, 47, 76–77, 125, 190–91, 23n4. *See also* learning networks

New City Writing, 59, 61, 84, 196–99

Ng, Meei Ling, 107, 108–9, 110

nonprofits, 11, 64, 79, 84, 105, 133, 180, 193–94, 164; Barefoot Artists, 91; and boards, 67, 197; community arts organizations, 83, 90; and funding, 75, 80, 112, 121, 197, 199; NY2X Coalition, 118; Urban Creators, 119

Northwest Arkansas Community College, 154, 157

Northwest Arkansas Community Correction Center, 161, 163

On the Row, 41, 52, 148, 161, 163, 166–73, 175–79. *See also* Prison Stories Project

Open Borders Project, Philadelphia, 197, 199

oral history. *See* Arkansas Delta Oral History Project

Osayande, Jeannine, 103, 104

Osterweil, Wendy, 105, 106, 182

Overcomers, 107, 109–10

Parks, Steve, 84, 192, 196. *See also* New City Writing

partnership, 67, 105, 106, 131, 190, 195, 196; building, 183, 191; for the Assessment of Readiness for College and Career, 38; Plant One Million, 121

Pennsylvania Horticultural Society (PHS), 112, 121, 122, 125

Philadelphia, 11, 79, 183; Art Institute, 108; Center for Literacy, 30, 75; City Harvest program, 121, 122, 125; Education Fund, 198; Flower Show, 121; Free Library, 75; Higher Education Network for Neighborhood Development, 29; Literacy Day, 66; LiveConnections, 81; Office of Adult Education, 30, 75; Orchestra, 79; Parks and Recreation's Farm Philly Program, 112; Point Breeze neighborhood, 116, 121, 125, 184; Prison System inmates, 121; Sunday Breakfast Rescue Mission, 79, 107; West Mt. Airy, 81–82; Youth Network, 30

Philadelphia Futures programs, 71, 72–73, 187
Philadelphia Inquirer, 82, 90, 95
Philadelphia Urban Creators, 66, 116–20, 125
poetry, 41, 80, 81, 148–49
poets: Greg Brownderville, 138; Günter Eich, 174–77; Nazim Hikmet, 170, 171–72; in the Schools, 60
Point Breeze. *See under* Philadelphia
politicians, 17, 25, 27, 48, 52, 140, 158–59, 182; mayors, 48, 66, 67, 75, 119; senators, 137–38, 143
popular education, 83, 85
postsecondary education, 135, 186; CITI Foundation's Success Project, 198
preschools, 153, 195
Prison Stories Project, 147, 157, 161, 162, 167, 168; funding for, 169, 194–95. See also *On the Row*
Puentes de Salud health clinic, 74, 75
Puerto Ricans, 94, 101, 182

racism, 17, 32, 67, 71; institutionalized, 21, 40, 42, 43, 100, 189
Real Conditions, 83, 84
Reid, Mike, 64, 65, 66, 67
religious institutions, 22, 23, 47, 58, 115, 117, 133, 138; African American churches, 41, 133; Church of the Redeemer, Philadelphia, 121, 122, 125; Episcopal churches, 169, 170; Saint Paul's Episcopal Church, 161, 162, 168–69; synagogues, 23, 47
Romero, Audrey, 154, 157, 158

school boards, 5, 49, 133
School District of Philadelphia (SDP), 31, 32, 186, 187
schools. *See* charter schools; college; elementary schools; high schools; magnet schools; music schools; preschools; school boards; School District of Philadelphia (SDP); universities
senior citizens, 23, 75, 134, 184, 191
Shakespeare, William: Chicago Shakespeare Theater, 143; *Othello*, 143; *Romeo and Juliet*, 143, 150; *The Tempest*, 150–51, 152.

See also Team Shakespeare; White River Shakespeare Festival
SISTA (Students Involved in Sustaining Their Arkansas), 46, 139, 188–90
Smith, Nyseem, 65, 66, 119
social justice activism, 79, 80
social media, 13, 62, 74, 84, 96n1
socially engaged art (SEA), 96, 97, 99–102, 104
Soil Generation, 119–20, 125
Spiral Q sponsors, 79, 80
standardized testing, 13, 25, 33, 39, 41, 97, 114; the ACT, 38, 51, 135, 137, 139; Keystone Algebra I, 32, readability scale, 17
Steans Center for Community-Based Service Learning, 34, 195
Stitches group, 146, 154–55, 156–61
Sullivan, Mecca Jamillah, 59–60, 61, 62, 66–67
synagogues. *See under* religious institutions

Team Shakespeare, 41, 52, 146, 148, 149–50, 153–54
Tejuoso, Olanrewaju (Lanre), 92–93, 94–95, 97–98, 100
Tempest Tossed, The, 41, 52, 137, 154
Temple University, 25, 27–29, 62, 68, 103, 196, 198; College of Liberal Arts, 64, 197; program in Rome, 9, 94; students, 61, 67, 69, 75, 118, 187
theater, 18, 23, 40, 153, 154n4, 167; at Central Florida, 152; at DePaul, 156; puppet, 79, 87; staged readings, 162, 169; TheatreSquared, 144, 148; at University of Arkansas, 137, 144, 150, 157. *See also* LatinX Theatre Project
Toyota, 38–39, 132
Tree House Books, 16, 25, 57, 58–68, 82, 119; board, 67–68, 71; development of, 75–76, 197, 198; lessons from, 68–71
Tyson Foods, 37, 130, 154

undergraduates, 5, 34, 70, 185, 197; DePaul, 34, 195; Temple University, 28, 63, 117; University of Arkansas, 16, 189
unemployment, 43, 91, 107, 115

unions: American Civil Liberties Union, 168; Actors' Equity, 148, 156; credit, 24; meat-cutters, 113; organizer, 161; Philadelphia Federation of Teachers, 31
universities, various, 27, 48–49, 169, 194
University of Arkansas, 46, 129, 130, 134, 138, 162, 168; Agricultural Extension Service, 184; College of Engineering, 36, 131; at Fayetteville, 181, 188; at Little Rock, 151; for Medical Sciences, 131, 136; Walton Family Gift to, 35, 194; Women's Giving Circle at, 195. See also Brown Chair in English Literacy
University of Illinois–Chicago, 83, 84
University of Iowa, 83, 136
University of Pennsylvania, 29, 103
urban agriculture, 24, 110, 113, 115, 116, 119, 122–26; Bartram Gardens, 111–12, 125; Greensgrow, 111; Growing Home, 112, 119; Growing Together, 23, 112, 116, 119, 120–22; Jewish Farm School, Philadelphia, 111; Mill Creek Farm, 111–12; Philabundance, 112; Refugee Urban Agriculture Initiative, 120, 121
Urban Creators, 117, 118, 124; website, 119
US Census Bureau, 30, 33, 37, 146n1, 181

Varner Supermax Prison, Gould, Arkansas, 147, 148, 161, 163, 167, 168
Vela, Sativa, 154, 156, 157, 158, 160
Village of Arts and Humanities, Philadelphia, 74, 75, 89, 93–94, 97–101; and funding, 91–92, 103; staff, 90, 95

Walmart, in Arkansas, 37, 130, 194
Walton College of Business Communication Center, University of Arkansas, 188, 190
Walton Family, 35, 156, 194; Arts Center, 155–56

Weavers Way Co-op, Philadelphia, 114, 125
Weiss, Jon, 58–59, 61, 68
Wenger, Etienne, 113, 114
Wenger-Traynor, Beverly, 113, 114
White River Rural Health Center, 133, 150, 182, 195. See also ARCare
White River Shakespeare Festival, 136, 139, 148
Wieseneck, Sue and Bob, 63–64, 66, 198
Wilhite, Erika, 151–52, 153
Wilhite, Rodney, 152, 153
Williams, Joseph (JoJo), 89, 91
Words on Wheels (THB), 65, 67, 76
writers: African American, 27, 42; David Bradley, 81; Caribbean, 85; college student, 86, 157; on death row, 52; Günter Eich, 171; high school student, 157; Jamaica Kincaid, 60; Mighty Writers, 82; Razorback Writers After-School Program, 194–95; Darcy Sebright, 61, 62, 63, 67, 68; Teachers and Writers Collaborative, 60; Writers in the Schools program, 157; Young Writers Program, 60. See also On the Row; writing
writing, 17, 103, 169, 195; at colleges and universities, 5, 86, 138, 196–97; courses, 102, 198; essays, 6, 41; groups, 85, 86, 97, 197; Neighborhood Alliance, Philadelphia, 83, 84; projects, 46, 83, 84, 103, 197; at Temple University, 61, 84, 197, 198; at University of Arkansas, 152, 157, 162; workshops, 73, 74, 102, 148, 154n4. See also grant writing; New City Writing; SISTA

Yeh, Lily, 89–90, 91, 92, 93

Zero System, 89–99, 101. See also Baez, Grimaldi

www.ingramcontent.com/pod-product-compliance
Lightning Source LLC
Chambersburg PA
CBHW061810290426
44110CB00026B/2845